Human values and ethics in the workplace

Praise for *Human values and ethics in the workplace*

At last, a book for all managers and leaders on how to walk the talk on ethical practice and decision-making. A must-read handbook for all those who are committed to raising the bar of integrity in their life.

—Alastair Rylatt, author of *Winning the Knowledge Game*

Any leader, in any walk of life, looking to develop strength of character in themselves and others will find many answers in *Human Values and Ethics in the Workplace.*

—David Penglase, author of *What's Ethical about Selling?*

I enjoyed reading the book and recognised the writer's heartfelt passion and belief in how a positive approach to ethics in the workplace can lead to better quality relationships and higher performance.

—Angela Lewis, book review for Australian Counselling Association's journal, *Counselling Australia,* Winter 2008

It is such a wonderful and thorough coverage of business ethics. I particularly enjoyed the section on "world views" and also the coverage of the high-profile corporations. Is your book being used at business schools and universities to teach ethics? It needs to be!

—Andrew O'Keeffe, author of *The Boss*

Human values and ethics in the workplace

Glenn Martin

Human values and ethics in the workplace
Glenn Martin

Copyright © Glenn Martin 2011

All rights reserved. No part of this publication may be reproduced or transmitted in any form or by any process without the prior written permission of the publisher, except for the inclusion of brief quotations for a review.

Glenn Martin asserts his moral rights as the author of this book.

Book layout and design by Glenn Martin
Front cover picture is of "Cat's Cradle", Rick Reynolds, Sculpture by the Sea Exhibition, Bondi, November 2006. Photo taken by Glenn Martin.

Typeset in Sylfaen 10 pt

First published 2007 by G.P. Martin Publishing.

Revised edition 2011.

Websites: www.ethics.andvalues.com.au
           www.glennmartin.com.au
Contact: glenn@glennmartin.com.au

Printed by Lulu.com

ISBN 978-1-257-01303-6

National Library of Australia
Cataloguing-in-Publication Data
Martin, Glenn.

> Human values and ethics in the workplace.
> Bibliography.
> Includes index.
> 1. Work - Moral and ethical aspects. 2. Employees - Conduct of life. 3. Business ethics. 4. Values.
> 5. Ethics. I. Title.
> 174

CONTENTS

Preface		vi
Introduction		1
PART A: Core human values: A framework for conduct		14
Ch. 1	The contemporary business environment	17
Ch. 2	The scope of ethics	34
Ch. 3	Ethics as core human values	57
Ch. 4	The development of personal ethics	80
Ch. 5	The Values Evolution Model	98
PART B: Workers and managers at work		119
Ch. 6	Working ethically in organisations	121
Ch. 7	Making decisions ethically	146
Ch. 8	Ethical leadership in organisations	183
Ch. 9	Personal growth and development	223
Ch. 10	Coda: Present perfect	261
References		280
About the author		291
Index		292

PREFACE

This book grew out of my efforts to understand personal experiences. It took shape over a number of years, and I spent 18 months writing it. I wanted to formulate a framework that responded to other people's ideas about ethics and extended them. I also wanted to provide a practical tool that addressed the muddy places in which ethical questions arise.

Some ethical issues are really quite plain; others attract different, and often doctrinaire, viewpoints. It helps to at least try and see where we and those "contrary" others are coming from. We all operate out of world views. Often we are unaware of our own or that of others.

Jon Anderson, from the progressive rock group Yes, said: "It seems there is no end to the bad or the goodness of man" ("Beside", *The friends of Mr Cairo*). Yet I hope this book makes some contribution to an understanding of values and ethics, and leaves the reader with an increased desire to experience the world from a more expanded perspective.

To:

To my children, Elvina, Holly, Andrew, Timothy and Rohan, who in their own unique ways reflect the core human values and the desire to experience the world from a more expanded perspective.

And to the many writers from whom I have drawn in exploring the ideas in this book – it has been good to wrestle with your thoughts.

And to the friends who have encouraged me throughout this process.

Glenn Martin, August 2007

Introduction

Author's note

When this book was first published, in late 2007, the business ethics issue that stood to the fore was the spate of corporate collapses around 2001 in the USA, Australia and elsewhere in the western world. Since then we have experienced the phenomenon of the global financial crisis, with a myriad of collapses of huge banking institutions around the world and the intervention of governments to support their economies, on an unprecedented scale.

The global financial crisis raises fundamental issues about the functioning of capitalism, and the role of governments in regulating corporate behaviour. Nevertheless, I continue to believe that the most serious issues facing society are not the design of a new "ism", be it "new capitalism", "social capitalism" or whatever, but the attitudes of people in business and in all types of organisations towards ethics and integrity in their personal and corporate conduct.

The physical environment has also come to the fore in just a few years (finally!) as a pressing social and economic issue. But governments do not yet have an adequate sense of urgency about this issue, as was demonstrated in Copenhagen in 2009.

The content of this book has been reviewed in the light of these events and other developments since 2007. Yet in essence it stands as it did then. The concepts in the book provide a framework for thinking about ethical issues, taking the perspective that there is a universal set of core human values. The framework incorporates the physical environment just as much as the economic environment.

It is implicit in the book that organisational change, and change in the business world, is predicated on personal change and growth. Leaders must first change themselves. The book also remains primarily directed towards people who are not in positions of power. It speaks to people who have to make ethical choices every day in the course of their work, from their place in the web of relationships in their organisation.

Sydney, May 2010

* * * * * * * *

Many people, unfortunately, do not believe it is possible to work ethically or with integrity. They believe that their employers – through managers and shareholders – prevent it, because revenue and profit targets dominate work decisions and behaviour. Alternatively, if they are managers, they believe the business environment forces them to act in ways that would be best not subjected to too much moral scrutiny. Perhaps it involves lying to customers (or just being a little bit cavalier with the truth). Perhaps it involves making decisions they know are unfair, because they just want to "get the job done".

So, a book that says it is possible to work with integrity – in the current business environment – is making a bold statement. There may be a view that says organisations have undergone a shift in recent times in response to the spate of corporate collapses such as Enron. This view says that new compliance regimes have finally made organisations take ethics seriously. But although it may not be fashionable to say so, there is a widespread feeling that compliance (and ethics) is just another burden and constraint on business.

The prevailing view, still, is that business is tough and, if you want to succeed or even survive, you have to be prepared to cut corners, be rough, package the truth for the occasion and squeeze what you can out of workers. Business is still widely seen in terms of football – you set out to defeat opponents, and you should not be afraid of getting and giving bruises.

Contrarily, despite the dominance of this view, people persist in expecting business to be fair. They continue to hope that companies will be honest and expect that employers will act with decency. As employees (workers or managers), they continue to feel the conflict between right conduct and what they see themselves, on a daily basis, being forced to do. In the face of this pressure they may adopt an attitude of resigned helplessness. But this can only ever be a temporary solution, because the issue of ethics never goes away, and living in a state of dissonance between our ethical principles and our behaviour is unhealthy.

And managers themselves, when asked why people would want to follow them, do not say, "Because of my single-minded focus on the bottom line". Rather, they refer to values like honesty, integrity, consideration for people and capacity to inspire them. There is an admission here of the importance of ethics and relationships to business success, even from the people who are directly charged with the responsibility for producing the bottom-line results through the struggle with competitive forces.

Objectives

It would be easy to be disheartened about the possibility of working ethically. The pressures of business are pervasive, persuasive and relentless. But the hope remains that business might be conducted successfully *and* with ethics. To nourish that hope this book aims:

- to articulate our persistent, intuitive feelings about ethics (which are to a remarkable extent shared with others)
- to propose a framework for ethics using a model of the person based on core human values
- to suggest ways of working that are in harmony with our conceptions of ethics but which also enable us to act powerfully and creatively.

Although we are all adept at rationalising our conduct when we suspect we are doing something dubious, we know that ethics still means something to us when large-scale business catastrophes occur. The opening years of the 2000s saw a number of huge corporate collapses in Australia and the USA, all of which threw up questions of ethics. In Australia, between 2001 and 2003, HIH, One.Tel, Ansett and Pan Pharmaceuticals all fell, with combined losses of close to $10 billion. In the USA, Enron and WorldCom were collapses of unprecedented magnitude. Enron then brought down Arthur Andersen's with it, one of the world's largest accountancy firms.

In all of these cases, questions of ethics were at the fore. In some cases the question was whether the corporation had been operating its affairs honestly and legally. Some of these corporations had been misrepresenting their financial situation. And of the executives involved, as well as breaking the law, some of them would seem to have inappropriately requisitioned enormous amounts of company funds for their own benefit.

Suddenly, society was reminded that running a large company carries moral responsibilities – to shareholders, employees, customers and society; it is not a game without rules for those who are sitting in the seats of power.

Pervasive ethics

The fact that these corporate collapses were immediately understood – across society – as ethical crises, demonstrates how deeply ethics sits within us all. It was clear that people generally share common ground on basic ethical values like honesty and fairness, and they expect people to abide by these values in business as well as in ordinary life, even in the intense, high-stakes, competitive world of big business.

The problem is, if we accept that those corporate disasters were failures of ethics, we are recognising that ethics is ever-present at work. Some people still try to quarantine ethics, by saying or inferring that it only applies to certain types of situations, but this is a flawed perspective. To maintain that there can be business decisions and actions that are "ethics-free" is to misconceive what ethics is. The reality is that ethics is a lens that offers its perspective on any situation, and hence it applies to any and all situations.

Ethics is therefore a pervasive element in business, because its perspective applies to any business decision. A manager may be faced with a decision to cut costs, which may involve making some employees redundant, but it is a mere bluff to say that this has to be looked at in economic terms only. Whether the manager acknowledges it or not, the human aspects of the situation are real, which is to say the decision has ethical implications.

Interestingly, once the lens is widened to embrace the human and ethical aspects, it becomes clear that the narrow economic view has multiple faults. The ethical perspective presented in this book highlights the role of imagination and innovation in addressing ethical issues. What we can observe here is that when the lens is widened to include people and values, a richer understanding of the problem emerges, and a greater scope for solution-finding ensues.

Being clearer about ethics has the potential to radically alter how we work and live. It is thus a very practical enterprise to examine our ethics and clarify where we stand. It is not a mere philosophical indulgence or a game of words.

However, the closer we get to daily work decisions and routines, the harder it becomes to agree on what it means to act ethically. The most challenging argument the would-be ethical worker or manager has to confront is, "we have to do this if we are to survive". How does the ethical perspective deal with this?

Ethics and success

It would be nice to think that working ethically is not an encumbrance but is actually the foundation for our business success. It would be nice to think that examining ethics will make it easier for us to deal with the complexities, quandaries and choices that organisational life presents us with. This book will indeed assert that there is a positive relationship between ethics and success, but it does not take the naïve, simplistic view that "good ethics is good business".

It would be foolish to create the impression that having an ethical perspective on organisational conduct will always smooth the path to success. The very point about ethical choices, in many if not most cases, is that they confront us with a choice between what seems advantageous and what seems costly. In fact, this is central to how Immanuel Kant, the 18th century ethical philosopher, defined ethics.

The distinction Kant made was between prudence (what is of tangible benefit to me) and ethics (what is my duty). The treatment of ethics and success in this book will show that the relationship between them is not as stark and contrary as Kant implied but it is, at the least, complex.

Presuming we accept that we are not primarily looking at ethics because we see it as merely another tool for success, what benefit might our examination bring? A preliminary answer is this – increasing our understanding of ethics is beneficial in a similar way to increasing our knowledge, or improving our physical fitness.

To take the latter, becoming more physically fit will not guarantee that we won't get knocked down by a bus. It might not stop us from getting the flu. And even the process of getting fit can be painful or hazardous – we might feel awful for a while when we start to train, and we might strain a muscle. But we know from the experience of other people that we will be better off if we get fit. We will be capable of doing more, we will feel better about ourselves, and we will be more prepared for physical adversities that come our way.

Similarly, we generally accept that increasing our knowledge is preferable to being ignorant and not learning. Learning is a basic inclination for all but those who are depressed or repressed. An assumption of this book is that it is part of people's nature to look at human conduct from an ethical perspective. We make ethical valuations of our own and other people's behaviour every day. The book builds on our latent need to understand ethics and to know that we are acting consistently with our own ethical principles.

Practical ethics and moral philosophy

Immanuel Kant was mentioned above, but it should be noted that this book does not take a "history of moral philosophy" approach to ethics. The intent is to provide a practical and useful perspective on how to work and manage ethically in the contemporary business environment. The book will start from shared notions of values and ethics, and build a framework that makes sense of our experience of ethics, as a basis for understanding people's behaviour. The outcome desired is that readers can foster their own development and act with strength and integrity.

The task of recounting the origins and the vicissitudes of ethical theories belongs elsewhere. Reference may be made here to key thinkers from time to time. The range of contributors to ethical discourse is nowadays extensive. Not only is there the considerable store of western moral philosophy going back to the Greek philosophers like Socrates, there is also a multitude of non-western works, both ancient and modern. Taoism, Buddhism, Islam and Hinduism, as examples, all provide ethical perspectives that influence current thinking.

One of the common shortcomings of the moral philosophy approach is that, as managers and workers in organisations, we are never dealing with philosophical issues at an abstract level. Organisational life is never simple or clinical. We are dealing with strategic and operational issues that

Introduction

demand decisions, and at the same time involve psychological and social questions.

Drawing out the ethical aspects of a situation can be all the more difficult when the main protagonists only want to focus on budgets and "hard data", confining the conversation to "knowledge and logic". So a first step is recognising that we have to take into account people and their psychological and social complexities. There is also the challenge of gaining acknowledgment of the fact that emotions, attitudes, beliefs and motivations do play a large role in business decisions, however much managers or workers might want to believe that this is not so.

The doorway to recognising that ethics is already present in organisations is the acceptance that actions affect people (and the environment). Business actions are not just a matter of dealing pragmatically with physical facts about resources and financial objectives. Nor are actions the result of manipulating cognitive knowledge, concepts and abstract models with logic and reasoning alone. Every action that happens in organisations is subject to the criterion of how it affects people – and the environment.

Nevertheless, we could say that a good deal of what we do in organisations involves philosophical work, such as clarifying issues and working towards consistency of words and action. Philosophy provides us with tools with which to work, but it does not overcome the need to decide and act in workplace situations that are both complex and involve conflicting ends.

Our purpose here is to start with common perceptions and concepts and build a framework that illuminates the daily dilemmas of the workplace, so our scope is therefore narrower and more instrumental than that of the philosophers. At the same time, we do not believe that a useful approach can evolve out of a succession of case studies. To quote Edgar Schein: "There is nothing so practical as a good theory". We need to explore concepts and frameworks to establish a comprehensive and consistent basis for dealing with ethical questions.

Moreover, in acknowledging this we must allow that social factors also intervene. The behaviour and the discussions of managers and workers are likewise influenced by what others think – their peers, supervising managers, team members, customers and clients, suppliers, the public, and whatever reference groups are significant to them. Hence, a practical ethics that is realistic and helpful has to grapple with issues of personal psychology, social psychology and organisational behaviour.

The book's title indicates that the concept of human values will inform the approach to ethics. Approaches to ethics can fall into a number of camps:

- they can maintain that ethics are universal standards, or alternatively they can argue that ethics are relative to context, such as cultural, national, industry or religious norms
- some writers also approach ethics as an absolute injunction about right and wrong, while others leave room for flexibility and variation in conduct according to situational factors
- other writers come from a legal perspective, relating conduct to social standards as expressed in law
- ethics can be viewed from a personal perspective, emphasising conscience and duty.

As in all matters relating to humans and their relationships, these varied approaches are not necessarily contradictory and it is not a question of whether some are true and others are false. It is, rather, a matter of articulating an approach that helps us to understand what happens in organisations and to make choices about what we are to do, choices that enable us to live with ourselves and in dignity.

Criteria for practical ethics

To be helpful, a practical approach to ethics should fulfil the following:

1. It should resonate with our experience, both our individual experience and our collective understandings.
2. It should be comprehensive, addressing the breadth of our ethical dilemmas, and capable of guiding and illuminating all the situations that we are likely to encounter.
3. It should be applicable to a society, by which is meant that it is communicable to people of different backgrounds, persuasions and cultures (and to the myriad of sub-cultures that constitute society and organisations).
4. It should bridge two vastly different conceptions of ethics, namely:
    a. the view that ethics in organisations can only usefully be about compliance – about satisfying a minimum common standard (the law or a company policy)

b. the view that ethics must also include aspiration – striving for high levels of excellence in personal and organisational conduct.

The human values approach to be pursued in this book can be applied to both the compliance perspective and the aspirational perspective. It can give us a common language for discussing ethics and a foundation for understanding organisational behaviour.

Human values

What do we mean by human values? The entry points for discussion of human values are the common words we use to describe qualities that we approve of in people, words that everyone is familiar with – honesty, fairness, respect, decency, generosity, integrity, kindness, courage…… Conversely, there are qualities of which we disapprove – deceit, cruelty, meanness, fickleness…..

We denote these qualities as human values for two reasons. Firstly, they generally arise as qualities of humans (although it is also open to us to talk about loyal dogs or disdainful cats!). Secondly, calling them "human values" distinguishes them from values as used in an economic sense. In business contexts this is an important distinction to make, as we are frequently called upon to "add value" or to "give value for money". Moreover, human values denote approval of a quality rather than the quantification of an economic outcome.

The human values mentioned above are familiar to us from the terminology of character education, although it would have to be said that most people in society now have a fairly stunted experience of character education. Given that most people nowadays do not belong to a church and were never subjected to systematic teachings about right conduct, and that the school system is reluctant to take on this role, most people owe their primary understanding and articulation of human values to informal education through parental guidance, movies and television dramas.

Nevertheless, a starting point is a starting point. In general, people have little difficulty conveying what they mean when they speak of love, truth, peace or courage. It is when complex situations arise, as they often do in organisations, that misunderstandings and disagreements eventuate. We shall venture in this book to present a framework for human values that explains why these misunderstandings happen.

A "core human values" model will be presented as the foundation for addressing ethical issues. The human values approach is an alternative to offering a smorgasbord of different approaches from moral philosophy. The contention is that human values provide a useful language and framework that is more accessible and practical than the sometimes arcane philosophical language of deontology, utilitarianism, justice theory and virtue ethics.

Core human values will not eliminate the dilemmas that face us in our organisational roles, especially when it appears that our choices involve pitting one value against another (as is always the case in an ethical dilemma, on our understanding). It is not a prescription for simple remedies or a promise that this approach will precipitate the ultimate triumph of right over wrong.

However, the book is written from a position of optimism. It cannot be said that embracing ethics will necessarily lead to worldly success, and sometimes the opposite seems to apply, but we would assert that the pursuit of ethics is worthwhile. The book will seek to make it clearer in what sense it is "worthwhile" to be ethical. It is written both for the doubters – those who would like to believe it is possible to work or manage ethically but who think it is an unrealistic fancy, and for the believers – those who maintain that living ethically is a necessity, come what may.

Outline of the book

The book is divided into two parts and is made up of ten chapters. Part A consists of chapters 1 to 5, while Part B consists of chapters 6 to 10.

Part A: Core human values: A framework for conduct, explains the ideas presented in this book. It discusses a practical and personally effective approach to ethics in the workplace, and explains a model of the person in terms of core human values. This model, along with a model of the different ways in which people see the world, forms the foundation for Part B, which looks at how to apply these concepts.

Chapter 1: The contemporary business environment looks at the pressures that are experienced generally by people working in organisations today. These pressures are generated by an environment of conflicting demands, where business imperatives commonly seem to be at loggerheads with ethical values and developmental goals. The chapter looks at why people act unethically, the psychological and sociological aspects. It asks why

Introduction

ethics is desirable and what possibility there is of fostering ethics in our organisational conduct.

Chapter 2: The scope of ethics tackles the problem of defining ethics, accommodating the ordinary senses in which we refer to ethics. It looks at three different "levels" of ethics – ethics as it relates to laws or other standards (codes of conduct and the like), ethics as it describes the impact of conduct on other people and on relationships, and ethics as it relates to deeper personal identity and integrity. The chapter describes the social process of articulating and formulating ethics in society and in organisations.

Chapter 3: Ethics as core human values looks at the concept of values as a basis for discussing ethics. It distinguishes values from emotions and attitudes. It presents a five-dimensional model of the person as the foundation for a common language for ethics, and a resolution of the problem of communicating and interacting with people who have different perceptions of the world. The core human values are based on the idea that a human being has five dimensions – cognition, emotion, valuing, spirit (energy) and identity (self, soul or psyche). Each dimension is linked with a core human value. This approach is contrasted with other approaches to framing social and organisational values.

The links between the model and the idea that there are three "levels" of ethics are explored. Some particular issues are addressed using the core human values framework: the relevance of job competency, and the disjunctions that occur between ethical rhetoric and actual conduct in the workplace. This raises the issue that different people often seem to hold differing sets of values, and perhaps we have to consider that people's values evolve through different stages.

Chapter 4: The development of personal ethics presents an account of how humans develop through different stages of understanding about ethics. It discusses different "stage" theories, such as the cognitive approach of Kohlberg and the needs approach of Maslow. The emotional side of moral development is examined, together with the development of attitudes in the moral area. This examination takes us into an exploration of how people make transitions from one perspective to another.

Chapter 5: The Values Evolution Model describes a model developed by Brian Hall and others to explain the differences in values that people exhibit. This model postulates that people's behaviour and perceptions of the world can be characterised as seven world views. The values that are associated with each world view are described. The five-dimensional model of the person and the corresponding core human values are looked at in the framework of values evolution.

The chapter describes how people develop and make transitions between stages, and the skills they acquire along the way. The possibility of having a shared understanding of ethics when people see the world differently is explored.

Part B: Workers and managers at work, explores how the concepts in Part A can be used in the workplace, both by managers and non-managerial employees. The chapters in this part look at roles, scripts and decision-making, and personal development of ethics using the core human values model.

Chapter 6: Working ethically in organisations looks at the social issues involved in applying an ethical approach in organisations, for both managers and non-managerial workers. It addresses ethical conduct in terms of the three levels of ethics – rules (right/wrong), relationships and personal identity. Two aspects of this investigation are: taking account of the effects of organisational roles and culture on behaviour, and the establishment and use of scripts to guide our conduct.

Chapter 7: Making decisions ethically focuses on the process of making decisions. Decision-making complements scripts as the method for dealing with work situations. The focus is placed on both the steps involved in decision-making and the criteria that need to be applied to make the process meaningful. The critical issue of conflicts in values is addressed.

Decision-making is seen to have a significant psychological dimension; it is not just cognitive. This leads to an examination of what we can call intuitive decision-making. This latter approach is reconciled with the former process model.

Chapter 8: Ethical leadership in organisations applies the core human values to organisational situations and dilemmas. The chapter recognises that much organisational behaviour is conditioned by culture rather than by explicit decision-making processes. It addresses the questions of organisational roles, power and influence, and the implications for managing change. It also discusses the wider issue of the purposes of organisations, and describes organisations using the framework of the Values Evolution Model.

Introduction

The question of whether it is possible to talk about the "ethical organisation" is addressed. The chapter provides some comments on the challenge of championing ethics in organisations, and characterises leadership using the core human values.

Chapter 9: Personal growth and development provides an action plan for assessing one's own progress and fostering personal growth and development. It offers strategies for working on ethics, considering it as the key to personal excellence, effectiveness and integrity. The question of beliefs – their origin, impact and evolution – is addressed. The chapter includes discussion of issues such as the exercise of judgement, incorporating the core human values into one's working life, and using the Values Evolution Model .

Chapter 10: Coda: present perfect returns to the question of the relationship between ethics and success, broached at the beginning of the book. This issue lies at the heart of ethics; it is often a haggling point among philosophers and just as often among people in business, whether they are CEOs or humble employees.

The chapter also explores the issue of personal style and seeks to clarify the distinctions between style and human values. It also considers how we can foster our personal development of ethics and overcome discouragement.

PART A Core human values: a framework for conduct

Part A presents the ideas that form the foundation of this book. It offers an approach to ethics in the workplace that takes account of all aspects of the person and the organisational context. The core human values are presented as a way of understanding the complex and pressured environment of organisational life, and of finding a way of working with integrity. This model is complemented by an explanation of the different ways in which people see the world – their world views – and how these world views evolve.

1

The contemporary business environment

The spate of huge corporate collapses that occurred in the first years of the 21st century has had a significant impact on the current business environment, whether in Australia, the USA, the UK or elsewhere. None of these collapses was a natural disaster. All of them were precipitated by the conduct of their own executives, conduct that was variously deceitful, cavalier, deluded, greedy and self-serving.

The corporate collapses in Australia included HIH insurances, One.Tel (heralded as a new age communications technology venture) and Ansett (the long-time national airline icon), all of which collapsed within six months of each other in 2001. Around the same time, these disasters were mirrored in the USA by its own corporate meltdown – Enron (the stodgy utility company that had seemed to transform itself into a darling of financial dealings) and WorldCom (a would-be marvel of the internet era).

The combined losses from these collapses have been measured in the tens of billions. While they did not precipitate a wider economic collapse, they certainly raised the alarm about the risks faced by investors, consumers and employees due to unethical conduct by executives. The losses have been significant enough for societies and their governments to call for explanations and accountability, and for the heads of the culprits.

The Ansett collapse prompted government intervention. A levy was imposed on all airline tickets sold, to create funds to pay the accrued entitlements of Ansett employees. One.Tel's collapse prompted an inquiry into the actions of its directors, particularly in the light of the fact that two executives were each paid $AU7.5 million as a bonus in a year when the company lost $AU291 million, and this occurred just eight months before the company's collapse.

The HIH debacle, to the extent of $AU5 billion, was the largest corporate collapse in Australian history. It led to a Royal Commission, which produced a report that was damning of the key players. Some of these key players were subsequently committed for trial on charges of misleading investors and boards of governance. Some executives, such as Rodney Adler and Ray Williams, were found guilty and given prison sentences.

The call for compliance

Unsurprisingly, in the wake of these multiple disasters there was a public outcry about the failure of compliance measures to prevent or even, it seems, to notice what was happening. Auditors and boards of management both came in for heavy criticism. In the USA, Arthur Andersens, which had audited the books for Enron, itself spectacularly crashed out of existence. It had been one of the five largest accounting firms in the world.

Critics were quick to observe that Andersens had also provided consulting services to Enron, and that the value of these services far outweighed the revenue from its auditing services. In retrospect, the temptations of this arrangement were suddenly very clear.

The responses of regulatory bodies and governments have been predictable enough. In the USA and in Australia, governments revisited corporate laws to try and ensure that directors fulfil their fiduciary duties to stakeholders, act competently, and receive proper information on which to base their decisions. The answer, it would seem from these actions, lies in heavier compliance requirements on companies.

Despite this, the actions of governments and regulatory bodies made it just as clear that laws alone will not prevent such situations from occurring again, as proved to be true in late 2008 when banking collapses began to occur in the USA as an outcome of dubious lending practices. As in 2001, the collapses of these corporations and banking institutions occurred as the end point of entrenched patterns of cavalier, self-serving and underhand behaviour on the part of their leaders. The slide of their corporations into ruin was a drawn-out affair, and it seems that it is only after the event that the law can act, bringing charges against executives for criminal offences. This eventuality also demonstrates that laws already existed which defined and prohibited their unethical conduct.

The implication is that we need to focus on the human values of people in organisations. The law will always do what it can, but it is a crude instrument. It is difficult for governments to achieve a balance of regulation such that compliance will ensure protection of stakeholders without unduly hampering wealth-generating activities.

Beyond the headlines

The huge losses involved in these high-profile corporate collapses have made those companies the subject of the headlines. But no one would argue that it was only these companies which have degraded our sense of ethics. Ethical discomfort is not confined to a few collapsed corporations. It is a part of everyday experience for many people in business and in the workplace.

What makes this reality all the more poignant is that many employees feel pressured into acting against their own personal ethical judgement. In one study carried out by the Josephson Institute (http://josephsoninstitute.org) on this topic, 50% of workers reported that they had done something unethical at work, and 30% of salespeople had lied to win business.

Human resource (HR) managers are another group whose views about ethics have been examined. In a survey of Australian HR managers carried out by the author (Martin, 1997), 66% reported that there was a moderate to very great need to address the problem of employees cheating on the company, while 64% felt that there was a moderate to very great need to address the problem of the company cheating on customers, employees and others.

When asked to name particular ethical issues which had been a concern in their organisation, over 70% of respondents named one or more issues. These findings suggest that managers are indeed aware that ethical issues exist in their organisations.

Another perspective is what employees say about their fellow workers. The US-based Ethics Resource Center (www.ethics.org) conducts periodic surveys of employees' views of ethics. The 2009 National Business Ethics

Survey found that 49% of employees had observed unethical conduct by other employees in the previous 12 months. The types of misconduct most frequently observed were:

- company resource abuse (23%)
- abusive or intimidating behaviour (22%)
- lying to employees (19%)
- email and internet abuse (18%).

The 2009 report (p 41) concluded that employees' experience of ethics in the workplace had improved over the previous 12 months. But looking back over 15 years of its surveys, it commented, "We are experiencing an ethics bubble. The positive results of this study are likely to be temporary. We are beginning to see an important connection between workplace ethics and the larger economic and business cycle: when times are tough, ethics improve. When business thrives and regulatory intervention remains at status quo, ethics erode."

An Australian survey by KPMG in 1999 (Lagan, 2000) ranked the top ethical issues as identified by managers and by workers. For managers, the top issues were:

1. Conflict of interest
2. Unauthorised use of company assets
3. Conducting personal business during working hours
4. Falsifying organisational records
5. Disclosure of confidential information
6. Sexual harassment.

For workers, the top ethical issues were:

1. Personal use of corporate assets
2. Falsifying sick leave or absenteeism
3. Conducting personal business during working hours
4. Sexual harassment
5. Disclosure of confidential information
6. Conflicts of interest.

Most ethical issues are confined to the workplace; they do not result in legal action. But an examination of legal cases in any area of business or employment law demonstrates the ongoing reality of unethical behaviour on the part of companies, managers and workers. To take a quick scan across this terrain, consider the following examples:

- a car salesman lying to a customer about the history of a vehicle – how many previous owners it had had, how many kilometres it had travelled, and the locality where it had been used;
- several businesses in the same industry holding secret meetings to make an agreement to fix the price of their goods at certain levels;
- a company relocating a manager to another office fifty kilometres away as a means of forcing him to resign;
- a job applicant being assured that the position he is applying for is permanent, but then being made redundant by the company six months later;
- a company having an established practice of employing workers as trainees and then terminating them when the training subsidy runs out;
- a company attempting to boost its end-of-year sales figures by hiring teleworkers who met their targets by sending out unsolicited goods to customers (much of which was returned in the new year).

This list merely indicates the scope and reach of unethical conduct in business. Every organisational and business stakeholder may be affected by stratagems such as these, or be pressured to participate in them – workers, managers, suppliers, customers and clients, unions, environmental groups, government departments, competitors. The list of unethical possibilities extends even further when we consider workplace safety and discrimination. Laws and regulatory bodies exist to monitor and enforce occupational health and safety, equal employment opportunity and freedom from workplace harassment.

In each case, the people involved are exercising choices, and these choices negate or undermine particular human values. The defences commonly offered are to characterise the action as a technical infraction against a legal proscription, to claim that business survival gave them no choice, or to maintain that other companies do the same sorts of things.

Mapping the ethical landscape

This quick scan of examples of ethical issues in the workplace indicates the range of areas that may be affected by ethical concerns. Every context in organisational life tends to have its ethical "hot spots". If we are to develop an ethical perspective that can be applied consistently across the extent of the organisational landscape, then it is helpful to understand the variety of situations that can throw up ethical questions.

Ethical questions tend to emerge out of communities of interest. These might be particular industries, sectors, occupations, managerial levels or stakeholder groups. Each of these communities of interest is described briefly below.

Industries. We can observe that particular industries tend to generate ethical issues that are peculiar to their context. For example, the mining industry faces a host of environmental issues – should companies be allowed to mine uranium? Should they be allowed to mine on aboriginal lands? What measures should they take to prevent or minimise long-term damage to the locality?

Other industries raise different kinds of issues. For retailers, advertising and promotional practices are ethical sensitive spots. For energy companies, their attitude towards sources of energy that are more conservative of non-renewable resources is a testing issue.

Sectors. The demands of the commercial sector raise different ethical issues to the public sector. The commercial sector may be asked to justify its level of profits, or pressured to demonstrate corporate social responsibility in a variety of ways.

The public sector may be subject to pressures because of how it decides to allocate its scarce resources. How much money should public transport systems devote to safety? How should hospitals decide where to locate their emergency facilities? In many ways, the not-for-profit sector faces similar issues to the public sector, but with a different environment and different sets of relationships to deal with.

Occupations. Similarly, different occupations face different critical issues. Construction workers and engineers must make sure that the safety of workers and the public is protected adequately. Doctors must exercise care in their diagnoses. News reporters and editors must take care not to misrepresent situations or show bias in their reporting. The existence of codes of ethics for different occupations and professions illustrates the different tensions they face.

Managerial level. Ethical issues also differ depending on where the person is located in the hierarchy of organisational responsibility. The knowledge and power, and the corresponding obligations of workers are narrower than those of higher-level managers.

Relationships between organisational stakeholders. Another way of mapping ethical territory is by looking at all the stakeholders connected with an organisation and the kinds of relationships they have with the organisation. To begin with, it is useful to consider the company itself as an entity separate from the people involved. As such, it has relationships with its own managers and workers, and with external parties.

A list of the key stakeholders might then include:

- managers
- non-managerial workers
- external contractors
- suppliers
- customers and clients
- regulatory bodies
- unions and other collectives such as environmental lobby groups.

As a further mapping exercise, one could then examine the kinds of ethical issues that commonly arise in each of these relationships. The fact that the business environment is constantly changing adds to the complexity of the issues to be identified. The kinds of change factors that are commonly cited include:

- rapid technological change, and its multiple effects on work roles and customer relationships;
- demographic change, as birth rates decline, the workforce matures in age, and ethnic diversity increases;
- organisational changes such as mergers, acquisitions and restructures and consequential changes to worker-manager relationships;
- changes in regulatory requirements in a wide range of compliance areas.

Having surveyed the range of contexts for workplace ethics and suggested the kinds of ethical issues that can arise in each case, we should remind ourselves that ethics is not a facet of particular kinds of situations. It is about applying a values perspective to *any* situation. However, if we are to develop a robust perspective on ethics, we need to have some idea of the kinds of situations we may need to address.

Frustration over ethics

The 2009 National Business Ethics Survey by the Ethics Resource Center found that 63% of employees reported acts of misconduct they had observed. In earlier surveys, the reasons employees gave for not reporting misconduct were primarily because they believed no action would be taken and because they feared that their identity would not be kept confidential.

In the 2009 survey, 15% of employees who reported misconduct perceived that they were retaliated against. The most common forms of retaliation were:

- other employees gave you the cold shoulder (62%)
- your supervisor of management excluded you from decisions and work activity (60%)
- you were verbally abused by your supervisor or someone else in management (55%)
- you almost lost your job (48%).

In one of the more positive findings, only 8% of employees felt pressured by their employer to commit misconduct. This percentage has declined steadily in recent years (from 14% in 2000). A strong correlation was found between perceived pressure to act unethically and the reported incidence of misconduct.

This survey reinforces the view that ethical challenges are widespread in workplaces, and are not just confined to the companies which came to our attention because they collapsed in spectacular fashion. The desire for ethical workplaces is widely shared. The problem is that the desire for ethics is frequently frustrated by the belief that it is not possible to improve matters.

One of the most common expressions of frustration is the view that it would only be possible if everyone adopted ethical practice together.

Managers argue that they have to cut ethical corners because "everyone else does, and we have to be able to compete". The problem this generates is that it forces regulators to move in and prescribe what can and cannot be done, introducing a regime of monitoring and penalties. The attendant costs and intrusions then become a source of complaint by companies.

Understanding unethical behaviour

Companies and their managers tend to defend their unethical conduct, when it is unveiled, on the basis that they have to cut corners in order to remain competitive. But this defence bears closer examination. For one thing, there are many varieties and gradations of unethical behaviour. In the case of many of the larger corporate collapses, the behaviour of senior executives appears to have been particularly egregious.

To understand unethical behaviour, we have to consider the motivations of the persons involved and the conditions under which they make their decisions. Five types of motivations can be identified (Frederick, Post & Davis, 1992; Walton, 1988):

1. **Selfishness.** The person is acting to maximise their personal interests, and other people are used to further this end. An example is the Australian senior executive (already well-remunerated) who diverted over $3 million of company funds to carry out renovations on his own house.

2. **Exclusive focus on company profits.** This person sacrifices honesty and other ethical principles in order to maximise the company's bottom line. It may result in the erosion of safety standards or the quality of products and services, or the exploitation of workers.

3. **Power.** This person, usually a manager, enjoys dominating others. Respect and compassion for others is minimal.

4. **Disregard for other cultures.** This person is not so much a brutal wielder of power. Rather, he/she is oblivious to the differences of others, and lacking in empathy.

5. **Tyrannised by trivia.** Again, this is more a sin of omission than a sin of commission. The person (usually a manager) is overwhelmed by the multitude of daily situations that present themselves for resolution. In this welter of little decisions, the big ethical issues are not considered properly and not handled well.

To this brief perspective on the reasons for unethical behaviour we should also add – if managers do not act to clarify and modify their values, their motivations tend to slide, over time, towards greater harshness and selfishness. Manager who are tyrannised by trivia will generally gravitate towards a fixation on power or bottom line profits in order to cope with their feelings of helplessness.

What has been described here is a psychological perspective. This needs to be complemented by the sociological viewpoint. Managers and workers are not only influenced by their own internal feelings and concepts, they are also influenced by the existing group norms and culture in their organisation.

Social influences on ethics

Probably the most dramatic illustrations of the influence of other people on a person's behaviour are the two series of experiments carried out by Solomon Asch in the 1950s and Stanley Milgram in the 1960s (see Myers, 2001). In these experiments, the behaviour of the subject was shown to be malleable in a social situation, where the influence of an authority figure or a social group operated, to a disturbing extent.

In Asch's experiments, the subject participated in a simple perceptual test, eg which of these three lines is the longest? When the subject was alone, the responses were invariably correct. Then Asch placed the subject in a group of seven. All of the other people had been coached to give incorrect responses.

After the first few responses, the group unanimously selected the same, incorrect answers. The effect was that many subjects went along with the group response. Overall, this occurred in 37% of the incorrect responses. Asch performed this experiment hundreds of times. His conclusion was, "It raises questions about our ways of education and about the values that guide our conduct".

Asch's experiments did not involve any wrongdoing by participants. Milgram's experiments, however, went further than Asch's. Milgram set up a situation where the subjects were told they were to teach pairs of words to a learner, and the goal of the experiment was to assess the value of punishment in learning.

The subject (the supposed teacher) was told that the learner would receive an electric shock each time they were wrong, and the voltage would increase by 15 volts each time. The learner was strapped into a chair on the other side of a glass panel and attached to the electrical apparatus, and the teacher had the controls of the apparatus. In fact, the apparatus was bogus, and the learner was coached by Milgram to pretend to be receiving the shocks. As the strength of the supposed shocks increased, the learner protested more, ending in screams of agony.

What did subjects do? The majority followed orders. As the learner made mistakes, they increased the voltage on the controls and administered the punishment. If the subject expressed a desire to cease the experiment, the researcher told them it was essential for the experiment to continue. In 63% of cases, the subjects continued up the maximum of 450 volts, a level which would not simply cause extreme pain, it would kill most recipients.

This series of experiments raises similar issues to Asch's, but in a much more disturbing way. It shows a readiness to suspend one's own moral sensibilities about causing harm to another person in the face of an authority figure's instructions. The experiments caused a huge public controversy about the level of moral independence of people generally. (As a side issue, there were also questions raised about the ethics of the experiments themselves, with Milgram defending what he had done.)

The question of the effect of social contexts on ethical practice is explored later in the book. The message at this point is that we need to include consideration of the effect of social contexts, group norms and authority and leadership if we are to understand ethical and unethical behaviour adequately. It is not sufficient to look only at individual ethical beliefs and reasoning.

This message has been recognised in different forums. One example is from the early days of the New South Wales government agency, the Independent Commission Against Corruption, in the 1980s. This Commission explores allegations of corruption in public life and public sector agencies. In the conclusion of one of its first investigations it asserted that leaders should be held accountable, not just for personal acts of corruption, but also for their part in creating "an organisational climate that is conducive to corruption". With Milgram's experiments in mind, this conclusion recognises the importance of the part that leaders play in steering organisational conduct towards virtue or vice.

The rewards of leaders

A focus on the role of leaders brings attention to the rewards they receive for their efforts. Mention was made earlier of the generosity of bonuses received by executives at One.Tel while it was careering towards collapse. A consideration of ethics would not be complete without a discussion of the rewards that managers and workers receive, and particularly, the relativities between top managers and operational-level workers.

This question is not about overtly illegal conduct. It is about the attitudes and guidelines that are adopted by senior managers and boards of governance, and how they reflect on values of fairness and social justice. This question is worthy of consideration for two reasons:

1. Over the last 25 years, the average level of CEO remuneration has increased enormously over their lowest level average workers' pay. Remuneration levels are heading in the direction of ever greater disparity.

2. Despite the rhetoric of "pay for performance", a number of studies from the 1990s onwards have found little or no correspondence between movements in company profits or share price on the one hand, and movements in CEO remuneration on the other.

US statistics from the early 1990s (Woldring, 1996) show that the differential between the average remuneration of the CEO of a large corporation and the average wage of workers was 157 : 1. Australian statistics from the same period show the differential to have been around 13 : 1. Since then, the differential has continued to climb in both countries.

With regard to the link between performance and pay, a study (ACTU, 2003) of Australian CEOs' remuneration for the top 100 companies found that there was no correlation at all between movements in profits and movements in their pay. This is a dramatic and disturbing finding, which makes a mockery of the rhetoric of performance and suggests that remuneration levels are purely the product of power and boardroom camaraderie.

Reticence to discuss ethics

Another factor in the contemporary business environment as it impacts on ethics is the phenomenon of managers' reluctance to discuss ethics. This reluctance often extends to workers as well. Apart from the infrequent times when the public fulminates against the leaders responsible for an

Enron or HIH, managers are generally unwilling to talk about ethics openly. Their comments are generally confined to a defensive protestation about the innocence of their own company.

Many companies have now produced a code of ethics. In her book, *Value Shift* (2003), Lynn Sharp Paine reports that an estimated 80% to 90% of America's large and midsize corporations have adopted written ethics guidelines. This sounds positive, but it often seems that the code is primarily a way of fending off discussion of ethical issues rather than a way of facilitating and guiding such discussions.

One insight into this phenomenon is the findings of a survey of members of the Australian Human Resources Institute (see Martin & Woldring, 2001). The survey was not about ethics. Its focus was on the issues which they saw developing in their profession. However, given that in the HR survey cited earlier, most managers identified that ethical issues were a concern, it could have been expected that ethics would surface in the AHRI survey.

Despite the number of responses (2,795 respondents), the issue of ethics was not mentioned at all. Taken together, what the two surveys suggest is that managers do not readily identify ethics as an issue, although if the question is put as an ethical one then they can recognise it as such.

There are many reasons why managers do not identify ethics as a management issue. These reasons may not be articulated – they are more in the nature of unspoken assumptions, but they explain the lack of discussion nonetheless. Two American writers, Bird and Waters (1994), have examined this phenomenon, describing it as the "moral muteness" of managers.

The reasons for this muteness are based on four types of beliefs or rationalisations about ethics:

1. **Ethics is simple, and everyone can be assumed to adhere to it.** Hence there is nothing to discuss. Unethical conduct is an exception, and the culprits are usually caught by the law or punished through public exposure and outrage.
2. **Ethics is irrelevant.** The goal of profit or organisational effectiveness is paramount, and apart from legal requirements and the need to maintain a good public image, anything goes.

3. **Ethics is too difficult to discuss.** Everyone has their personal view on ethics, and to start discussing it would be to waste time on a futile task, trying to reconcile all these views. Better to let it lie and get on with the job.
4. **Ethics is nice but impractical.** This is another slant on the above views. It maintains that we should be ethical in the workplace, but the truth is that many business people are not. So, you would not be competitive in the marketplace if you tried to apply "pure" ethical standards.

Comfort in compliance

Recent years have seen overriding emphasis in business given to the need to be competitive and to produce ever-increasing profits. This drive has been fuelled by the short-term results focus of the stock market. But the spate of corporate collapses around 2001 and the wider global financial crisis that erupted in 2008 have shown how this unbridled management mentality can spiral out of control, jettisoning any sense of prudence, morality or concern for people.

A renewed concern for ethical standards has highlighted the importance of compliance measures in organisations. As a consequence, compliance training is being heralded as the next issue to rise to the top of the executive agenda. Compliance is applicable across a wide range of corporate and employee conduct. Organisations are subject to laws and regulation in areas as diverse as trade practices, accounting standards, occupational health and safety, environmental standards, equal employment opportunity, sexual harassment, industrial relations and privacy, as well as legislation that affects their specific industry, like financial services.

Along with this heightened awareness of compliance, some senior executives and business observers are coming around to the view that compliance measures must be accompanied by efforts to foster and enhance the organisation's ethics. According to this perspective, just focusing on compliance can create a mindset where employees ask, "what is the least I have to do to comply?" This approach can have two results:

- organisations are still likely to make decisions that fall foul of the law, because they misjudged the situation, and

- organisations are still likely to act unethically, even when they manage to stay on the right side of the law.

The appropriate metaphor for the compliance approach is the archer who fails to reach the target because he aims too low. The message is, if you want employees to always abide by the law, you have to aim higher – employees have to actually seek to do the right thing.

One of the great ironies of Enron's collapse was that it had a large and well-funded compliance department: 150 staff and $US30 million a year as a budget. Professor Fred Talbott of Vanderbilt University's Owen School of Business Management in Nashville, has said (quoted in the *Toledo Blade*, 15 February, 2002) that until after 2001, compliance officers in companies had a low-key role, mainly check-listing things internally. In the wake of Enron, their role "was going to be the key to companies retaining the all-important trust of investors".

Talbot said that if companies are to get the trust of shareholders or employees, "they have to be open, above-board, transparent and easy to understand". These qualities shift organisations into the arena of the ethical. The inference is clear: if organisations do not cultivate ethical values such as transparency and integrity, they will be regarded as investment risks.

Employees believe in ethics

It might be expected that employees are cynical about the part that ethics plays in contemporary organisational life, but a survey of Australian employees has found very strongly otherwise. The 2009 Annual Business and Professions Study conducted by the St James Ethics Centre in Sydney found that 89% of employees surveyed (with a sample size of over 15,000) believe that their organisation has an ethical obligation to act with integrity towards the individuals the organisation serves. This is an overwhelming majority.

An even higher percentage (93%) believe that organisations should make a formal commitment to ethics, and act ethically even if it occasionally harms their profits. Three-quarters of respondents believe that all organisations should have a code of ethics, and should also measure and report on their performance in adhering to it.

This leaves the question of whether employees believe their organisations are actually operating ethically. The survey found that 82% of respondents felt that their personal code of ethics for their working life is very well aligned with their organisation's code of ethics. At the same time, 86% reported that they have a personal code of ethics to which they adhere in their working life, even if it means risking their job.

This is not to say that employees perceive their situation as being ideal ethically. Over one-quarter (27%) believe their employer is not doing enough to promote ethical behaviour in the organisations, and 25% regularly experience people behaving unethically towards one another in their organisation. Further, 22% believe that other employees would not adhere to the code of ethics if they thought that profits or funding would be harmed.

Another significant finding from the survey is that 80% said they are willing to put in extra effort at work if they know that their organisation is run ethically. Conversely, 77% said they would definitely leave their organisation if it acted in a way that contradicted their core principles.

Acknowledging the role of ethics

This chapter has been intended as an introduction to the general features of the contemporary business environment, from the perspective of how these features impact on ethical practices and ethical discourse. Ethics has been catapulted back into the limelight by the global financial crisis, as it was in 2001 by a succession of large-scale corporate collapses. There have been previous times when spectacular ethical misadventures in the business world have captured society's attention, but the recent dramas have afforded us again a new opportunity to reflect on the part that ethics plays in executives' and employees' exercise of corporate roles.

The experience of pressure to act unethically continues to be a commonly shared feeling of workers and managers. The pressure is on for higher performance and productivity, driven by the spectre of competition. The continuing advance of globalisation, assisted by rapidly evolving computer and communications technologies, feeds the perception and mythology of competition as well as its reality.

In the wake of the global financial crisis, the 2009 Ethics Resource Center survey found that the US recession has taken its toll on ethics in American business. Asked about the effects of the recession, about one-quarter (22%) agreed that "the recession has negatively impacted the ethical culture within my company." And 10% said that "to stay in business during the recession, my company has lowered its ethical standards."

It would be wrong, however, to imply that the workforce is comprised entirely of people who are operating wholly at a desperate, survival level. Pressures exist and are widespread, yet workers continue to aspire to do right, to work competently and to develop their talents.

The contemporary business environment may be difficult for many managers and workers. The scale and rapidity of change now may be greater than anyone has experienced in their lifetime, with all the fears and uncertainties that that generates. However, what is important in terms of ethics is that the desire to work ethically and with integrity remains strong across the workforce. The following chapters will explore how we can make this quest clearer and pursue it with more assurance and vigour.

2

The scope of ethics

So far we have taken a casual approach to the meaning of "ethics". We have been content to imply a definition of ethics by extension, that is, by presenting a range of situations where people apply the word. We have, however, noted that these uses seem exceedingly broad, and unless we refine our meaning we might easily descend into confusion. Hence, the object of this chapter is to work on defining and describing ethics in a way that clarifies and bounds the concept but still resonates with how we ordinarily use the term.

In the previous chapter we presented some examples of unethical behaviour or, at least, behaviour that most people would agree is unethical. To commence the task of moving from examples to a description of ethics, we offer the summary in Table 2.1 (Martin, 1998). The table could be the result of your own brainstorming, if you had sat down and asked: what would a business acting ethically do and what would it not do?

Table 2.1: Qualities of an ethical business

A business acting ethically would not…..	A business acting ethically would…..
lie to or deceive customers or the public subject customers, employees or the public to undue risk of harm – physically, financially, emotionally or in any other way exploit customers or employees be greedy damage the environment waste natural resources	obey the law adhere to contractual obligations be fair, respectful and humane to employees, customers and suppliers be socially and environmentally responsible actively establish safety systems and promote a safety culture observe and respect social and cultural norms produce goods or supply services that meet legitimate human needs support and develop employees' skills and well-being

The list in Table 2.1 gives us a canvas to map, so that we can understand ethics in terms of some core principles and features. If the major ethical issues that attach to organisational actions are covered by the above list, then we can begin to make some observations about ethics. Some of these observations will no doubt be obvious, but they will set some parameters for our understanding of what ethics is. Our observations will also enable us to distinguish between different kinds of judgements that we lump together as "ethics" in our day-to-day conversations.

The first observation that might be made is that all of the qualities in Table 2.1 concern relationships. They concern relationships within the organisation (between employees and managers) and relationships the organisation has with external parties – customers, suppliers, external contractors, shareholders/owners, competitors, trade unions, customer advocacy groups, environmental lobby groups, government agencies, regulators, financiers, the media and industry associations.

The question we need to ask, then, is how do relationships enter into a definition of ethics? First of all, we need to recognise that the list of qualities in Table 2.1 makes several assumptions. It assumes and accepts:

- that organisations are sanctioned as entities in society, and they serve a variety of acceptable purposes (from charitable works to government functions to commercial supply of legitimate goods and services);
- the economic basis of organisations, that is, they are funded in some legitimate (legal) way to fulfil their purpose and continue to exist, eg through sales, donations, fees or taxes.

What we want to propose here is that ethics is best described as comprising three levels of understanding (see Figure 2.1):

1. the law,
2. quality of relationships, and
3. identity.

The levels refer to an increasing understanding of ethics and an increasing commitment to high ethics in one's actions. We are discussing organisations at the moment, but this clearly also applies to individual persons and their actions as well. We recognise that some people will have difficulties with the issue of how we can make judgements about the actions of organisations (ie entities which are not persons in themselves), and we will address this later.

Figure 2.1: Three Levels of Ethics

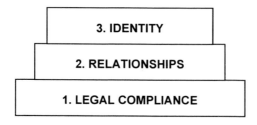

Ethics as legal compliance

For an organisation which seeks to be ethical, complying with the law is a threshold issue – as a minimum, it will comply with the laws and regulations that apply to it. If we refer back to the list of actions of ethical organisations in Table 2.1, we can see that acting lawfully relates directly to several of the items on the list. The list serves to explain a number of different ways in which an organisation will show that it seeks to comply with the law.

Laws and regulations

The organisation will observe the laws and regulations that apply to it, including taxation laws, corporate reporting requirements, local government zoning regulations (eg noise at night time) and privacy laws.

Contracts

The organisation will adhere to the obligations it has entered into contractually with other parties. For example, it will fulfil the terms of contracts with suppliers for the purchase of goods, and pay its accounts promptly. It will observe contracts with its own employees, for example, by not expecting them to work long hours of unpaid overtime.

Trade practices

The organisation's goods will not be of sub-standard or unsafe quality, and it will not make false representations in its advertising. It will not use pressure tactics to sell goods or misuse its power over customers or the market.

Safety

The organisation will observe legal requirements for occupational health and safety in the workplace.

Environment

The organisation will not contravene environmental laws. This would include laws relating to pollution, disposal of waste products and handling of hazardous substances.

Equality in employment

The organisation will have systems and policies in place to ensure that discrimination and harassment do not occur in the workplace, and that any instances of such behaviour on the part of employees are dealt with so that the principles of equal employment legislation are upheld.

General

Generally, we would expect a legally compliant organisation to follow proper procedures in fulfilling its legal obligations, to demonstrate this through appropriate mechanisms, including training and information, and to cooperate in investigations into any alleged violations of laws.

While we say that legal compliance is a threshold ethics issue – it is concerned with the minimum that an ethical company would do – we can readily see that organisations can approach compliance from a minimalist stance or from a commitment to fulfil the spirit of the law. The organisation that has scant respect for ethics will ask, what is the minimum we need to do to comply? Moreover, their purpose will be to minimise the risk of punishment, not to fulfil any higher purpose of the law.

Comparing what we have described here with the qualities in Table 2.1, we can conclude that acting lawfully covers some of what we mean by "ethics", but it is not sufficient to distinguish between organisations that see ethics in terms of minimal compliance with the law and organisations that have a much stronger commitment to ethics. "Being ethical " is not just about obeying the law.

Ethics as high-quality relationships

Organisations which have a higher commitment to be ethical will take a broad view of obeying the law rather than a minimalist view. But the legal perspective does not explain why this is so. To explain this distinction, we need to talk about their different attitude towards relationships. To return to the list in Table 2.1, organisations which are ethical will show the following qualities:

- They will be fair and humane to employees, customers and suppliers – they will not confine their consideration of these parties merely to what the law requires of them. They will demonstrate qualities of fairness and respect in all their actions and dealings;
- They will observe and respect social and cultural norms – in managing their own employees, in dealing with ethnic groups in

their own society, and in dealing with companies and markets in other countries;

- They will be honest in their dealings and their communications, internally and externally, even where the law does not impinge on their actions;

- Their pursuit of high-quality relationships will extend to a respect for the physical environment – minimising their negative impact on the environment, conserving resources and contributing positively to the environment where possible, above and beyond legal requirements;

- They will be considerate of the well-being of their employees and their security of employment, and they will remunerate their employees fairly and equitably.

This list of qualities seems to deal with the items in Table 2.1 more comprehensively. To distinguish organisations with a commitment to high-quality relationships from those which comply minimally with the law, we have to begin to use the language of human values. The qualities demonstrated by organisations driven by relationships include fairness, respect, consideration of others, awareness of diversity, and a sense of justice that goes beyond the law.

And yet, the qualities described here do not exhaust all of what the list in Table 2.1 tries to capture. That list describes qualities and purposes that seem to go further than fostering good relationships with others.

Ethics as realising deep identity

The indicators of another level of ethics – from our list in Table 2.1 – are:

- avoidance of greed;
- produce goods or supply services that meet social needs; and
- contribute to the development of employees.

What is it that these qualities suggest, over and above high-quality relationships? They suggest a greater, and more explicit, moral awareness by the organisation, an awareness of itself as an agent for good in society. In saying this of organisations, we maintain that the actions of an organisation are the outcome of the actions of the persons who are its managers and workers. There can be plenty of discussion around the issue of whether it is reasonable to be anthropomorphic about the actions of organisations, but in general conversation most people allow it, and we shall do so here.

We began by saying that to be ethical, an organisation had to at least be law-abiding. We then recognised a higher level of ethics, where the organisation is concerned to build high-quality relationships with its various stakeholders, based on human values such as fairness and respect. What we are saying now is that some organisations, whom we would want to distinguish as being most highly ethical, act as if they are pursuing high moral goals and they are bringing to realisation an identity as a positive social agent for good.

To be comprehensive, then, we need to have a definition of ethics that is broad enough to rope in all that we allude to in our ordinary use of the term. This would seem to embrace conduct that lies on a continuum from behaviour that complies with law through to behaviour that is highly aspirational and pursues positive social good.

Each of the higher levels subsumes the levels below it. We have already observed that the organisation which cultivates high-quality relationships will comply with the law in a stronger way than organisations who comply merely with the intention of avoiding risk. Likewise, the fact that an organisation pursues a moral identity will affect its relationships.

For example, an organisation which cultivates high-quality relationships will treat its employees well. It will ensure that the workplace climate is respectful, so that discrimination is unlikely to occur. What might be different about the organisation that is aware of a deeper sense of identity? One would expect that it has a broader view of employees' career development. It will not only ensure employees' maintenance of skills and employability, it will also recognise their need to develop and fulfil their talents and potential, and be imaginative in how it creates opportunities for this to occur.

Much more can be said about how organisations can be identified at different ethical levels, and this topic will be developed further in Chapter 8. The task at this point is to see where we have arrived in our quest to define ethics.

Defining ethics

At its most elementary level, ethics is about moral principles, which concern judgements about right and wrong, good and bad (or evil). A common dictionary definition of ethics is "the study of human moral values and conduct". The Macquarie Dictionary defines ethics as "a system of moral principles by which human actions and proposals may be judged good or bad or right or wrong".

We would like to offer a definition that is more descriptive of our common use of the term. The clues for such a definition lie in the roots of the two words "ethics" and "moral". The word "ethics" comes from the Greek, *ethika*, from *ethos*, meaning character or custom. The word "moral" comes from the Latin *mores*, meaning customs. Drawing on this ancestry and our previous discussion of what ethical organisations look like, we can argue that ethics has the following features:

- it is concerned about the *agreements that societies reach* about what is right and wrong (customs or norms);
- it is concerned with *the process of valuing actions* as right/wrong or good/bad, which is distinct from other types of opinions (like or dislike, aesthetically attractive or ugly) and also implies the ability to distinguish moral reasons from what other people think (social conformity);
- ethical actions *reflect back on what we think of persons* (or organisations) (character), which implies that people recognise themselves as moral agents who are responsible for their actions;
- it is concerned with *principles*, which are *universal* and which are more than a fixed, blind set of rules of behaviour, so it entails reasoning about behaviour and choices;
- moral or ethical behaviour is distinguished from selfish actions which are aimed at the person's own success, which is to say that ethics is about altruism, unselfishness or a *concern for the welfare of others*; and
- it is concerned with *how people act*, that is, it is not just of theoretical interest – it is a motivation for choices of action and conduct.

The discussion in the rest of this book recognises these six aspects of ethics and addresses the questions that each aspect raises. In the latter part of this chapter we will look at the first aspect – what is this process whereby societies reach agreements about ethics, and what issues does that process itself raise?

A working definition

There are, of course, hundreds of definitions of ethics that have been offered by writers on ethics. The following small selection gives a feeling for the ethical terrain that one experiences in organisations.

James Rachels (1993) emphasises the importance of reasoning in ethics: "Morality is, at the very least, the effort to guide one's conduct by reason, ie to do what there are the best reasons for doing, while giving equal weight to the best interests of each individual who will be affected by one's conduct."

Lawrence Hinman (1994) emphasises the social agreement aspect of ethics: "Morality amounts to guidelines that set the boundaries of acceptable behaviour – concerned with not harming others, paying the proper regard for others' well-being, and treating persons with respect."

Peter Singer offers a couple of definitions of ethics. The first emphasises the universality of the principles that underlie ethics: "Morality is concerned with rules, principles or ways of thinking that guide actions. It refers to values, rules, standards, or principles that should guide our decisions about what we ought to do."

Peter Singer's second definition points to the shift in focus from concern for self to concern for others that is central to ethics: "The notion of living according to ethical standards is tied up with the notion of defending the way one is living, of giving a reason for it, of justifying it. Ethics requires us to go beyond 'I' and 'you' to the universal law."

The Dalai Lama (1999) provides a definition of ethics that highlights the Buddhist perspective on the causes of human unhappiness: "Ethical acts are those which seek to foster the happiness of others and prevent their suffering."

Another definition that succinctly encompasses much of the six aspects of ethics identified above is given by Albert Schweitzer (1876–1965), a German theologian, medical missionary in Africa, and philosopher. His definition (quoted in Hill, 1976, p4) recognises the centrality of the valuing process in ethics, the shift of concern from self to others, the reflection of conduct on self-perception (character), and the role that both reasoning and social processes play in formulations of ethics.

Schweitzer's definition is presented here as a reasonable basis for describing what we are talking about when we use the term "ethics". We have added just one element to his formulation, a consideration for the natural world as well as other for people and society.

> **A working definition of ethics**
>
> In a general sense, ethics is the name we give to our concern for good behaviour. We feel an obligation to consider not only our own personal well-being, but also that of others, society as a whole and the natural world.

The first question we might ask about Schweitzer's definition of ethics is: does it accommodate the three levels of ethics we described earlier? Can we see in the definition that people and organisations might operate at the three different levels? Let us look at each of the levels.

Acting lawfully. In terms of Schweitzer's definition, a person or organisation that is sufficiently concerned about ethics to act lawfully can be said to have a "concern for good behaviour". We might also say they show consideration not only for their own survival and success, but in complying with the law they consider the well-being of society.

High-quality relationships. On Schweitzer's definition, a person or organisation that seeks good relationships with its stakeholders could be said to have a heightened concern for good behaviour. Their notion of good behaviour is that it gives strong consideration to the well-being of others and seeks to establish and sustain good relationships thereby. These people and organisations see the well-being of society as an extended web of mutually considerate relationships.

Deep identity. At this level of ethics, the aspect of Schweitzer's definition that comes to the fore is that the person or organisation "feels an obligation", not just to particular others with whom they interact, but to "society as a whole". The person or organisation holds a deep belief that this is the only way to operate and to be.

Underlying assumptions

At this point it would also help to note that the above features of ethics have been based on certain assumptions about people and how they deal with issues such as ethics. The most relevant assumptions are the assumptions of rationality, autonomy and responsibility. These assumptions underlie any discussion of ethics.

1. The assumption of **rationality** is the assumption that reasoning makes sense, that it is possible to follow a chain of reasoning through to a conclusion in a consistent and reliable way, and that this is linked to behaviour. This is a necessary assumption, even if one believes that the knowledge of right and wrong is immediate and intuitive, because people confess doubts about ethical issues and they often disagree with one another. Discourse about ethics is vitally concerned with these doubts and disagreements, and such discourse would not be possible without a shared language and agreement about the validity of reasoning processes.

2. The assumption of **autonomy** is also necessary. There would seem to be little point discussing ethics if one believed that people did not have any understanding of or control over their own actions. One might still have strong views about the power and influence of social systems over the individual, but there must nevertheless be room left for the free will of the individual to operate, or ethics becomes irrelevant.

3. Allied with the assumption of autonomy is the assumption of **responsibility**. This follows from the previous assumption, because it affirms that, having acted autonomously, persons can then be held accountable for their actions.

Motivations and ethics

One aspect that is inferred by the discussion of Schweitzer's definition of ethics is the importance of the role of motivation in ethics. Motivation is an aspect of ethics that can be troubling. This is especially so when it is the conduct of organisations that is in question, although individuals can suffer similar dilemmas.

Suppose a company donates large sums of money to a local community organisation. This would seem to be generous and laudable. But why does the organisation do this? Think of the possible reasons:

- The company receives a tax deduction as a result, which lowers the cost of the donation. There is also a benefit to the company in positive publicity, which assists its position in the market and contributes to its profitability.

- The company receives a tax deduction, but it has a regular pattern of donations to local causes, and it reviews its donations to ensure that its support goes to the areas of greatest social need.
- The company receives a tax deduction, but the real gain for the company is that a board member of the community organisation is influential with the local council, and the company's plans for future development will be treated favourably by the council.
- The money is used by the community organisation to build new facilities, so the community organisation is unlikely to notice or complain about the fact that the building site contains waste that the company dumped there illegally.

The point of these different scenarios is that companies may perform the same actions for a variety of reasons, and often for a whole complex of reasons that may be difficult to untangle. The company gives a donation. Is it being ethical?

One response to this question has to do with the purposes of commercial companies. Is it the business of companies to give away *any* of their profits to charitable causes? This is a position that has been argued heatedly since the 1970s. However, this question is peripheral to the question of motivations for actions, and it is taken up in Chapter 8 rather than here.

Can an organisation's action be ethical if the motivations for it are not all "pure"? We tend to think of ethical acts, particularly acts of generosity, as having to be driven by solely generous motives – with no thought of returns. In some of the scenarios painted in the example, the motivation was decidedly unethical – to use improper influence with the local council, and to seek to cover up its illegal, and probably unsafe, dumping of waste. In some of the other scenarios, the motivation could be described as strategic and astute, but hardly improper.

Let us consider the case where the company gains a tax deduction and a good reputation in the community. What is it that gives us reservations about the ethics of this company? We suggest that it is a transfer of concepts from the domain of personal ethics, the idea that "good works should be done in secret" as well as "without thought of return". As Jesus said in the Sermon on the Mount, "Be careful not to parade your good works before men to attract their notice" (Matthew 6:1).

This issue brings out some of the differences between how individuals and organisations have to be evaluated. There are two key factors to consider:

- It is not satisfactory for a company (let us assume a public company for the sake of this discussion) to give secret donations. To do so would mean that the money was not publicly accountable, meaning that it could just as easily be used for inappropriate purposes – funding terrorists or going into the pockets of the executives. Companies are obliged to be public in a way that individual persons are not.

- Managers of companies are obliged to be strategic in all that they do. Their job is to fulfil the strategic purposes of the company and to be aware of the possible effects of all their actions, including the making of donations. It would be naïve of them to give donations and not to think of the possible and likely effects of this for the company and in the community.

These two factors tell us that there are some inescapable differences in the ways that individuals and organisations operate, and we have to take account of this when judging the ethics of organisations. Let us accept that an organisation's donation has to be public, and it will also be the case that it receives a tax deduction for it, as a simple matter of law.

If we want to evaluate "how ethical" the company's action is, then we would need to compare its action with other companies rather than individual persons, we would need to consider its donation in terms of its capacity, and we would need to consider it in terms of the three levels of ethics we have described.

We should recognise that we need to exercise some caution in talking about "how ethical" a company is in the context of a discussion about donations to charity. What is clear from the list of qualities in Table 2.1 is that saying a company is ethical or unethical is an extremely broad concept. What we frequently intend to assert is that a company's action in a particular area – eg how it treats its employees, what representations it makes to customers about its products – is ethical or unethical.

Charitable donations are an aspect of that area called corporate social responsibility, and we should observe that it is possible for a company to give "generous" donations to charitable causes and yet be unethical in other aspects of its conduct, eg by having inferior levels of workplace safety. This point will be taken up in Chapter 8.

Applying our definition of ethics and the concept of three levels of ethics can help to explain how an assessment of an organisation's motivations affects our assessment of the ethics of its actions. To start with the idea that ethical actions concern good behaviour and the well-being of others, we can say that the donation assists a community cause and this is a good thing, leaving aside arguments about why the particular organisation was chosen.

We can also assume that the donation is voluntary and thus is above what is legally required of the organisation, that is, our minimum level of legal compliance. To assess the level of generosity we could resort to statistics about the ratio between the donation and company turnover or profits. An exercise of this kind was carried out in Australia in 2001 on a nation-wide basis as part of the Federal Government's Industry-Community Partnerships Program.

The initiative compiled figures on the level of corporate support for community causes. It concluded that it was difficult to be precise because support took many forms other than direct donations. However, one measure was that individual donations to community causes in Australia in 1997 amounted to $3 billion, and donations by businesses amounted to $2 billion (37% of the total). As a proportion of GDP, the combined individual and business donations constituted less than 1%.

It is therefore a question of how the donation evidences a company commitment to high-quality relationships in the community or how it reflects a conscious commitment to a role as a positive contributor to social good – our two higher levels of ethical conduct. This is where the issue of motivation becomes of interest.

To answer this question we can ask, what is it that reveals motivation? Taking one of the scenarios above, what fact or event would reveal that the company's donation was intended to influence the local council? It would be when the company's plans for development seemed to glide through council in an unusually smooth, silent and brisk manner. The point here is that motivations are not always evident until later.

If we had to try and establish that the donation was evidence of building good relationships rather than an untoward stratagem, then we would work on the basis that an organisation which does things properly or fairly will establish mechanisms that demonstrate it is open to verification. In this case, it may establish a committee which has representatives from the local community to determine needs and priorities and make decisions about donations.

Looking for motivations is important because motivations do demonstrate the level of ethics of an organisation's actions, even if the motivations are not immediately evident. Even where motivations are complex, nevertheless, organisational actions reflect a given complex of motives. They reflect a decision to follow one course of action rather than another, and motivations can be attributed to these courses of action.

Motivation is implied by all the ethical judgements we make about actions. For example, in Table 2.1 we say that an ethical company will be socially responsible. In saying this we imply that a company that acts in a socially responsible way, say, by donating money to a charitable cause, is intending to be socially responsible. The fact that a company may be using the donation for a nefarious purpose does not undermine the idea that ethical actions are related to ethical motivations. When we found out the true reason for the donation we would quickly re-evaluate our ethical assessment of the act.

The only real concern about the motivations of companies is that their generosity is generally inseparable from benefits that the company itself obtains, such as enhancement of its reputation. However, if the community is vigilant to the improper uses of donations and guards against that, there seems little problem. The generosity of the company is public, and it becomes accountable for its ongoing reputation as a supporter of community causes.

We can understand this in terms of the company building high-quality relationships. The donations broaden its stakeholder base to include charitable concerns, and relationships with other stakeholders are generally affected by extension. How does this work? A donation to a charity is a mark of respect shown towards more vulnerable people. If the company gives to a charity, then customers, clients and suppliers of that company expect the company to behave towards them in a similarly respectful and ethical way.

This connection is not always evident, and in fact there are manifold examples of disconnect or contrariness between the two, and some companies could even be said to trade on the fact that they contribute to charity. So, a customer or client might be tolerant of high prices where they might otherwise be stricter about demanding value for money.

This criticism is not new and is not denied here. What is asserted is the possibility of a virtuous cycle where the company's charitableness fosters its self-concept as a company that sustains high-quality relationships with its stakeholders and that contributes positively to social good. This self-concept then governs its employees' behaviour and company decisions. To the extent that a company achieves consistency between its charity on one hand and its business operations on the other, its employees and other stakeholders will generally show higher morale and commitment.

The social process of ethics

We recognised from Table 2.1 that some of these qualities were subject to different kinds of evaluations from a social perspective. Some qualities concerned laws, and therefore there is little scope for disagreement about qualities related to that criterion. But other qualities in the list left more room for disagreement.

There is more likelihood of disagreement, for example, about what constitutes being "socially and environmentally responsible" and about how much we should expect organisations to do in this area. Likewise, what does it mean for a company to be greedy? The banks in Australia are frequently accused of greed when they announce their annual profits, which routinely exceed a billion dollars for the major four banks. The banks argue that they have to compete with international banks, and if they do not perform at this level they are vulnerable to takeover.

Moreover, community judgements about what is ethical shift over time. What was environmentally acceptable in 1970 is in many cases unacceptable today, or even illegal. In Sydney it was known for many years that industrial companies along the banks of the Parramatta River ran their toxic wastes straight into the river. Public opinion eventually galvanised to the point where these practices were outlawed. Companies changed their environmental practices and/or moved, and the quality of the river water improved.

There are many other areas concerning human values where social consensus has shifted over time and laws have been passed to reflect the changes. Some of these are:

- occupational health and safety laws, where the evolution in laws can be traced back to the beginnings of large scale industrialisation in England in the early 1800s;
- equal employment opportunity laws, which were first enacted in Australia in the 1970s;
- more recently, and with the impetus of the advance of digital storage of information and the internet, laws have been passed relating to companies' treatment of individuals' privacy.

This section is thus concerned with the process whereby societies subject ethical issues to discussion, and with what happens as a result. In opening this topic for discussion we are acknowledging that the scope of ethics extends beyond philosophy. The discussion of ethics takes place in a social context, leading to social actions which include law-making and other social arrangements.

If this is so, then the scope of ethics includes consideration of psychology, particularly the role of emotions and motivation. As well, it includes consideration of social factors as examined in the fields of social psychology, sociology and organisational behaviour. We may remind ourselves that ethics is concerned with *how people act*, not just what our philosophical position might be on the nature of reality.

Figure 2.2 illustrates the three major fields which need to be explored if we are to make sense of ethical conduct in organisations – philosophy, psychology and sociology.

Figure 2.2: Making sense of ethical behaviour in organisations

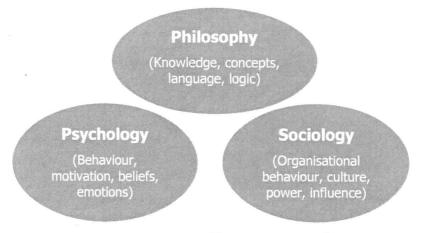

Ch. 2 | The scope of ethics

A description of the social process of establishing ethics has been given by Verne Henderson (1990). He sees it as a dynamic, ongoing process, as we have noted above. Figure 2.3 illustrates the process. The process begins at the centre. An issue, experience or event is like a stone falling into a pond, sending ripples outwards.

What happens as a result of social discourse falls into three zones:

Zone 1. When experiences and events occur, or social changes occur, they generate social debate. The events could be sudden and unanticipated, as the September 11 attacks in America were. They could be planned, as the Sydney Olympics generated similar discussions on the balance between security precautions and people's enjoyment of the Olympics. They could be the result of technological changes, such as developments in genetics and experiments in stem cell research.

In this zone, people are still feeling the direct impacts of the event and are yet to start to think about its ethical implications. But they are aware that the event does have ethical implications.

Figure 2.3: The social process of establishing ethics

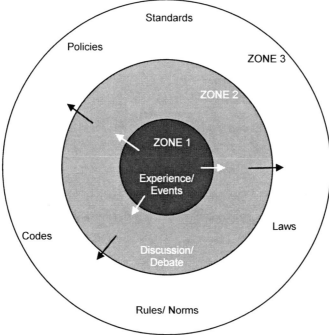

Zone 2. People discuss and debate the moral implications of the events or developments. This is the zone where alternative perceptions joust, and different ethical frameworks are applied. Proposals for a response are aired, and prominent individuals may be busy trying to persuade the populace to adopt a given stance. There is conflict between prevailing attitudes and those who challenge society to think about it differently.

There have been many instances of such shifts in attitudes in recent centuries (even given all the imperfections of the present) – how people have come to reject the slavery of black Africans in the USA, how it is no longer accepted that wives are the chattels of their husbands, how women in the workforce should earn equal pay for work of equivalent value, how people with disabilities should not be locked away from society.

In Zone 2, people are contending with alternative possibilities and wrestling with how to reconcile their current beliefs with new situations.

Zone 3. In many cases, people (societies, organisations) reach a consensus about the ethics involved in the novel event. At this stage their ethical judgements may be expressed in social mores and norms, or they may be enshrined in law, with penalties applied for transgressions. At organisational or industry levels, codes of practice may be devised as a voluntary measure to encourage adherence to agreed standards of corporate behaviour.

In Zone 3, new, shared perceptions about ethics or the application of ethics to new areas emerge. This can be like an uneasy truce until further experience allows people to trust that the new standard is workable. An example is the extension of equal pay to female teachers in New South Wales in the early 1960s. Critics at first cried that it would bankrupt the State. It was apparent after a while that this would not occur, and it was also generally accepted that the move had altered the teaching culture for the better.

Debating ethics and the law

One aspect of the social process of establishing ethics bears closer scrutiny. When events and social change precipitate discussion of the ethics involved, there are actually two related debates taking place. One debate concerns whether certain actions and practices are ethical, and the other is whether laws should be passed to enforce or prohibit certain conduct.

Figure 2.4 shows the four possible outcomes of these linked debates.

Figure 2.4: Two dimensions of social debates on ethics

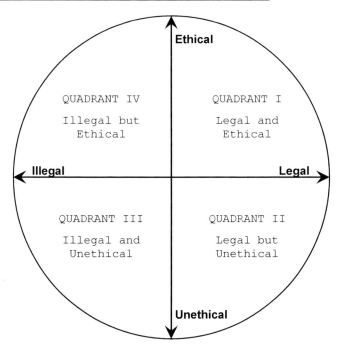

In a simple world, all actions would lie in either Quadrant I or Quadrant III – they would be either ethical and legal, or unethical and illegal. However, this is not the case for three reasons:

- Firstly, the law is a crude instrument and is not subtle enough to capture all of the situations that it would need to cover to ensure that all unethical conduct was proscribed. And if it did manage to achieve this goal, it would be impossible to police.

- Secondly, we live in a society that is ideologically committed to freedom, so governments are loathe to pass laws to constrain behaviour unless there is a strong demand from the public to do so. This attitude extends to corporate life as much as personal conduct, in accordance with the ideology of capitalism.

- Thirdly, the intent of law is generally to set a minimum standard for behaviour. That is, it is concerned with compliance rather than prescribing higher aspirations for people.

As a result, we are left with conduct that inconveniently falls into Quadrant II (ethical but illegal) or Quadrant IV (unethical but legal). It is perhaps Quadrant IV conduct that presents the most dilemmas for managers and workers in organisations. Quadrant II situations probably do not arise as often.

An example of an ethical but illegal action in the personal sphere is a driver breaking the speed limit while they are taking a critically injured person to hospital. A business example might be a bus driver granting a youth a concession ticket even though they do not have their concession pass with them, because the driver knows they have one. We often explain such conduct by saying it was "only technically corrupt". Indeed, a former Premier of New South Wales appealed to this defence when he was found guilty of improper process in the appointment of a public official.

However, the area where organisational behaviour comes in for most criticism is Quadrant IV behaviour, when people judge conduct to be legal but unethical. These situations are easy to identify, because invariably the organisation will make a public statement proclaiming that its conduct is legal. This statement is the red flag warning sign that something unethical has taken place.

A wide range of conduct can fall into Quadrant IV. Bullying by managers is one of these. Although difficult to define, bullying is generally a systematic form of behaviour that offends, humiliates or intimidates someone (Lowe, 2009). The perpetrator is usually someone who has authority over the target person, and the behaviour can include regular verbal abuse, the imposition of onerous workloads and making it difficult for the target person to carry out their work in peace.

Bullying is essentially harsh and unfair, and involves a cruelty that cannot be justified by any job or task requirements. The perpetrator generally argues that the work environment is tough or robust and their behaviour is justified. From our ethical perspective, such conduct is often unable to be "caught" by legal regimes. Occasionally people are successful in obtaining relief under harassment laws. In general, however, we must ask how such behaviour appears against the second level of ethical standards, that of high quality relationships.

Seen in this light, it is clear that bullying constitutes a failure in respectful relationships. In the next chapter we will pursue the reasons why managers and supervisors may act in these ways.

Another area where lawful but unethical behaviour may occur is in the area of marketing and selling, although it should be said that if the law had the chance to examine many of these situations, it would often conclude that the sales tactics and advertising messages involved did indeed contravene the law. This is an area where it can be difficult to draw the line between what is acceptable marketing and illegitimate pressure.

Again, the law can be helpful in establishing what the accepted guidelines for behaviour are as a minimum. However, the test we would want to bring to bear is what effect the behaviour has on the quality of relationships between the company and the client, customer or supplier. If the customer, for example, is left feeling deceived and cheated, then even if the company cannot be held legally liable for its conduct, we would argue that its ethical standards do not meet the "quality of relationships" test.

Philosophy, psychology and practical ethics

We have discussed the social process of establishing ethics in society. We could have said that similar processes also go on within organisations. In some organisations, this process occurs explicitly and with leadership and encouragement by senior management, while in other organisations the process is mediated implicitly. Workers and managers observe how senior managers act, and what behaviour gets rewarded, and do likewise. Hence, social processes are an inherent part of ethical conduct.

We have also intimated that personal ethics is not just the product of philosophical reflection. It is the result of a dynamic interaction in the person between their (philosophical) reasoning about ethics and their (psychological) feelings and motivations. The social process is the third factor in the equation.

The extent of the importance of social context can be gauged by a comment made by the Chief of Police in London in the 1990s. He said that he worked on the basis that 5% of people were always corrupt and 5% were never corrupt. The other 90% could be influenced by the situation and the social context. This gives an awful weight to the power of social pressures and circumstances.

As a counterfoil to this view, we can offer the findings of Lawrence Kohlberg (Sprinthal, Sprinthal & Oja, 1994), in his work on moral development. He found that people who had been assessed at higher stages of moral development were more resistant to cheating in a variety of test situations. This is one indicator that there may be some benefit in fostering moral development.

The next chapter will look at an account of ethics in terms of human values. This is the philosophical aspect of our quest. We can then look (in Chapters 4 and 5) at the development of ethical awareness at a personal level, the psychological aspect. These chapters will move from looking at how we think things should be to how they actually happen to be, and what we can do about that.

In Chapter 6 that will be followed by an examination of the social aspects of ethics in organisations. Again, that will concern the common realities of ethics for people working in organisations, and what we do to foster human values – and thereby improve our experience of work or managing others.

3

Ethics as core human values

It is becoming more common in business literature for writers to talk about values. It seems to strike a chord with managers and workers, and it also seems to offer an explanation for the widespread discord that exists in organisations. However, much of what is written about values is very poorly defined and does not add to our understanding. The term "values" is commonly used to mean anything from an attitude to a belief, a goal, a strong emotion, a desire or a mere preference. And the content of these "values" could relate to anything from moral principles to market domination, from codes of behaviour to organisational image.

The intent of this chapter is to look at the assortment of concepts that is commonly thrown into the same bag and called values, then to build a coherent framework for values – based on an understanding of the person. We will discuss how values are distinguished from related concepts such as attitudes, beliefs, needs and motivations, and explain how these concepts relate to one another. The place of ethics in the realm of values will become clear in this context.

A foray into values

As we did with the concept of ethics in Chapter 2, we want to start with commonly expressed ideas about values as a starting point for building a coherent approach to the subject. The appeal to values as an important aspect of personal or organisational functioning is expressed by Ken

Richard and Michael O'Connor in this way: "When aligned around shared values and united in a common mission, ordinary people accomplish extraordinary things" (1997). The idea promoted here is that values are a strong motivator for action; this is true at both the personal and the collective levels.

A picture of an organisational climate where values are not articulated or coherent, and behaviour does not exhibit commitment to a clear set of values, is painted by Susan and Thomas Kuczmarski (1995). They employ the concept of anomie (from the sociologist, Durkheim) to explain the sense of lack of energy and lack of purpose that are characteristic of such an environment. The qualities they identify include:

- low employee morale
- lack of loyalty
- lack of professional passion
- weak leadership
- meaningless work design
- lack of esteem
- no sense of belonging
- inadequate employee advocacy
- lack of opportunities for learning.

In fact, the Kuczmarskis go further than this, citing Karl Marx's views on the alienation that workers experience in the workplace when there is no shared, inclusive set of principles and values governing the enterprise. In organisations, the critical factor for productivity and morale is not just the existence of a coherent set of values; it is that these values are consistently practised by both managers and workers. The organisation must establish all the practices that are required to foster and support the values, such as appropriate reward systems, feedback on performance, and mentoring.

In organisations, a strong values basis exhibits itself in managers who recognise workers' efforts through positive feedback. Trust is built and sustained between workers and managers. Workers are recognised and respected as people, and there is a climate of caring that moderates the organisation's focus on tasks and achievements. Workplace behaviour and practices are continually scrutinised for inconsistency with espoused values. Workers and managers operate more openly and with more commitment, because there is no gulf between their personally held values and the organisation's values.

Barry Posner and Warren Schmidt (1992), who have researched and written about leadership and values for many years, refer to values as "the silent power in personal and organisational life. Values are at the core of our personality, influencing the choices we make, the people we trust, the appeals we respond to, and the way we invest our time and energy. In turbulent times, values can give a sense of direction amid conflicting views and demands."

It is not difficult to accept that values are the silent power behind people's actions. It is when we try to identify whether there is a common set of values, and what they consist of, that we run into differences of opinion. For example, one book on values in the workplace (Henderson and Thompson, 2003) lists the following values: productivity, profitability, vision alignment, team culture, passion, empowerment, commitment, innovation, energy, joy at work, success consciousness, motivation, consistency, parameters (standards) and aligned decisions.

Trying to make sense of a list like this in terms of an understanding of either individual persons or the organisation, can be difficult. How do we distinguish ethical values here, and what other sorts of values are we distinguishing them from? How do we distinguish between the values of the organisation and values of individual persons? Should we be distinguishing between values that refer to how we conduct ourselves (ethics) and "values" that refer to goals and objectives (either the individual's or the organisation's)?

Another approach to identifying values is offered by Hyrum Smith (2000). He poses a number of questions:

- What things seem important about each of the life roles I have played?
- What people, activities or things have real importance for me?
- What do I like to do when I am not under pressure to do other things?
- What would I do if I knew I only had six months to live?
- What talents or special abilities do I have?
- What do I enjoy sharing with others?
- What things do I do that give me the greatest sense of harmony and inner peace?
- To what do I want to dedicate my life?

Smith's is an altogether different approach to values. This is the life-mission, career-aspiration angle. This points us towards Edgar Schein's (1998) work on "career anchors". He explored the different motivations that people exhibit in their careers, concluding that there are eight main career anchors.

Schein defines a career anchor as a self-concept consisting of self-perceived talents and abilities, basic values and an evolved sense of motives and needs as they relate to the person's work life. He says that career anchors evolve as the person gains occupational and life experience. They are called anchors because they operate as a stabilising force. They are the values and motives the person will not give up if they have to make a choice.

Schein says that most people discover that one of these eight categories forms their career anchor, but most careers permit the fulfilling of the needs that underlie several of the anchors. The eight career anchors are:

1. Autonomy/independence
2. Security/stability
3. Technical-functional competence
4. General managerial maintenance
5. Entrepreneurial activity
6. Service, or dedication to a cause
7. Pure challenge
8. Lifestyle

Schein describes these categories as anchors because they are relatively stable, which is also a characteristic of values as explored by many researchers. But for our purposes we might see career anchors as a narrower concept than values in two respects: (1) career anchors refer to preferences and choices about types of work, not to broader life decisions, and (2) career anchors refer to purposes or vocations rather than ethics, ie our standards of conduct.

Mapping human values

There have been many large-scale research projects which have sought to map human values. We will present the results of three of these projects, to see how much consistency there is between them, and to see how these efforts illuminate the concept of values. Milton Rokeach has investigated values in the USA from the 1960s onwards. Shalom Schwartz of the Hebrew University in Jerusalem carried out studies in the 1990s that traversed 44 countries, coming up with a common set of values. Sheila Ritchie and Peter Martin from the UK investigated motivational factors with managers in over 20 countries in the 1990s, determining a set of common factors.

Milton Rokeach

Rokeach's (1973) definition of value was "an enduring belief that a specific mode of conduct or end-state of existence is personally or socially preferable to an opposite or converse mode of conduct or end-state of existence". He grouped values into two basic types: terminal values and instrumental values. The terminal values are ideal end-states of existence, while the instrumental values are ideal modes of behaviour.

He conducted his studies by surveying American adults, beginning in the late 1960s. A set of values was initially identified through interviews and focus groups. The resulting set – 18 terminal values and 18 instrumental values – was then presented to respondents, who were asked to prioritise the values in order of their importance to themselves as guiding principles for their lives. The values are shown in Table 3.1.

Table 3.1: Values of American adults

Terminal values	Instrumental values
A comfortable (prosperous) life	Ambitious (hard-working, aspiring)
An exciting (stimulating) life	Broad-minded
A sense of accomplishment	Capable (competent)
A world at peace	Cheerful
A world of beauty	Clean (neat, tidy)
Equality	Courageous
Family security	Forgiving
Freedom	Helpful (helping others)
Happiness	Honest
Inner harmony	Imaginative
Mature love (intimacy)	Independent (self-reliant)
National security	Intellectual (intelligent)
Pleasure	Logical (rational)
Salvation (eternal life)	Loving
Self-respect	Obedient (dutiful, respectful)
Social recognition	Polite
True friendship	Responsible (reliable)
Wisdom	Self-controlled

Shalom Schwartz

Schwartz's studies (1992; 1994) extended the work of Rokeach, exploring people's values across many different cultural contexts. He produced a list of 57 personal values, which he grouped into ten motivational domains. These are shown in Table 3.2.

Table 3.2: Schwartz's set of personal values

Security	Cleanliness, country/nation, reciprocation of favours, social order, family, sense of belonging, health
Hedonism	Pleasure, enjoyment, self-indulgence
Conformity	Obedience, honour, politeness, self-discipline
Tradition	Acceptance, devotion, humility, respect for tradition, moderation, privacy
Benevolence	Helpfulness, honesty, forgiveness, loyalty, responsibility, spirituality, friendship, love, meaning in life
Achievement	Capability, ambition, influence, intelligence, success
Power	Social power, authority, wealth, public image, social recognition
Stimulation	Daring, variety, excitement
Self-direction	Curiosity, creativity, freedom, choosing own goals, independence, self-respect
Universalism	Environment, nature, beauty, broad-mindedness, social justice, wisdom, equity, peace, inner harmony

One of the interesting aspects of Schwartz's set of values, compared with Rokeach's, is that Schwartz does not attempt to group values into those that are terminal and those that are instrumental. For example, the motivational domain he called Benevolence contains Rokeach's "friendship" value (an end-state) as well as "honesty" (an instrumental value). Schwartz would appear to be saying that it makes more sense to group values in terms of aspects of personal existence.

While the distinction between end-states and instrumental values seems to have some merit, signalling "how I would like things to be" in contrast to "how I would like to act", it is likely that many people will see some instrumental values as end-state values. For example, it would be quite understandable for a person to say that being loving is a terminal value, not merely as a means to an end-state.

Many of Schwartz's motivational domains also echo Schein's careers preference perspective – Schein's career anchors of security, lifestyle, service and pure challenge all have their correspondences under Schwartz's framework. Given that Schein's study is work-focused, we can observe that many of the values are concerned with skills, competence, mastery and achievement at work.

Another factor that might make the Schwartz and Schein frameworks more compatible is the idea that people may progress through stages. Perhaps a person's career anchors evolve, and a person who is engaged initially with power and achievement may become more focused on universalism as their life experiences accumulate and affect them. This idea of the evolution of values will be taken up later.

Sheila Ritchie and Peter Martin

Ritchie and Martin's study (1999) was carried out among groups of managers. Its focus was identifying what motivated the managers at work the most, using a series of forced-choice statements. The technique allowed the respondents to distribute 11 points at their discretion between four different statements, and this was carried out for 33 sets of statements. The result was a set of scores for each person covering 12 motivational factors.

The 12 factors are:

- Money/rewards
- Physical conditions
- Structure
- People contact
- Relationships
- Recognition
- Achievement
- Power
- Variety
- Creativity
- Self-development
- Interest/usefulness

Again, there is an extensive overlap with the other studies in the factors identified. Power, achievement, variety, creativity all echo Schein's career anchors, Rokeach's values and Schwartz's alternative set of values. We could say that what is different about Ritchie and Martin's study is that it is oriented more towards people's needs than their values. We can flag this as a distinction to explore.

So far, this discussion has been dominated by the idea of values as expressions of individual interests, preferences or propensities. This by itself does not illuminate what we mean by moral, or ethical, values – except that we might assert that people have a moral duty to make the most of the talents they have been given (which is certainly what Hyrum Smith is saying). And we still need to find a model that makes sense of the plethora of values we seem to be faced with.

The associations between needs and values

We noted that Ritchie and Martin's study was more directed towards needs rather than values. It is worth exploring the relationships between needs and values, because this starts to clarify what values are and what they are not. In saying that the motivational factors study was about needs, we are saying that people experience themselves in different ways from each other. One person experiences money and power as being important, while another experiences creativity and self-development as important. These motivational factors, then, are personal psychological needs. People expend their energy trying to fulfil these needs.

One of the points that Ritchie and Martin make in their study is that it is more productive for people to cultivate their strengths rather than try to force themselves to operate against them. This is not how we think about moral values. We think of moral values as having some prescriptive weight, regardless of whether people feel like acting in a particular way.

But we can also see how moral values are still required to moderate people's motivational factors. A person who is fulfilled through the exercise of power, for example, may do this in a moral way or an immoral way. So it is clear that moral values are something other than motivational factors, or psychological needs.

Another person who investigated human needs was Abraham Maslow. His hierarchy of human needs is well-known:

- Physiological needs for food, water, shelter
- Safety from physical and emotional harm
- Social needs for acceptance, belonging and friendship
- Self-esteem, including autonomy, achievement, status, recognition
- Self-actualisation, achieving one's potential.

Maslow maintained that people are motivated to action in order to satisfy these needs, and that when a lower level need is satisfied, people are freed to focus on the next level of need. Self-actualisation is thus approached through stages, as the lower-level needs are satisfied.

Maslow's theory (which remains very popular but has been criticised as lacking in empirical support) may provide some explanation for people's behaviour, but not the justification for the behaviour that a framework of ethical values would put forward. A person's act of lying about their credentials in order to win acceptance could be explained in terms of their needs, but it does not provide a moral justification for their act. The needs theory explains why people focus their attention on the things they do; we have to look elsewhere for the moral values which act to moderate the actions people take in the course of fulfilling those needs.

However, once we recognise the concept of needs, a review of the values sets identified by Schwartz and Rokeach suggests that many of these "values" may in fact be needs. So too the career anchors of Edgar Schein – they represent personality traits of a person which lead to the need to express or fulfil those traits.

What remains compelling about the concept of ethical values is that they play the role of moderating or qualifying the effect of people pursuing their personal "needs" in an unrestrained way. Only in economics do we tolerate the pleasant fiction that a successful economy is the product of people all pursuing their selfish interests, guided by an "invisible hand" that ensures the general welfare of society. Unfortunately, this fiction, attributed to Adam Smith, ignores his parallel endeavours to assert the necessity for a moral framework for society.

According to Rokeach (1979, p 48), values are cognitive representations of underlying needs *after* they have been transformed to take account of societal goals and demands. Unlike a person's needs, all of a person's values can be openly admitted, advocated and defended, to oneself and to others.

We have said that it becomes problematic to try to divide values into terminal (end state) values and instrumental values. Another way of differentiating between values is to distinguish between values concerned with competency and values concerned with ethics. This makes room for a framework that incorporates both the ideas that Schein and Maslow were concerned with – developing one's potential – and the values that do not fit into that mould, values such as honesty, love, forgiveness and peace.

The competency values are exhibited by different people according to their talents, while the ethics values apply across the board. The ethical values then also perform their function of modifying the conduct of people pursuing their needs or propensities. Hence, the person who desires power may do so, but not at the expense of mistreating other people.

Nor do we forget that people generally pass through stages of personal growth, and their values will reflect the issues that are important to them at each stage of their development.

Defining human values

There are other aspects of human values that will emerge as we address the defining of values. Our rough sketch of the values terrain has prepared us to attempt a definition, but in doing so we will become aware of other related and potentially confusing concepts – beliefs and attitudes.

The sociologist Robin Williams (1979) defines values as expressions of what is socially desirable which are formulated by social groups and societies. Values are cognitive and emotive, and they affect action, containing criteria for acts to be taken or avoided. They are not mere preferences.

Values also embody beliefs, about the nature of reality and of people. For example, the treatment of people with mental illness is conditioned by current beliefs (or knowledge) about the causes of their behaviour. When it was believed that certain behaviour was caused by demon possession, treatment of those people was conditioned by this belief.

However, values themselves should be distinguished from cognitive beliefs. Values are not provable as true or false; in that sense they are better described as preferences, assertions, behavioural standards or expressions of commitment.

Values are also general statements, not attached to specific objects. This distinguishes them from attitudes, which always relate to specific objects or classes of people. Values are considered to lie at a deeper level than attitudes, and to be more influential on behaviour. Attitudes are based on beliefs about particular objects or classes of person, and if these beliefs shift, so too can the attitude. Examples include attitudes about links between race and intelligence, or a person's age and their ability to learn. These attitudes can change as a consequence of new knowledge about the objects or classes of person. Values are not so easily changed.

Values perform the functions of selecting courses of action, resolving conflicts, invoking social sanctions, coping with needs, or making judgements or defences of choices. The values that individuals or social groups hold are organised into sets which provide preferential standards that guide conduct. These sets constitute selections of individual values and the prioritisation of those values.

Another perspective on values asserts that people's perceptions are themselves subject to the values and beliefs one has. For example, we may have beliefs about competition as an aspect of social reality. The consequence of this may be that we place a high value on competence, as being needed if we are to compete effectively in the world. The fact that values and beliefs in turn affect perceptions about situations goes some way towards explaining the persistence of values and their resistance to change. This is summed up by the saying, "to the person who has a hammer, everything starts to look like a nail".

Another insight into the nature of values is given by Brian Hall (1986). He describes values as priorities held by a person, but he adds that these priorities reflect the internal images and world view of that person. The dependence of values on a structure of beliefs is thus emphasised. He refers to the work of Paolo Freire on language and education in South America in the 1960s. Freire observed that among a group of people, certain words, which he realised were values, would be emotionally charged and would elicit passionate discussion. He began probing for these words – work that Hall continued.

Hall (2003) came to describe values as "elemental pockets of energy that cluster as the primary ideals common to all human beings. These ideals are also found as images in the conscious and unconscious, and experienced as energy through 'will' when we make a decision or tell stories." Values are thus the mediator between the internal world of images and the observable world of everyday life, and they are a way of understanding both our internal life and our external behaviour.

To bring this discussion together we can offer to define values for our purposes, drawing from the various writers mentioned.

> **A working definition of human values**
>
> Human values denote a person's or society's deep preferences and commitments for particular end-states of existence or modes of behaviour. They motivate our choices and judgements across the full range of human situations, and concern both mastery (or competence) and ethics (or morality).

Beliefs and values

The relationships between beliefs and values can be explored further. If it is true that values arise out of beliefs, then it is of interest to know what beliefs are concerned with. Edgar Schein (1984), the proponent of career anchors, identified five areas where people develop beliefs:

- the nature of reality and truth – dealing with questions such as, what is real? what is fact? how is truth determined? is truth revealed or discovered? is time linear or cyclical? is space limited or infinite?

- the nature of human beings – what does it mean to be human? is human nature good, evil or neutral? are humans predictable or not?

- the relationship of humanity to the natural world – is humanity intended to dominate nature? is harmony with nature possible?

- the nature of human activity – should humans be passive or fatalistic? what is work and what is play? how should humans engage themselves with the world?

- the nature of relationships with other human beings – what is the right balance between power and love? are relationships with others inherently competitive or cooperative? should we be individualistic or communal? what is the role of tradition and authority?

Beliefs about these matters give rise to values that traverse the entire field of human actions, including orientations towards power, harmony, fun, cooperation, obedience, predictability and passivity. The fact that values are based on beliefs also brings the notion that values, although they may be relatively stable over time, are not fixed eternally. Experience that impacts and moulds beliefs will likewise influence values.

In fact, the evolution of values is a function of the development of a person's beliefs, according to Brian Hall (1986) and Clare Colins and Paul Chippendale (1995). These writers subscribe to a stages model of values development which we refer to in this book as the Values Evolution Model. This model is explored in the next chapter.

What we want to work towards here, however, is a model of the person which gives some coherence to the clusters of beliefs and values that characterise a person. We accept that values are grounded in beliefs, and that these beliefs arise because people experience themselves as humans located in a physical world along with other humans. Somehow, people derive sets of preferences and standards which concern the "oughts" of life, the things that are true, good or beautiful. These values trigger some specific behaviour and constrain other behaviour that contravenes the values.

Values and the person's experience of the world

We have been content, thus far, to accept the distinction that Rokeach introduced – that there are values related to competency and values related to ethics. However, it would be unfortunate if the impression was created that these domains are unrelated to each other. On the other hand, if they are related, how is the quest for social recognition, for example, reconciled with benevolence? Does one simply say, "Oh, I'm not very good at benevolence"?

One way to approach this question is through a framework offered originally by Will Schutz in the 1950s. His framework was picked up in the 1990s by an organisational consultant and applied to "reading the mind" of organisations (Garden, 2000) (see later in this chapter). Schutz formulated a theory of interpersonal experience that looked at the struggle persons have to go through to make sense of the world and themselves, and figure out how to relate to it.

Schutz concluded that this encounter with the world can be explained using three categories: identity, competence and relationships. A person's values develop through their struggles to develop a sense of mastery and balance within each of these categories that they find satisfying. This is explained below for each of the three categories.

1. Identity. The ideal is that the person recognises him/herself as a person with their own innate right to exist. They are comfortable within their own space and can interact with others, they maintain their integrity as an individual and they assert their uniqueness.

In fact, the person begins with a strong need for self-preservation, which can easily become self-centredness. What counter-balances this tendency are the twin values of creativity and harmony. With these values, the person recognises that other people are necessary to their own survival and development. Through the exercise of these values, in tension with the fear about one's identity, the person learns to lose their fear and act creatively and harmoniously with others.

2. Competence. The ideal is that the person is effective in the world in relation to others. They have means of expressing themselves and developing their talents in order to achieve goals. They can influence others and maintain a feeling of being in control. They can establish goals to aim for, they can adapt to changed circumstances and they are confident of achieving the goals they set.

In fact, the person begins without competence and with the anxiety that that generates. They seek mastery through achievements and controlling behaviour. The antidote values are understanding and justice. These values temper any excesses generated by the strivings for competency, excesses which could materialise through anxieties and, as competence does develop, through pride and hubris.

3. Relationships. The ideal is that the person creates a manner of engaging with others that is real and genuine. They can establish relationships that are sustainable and mutually beneficial, and can work with others to accomplish tasks. They can develop loyalty, trust and commitment with other people.

The initial reality is that the person, fearful of not finding positive relationships, seeks to possess and control the other person. The values that neutralise this tendency are love and respect. These values enable the person to persevere in establishing genuine relationships, thereby enabling the expression of their need for intimacy and communion with other people. Along the way, the person learns other values, such as restraint, self-discipline and humility.

Ethical values have thus made an entrance into this scheme because there is tension within each of the categories. On the one hand, the person has a natural propensity in one direction within the category; what moderates the person's behaviour is a counter-balancing ethical value.

Exploring each of these dimensions has again raised the idea of stages of development, and the suggestion that certain values may be more influential with a person at certain stages of their development. Some values will not show up on their radar until they have reached a given level of awareness. There is much support for this idea in the Values Evolution Model, as we will see in the next chapter, but we might have one objection to this idea.

One of the qualities of values which seems necessary is that they have universal application. They are not relative to certain people, or situations, or types of people. Particularly in the area of ethical values, does a stages model of values development fail this test of universality?

This question may not be such an obstacle. If we consider again what the studies of Rokeach and Schwartz set out to do, they sought to map the espoused values of whole populations. In doing so, they identified all of the values which occurred, and the extent of their incidence. For example, Rokeach's 1971 study found that the values which ranked highest were "Imaginative" (daring, creative) and "An exciting life" (stimulating, active).

Both Rokeach and Schwartz recognised that the values profile of individuals could differ significantly from that of a society generally. Rokeach observed that the particular values which were most significant to an individual, and their prioritisation, can differ markedly between individuals, as well as for individuals at various times of their life.

The variation between individuals was a feature of the studies that Ritchie and Martin carried out. The extent of importance individuals placed on the twelve motivational factors differed to an enormous extent between individuals. For example, the highest score assigned by an individual to Money was 96, while the lowest score was zero (the median was 19, and roughly two-thirds of the scores fell within ten points of the median). The highest score on Self-development was 84 and the lowest was seven, with a median of 32.

If we accept as fact that individuals can differ widely in their awareness and their foci of interests, then we have to review our requirement for a set of values that has universal application. The avenue is the levels of ethics we introduced in the previous chapter. A person's understanding of ethics evolves through three levels:

- concern with laws, rules and compliance
- concern for strong and healthy relationships
- concern for the development and fulfilment of personal identity.

With this perspective, we posit a universal set of ethical values, but we understand that individuals will (a) interpret them differently according to their level of development, and (b) give varying weight to particular values, again, according to their level of development. For example, for a person who is focused on duty and obedience to institutions, the principle of equality may be seen primarily as a rule to follow – the organisation has a policy about equal employment opportunity, and this should be followed. This person's appreciation of people from different ethnic groups is probably not a central focus of interest for them.

Allowing this approach, what can we say stands as a universal set of ethical values, and can we relate this to a concept of the person?

Core human values and the person

Our concern is with values that relate to ethics. We see that many of the values identified in the studies discussed above relate to the development of talents and competencies. In the discussion that follows, we will leave these values aside and address instead the subset of values concerning ethics.

There are numerous ways we could approach these values. One approach would be to arrange them according to the three levels of ethics. However, we expressed reservations about that approach, for fear of creating a relativistic framework where people could say some ethical values did not apply to them.

Another approach would be to view ethical values in terms of the areas of experience people encounter – identity/self, competence and relationships. As a tool of analysis, this opened our eyes to the tensions that permeate individuals' experiences, and to how ethical values enter into every domain of a person's life. However, what we are looking for now is an ethical framework that focuses on the person rather than on the domains of their experience.

The person operates in a wide variety of contexts – self-functioning, participating in institutions, interacting with people and dealing with objects and the material world. Rather than attempting to create an ethical map for all of these types of dealings, the approach adopted will be to present a model of the person.

Each dimension of the person under this model will attach to a key value, and each key value can open out into a collection of related sub-values. With this model, the activities of the person can be addressed consistently. The values will have their application whether the person is relating to institutions, people or the material world.

The model proposed sees the person as consisting of five dimensions:

- Cognition
- Emotions
- Valuing
- Spirit/energy
- Identity/psyche.

One interesting place to see how this makes sense is in management theories. If we view management from the perspective of the dimensions of a person, then through the 1970s and 1980s the major focus was on the rational aspects of management – activities like devising strategy, analysing the organisation and its market, and making decisions were the target of discussion. The cognitive focus of management began to shift from the late 1980s onwards, but retained its prominence in the form of knowledge management. As commentators became aware that the basis of wealth creation was shifting from physical resources such as land and machinery towards the intangibles of knowledge and information, efforts began to be devoted to how managers could harness and cultivate these qualities.

Then, in the 1990s, Daniel Goleman (1998) (and others) challenged the current management agenda by saying that rationality was inadequate for carrying out the management role effectively. He asserted that managers also need to understand the emotional aspects of the role, so emotional intelligence (EQ) became part of discourse about management. Interestingly, this new perspective has even affected approaches to knowledge management, as observers noted that having excellent databases and data-capturing systems is not sufficient in itself to achieve effective management of knowledge. Employees' relationship-building skills are required, as company-critical knowledge arises and flows among people who work together as a community.

More recently, some writers have started to cast the focus onto values (eg Fairholm, 2003; Kuczmarski & Kuczmarski, 1995; Henderson & Thompson,

2003). They maintain that rational skills and emotional intelligence are not sufficient to create a high-performing organisation. A strong and explicit values orientation is required. The values they are talking about are not just competency values (like excellent skills, products and services), but ethical values (like respect for customers and employees).

How do the final two dimensions come into play? The fourth dimension – spirit, or energy – refers to what starts to happen when the first three dimensions are cultivated. As values are clarified and commitment around them develops, buttressed by the rational and emotional dimensions, energy starts to develop in organisations. Two of the more significant organisational studies of the 1990s recognised this aspect. Jim Collins in *Good to great* (2001) and Jim Collins and Jerry Porras in *Built to last* (1994) demonstrated that when the leaders in a company establish a foundation of clarity around operating values and strong relationships, the energy of the organisation starts to build, generating its own impetus for success. This energy is connected with the development of a sense of community among the participants.

The fifth dimension is a further outflow of the establishment of a foundation of values combined with rational and emotional skills. As organisations (and their managers) persevere in their purpose, they begin to develop their own sense of uniqueness, their own style and identity, or psyche. Annamaria Garden (2000) explored this phenomenon in organisations, using a psychological perspective. This aspect may be experienced, both in organisational life and at a personal level, as an overtly spiritual phenomenon (Zohar & Marshall, 2000; Hawley, 1993).

The core human values attached to the five dimensions of the person are shown in Table 3.3.

Table 3.3: Core human values

Dimension of the person	Core value
Cognition	Truth
Emotions	Peace
Valuing	Right action
Energy/spirit	Love
Identity/psyche	Insight

These five core human values can be regarded as the foundation of ethics among people. They embrace personal actions and social activity, and they operate in the way that values should, namely, by providing the benchmark for the formulation of more specific rules, codes, policies or norms. Thus it accommodates cultural differences, although at the same time it avoids cross-cultural relativity by asserting that these values serve to judge a specific society's norms. And from the studies of Schwartz discussed above, it would seem that the core human values are shared across cultures.

The five core human values also address individual differences within a society or group. We know that people differ in their experience and understanding, and we want an ethical standard that meets society's compliance needs as well as positing aspirational goals. The core human values can be represented as the basis for the laws and rules of all social groups, applicable to everyone, and they can also be interpreted more deeply, as a basis for exploring personal and social growth.

How would the five core values be explained as the basis of social rules? Each dimension can be viewed from the perspective of how a legal official (eg police or court) would evaluate a person's conduct. The following situations illustrate each dimension.

1. Cognition: Truth. It is clear that the law expects people to be truthful. When a person stands up in court to give evidence, they are asked to swear or affirm that what they will say will be "the truth, the whole truth and nothing but the truth".

2. Emotions: Peace. It is similarly clear that as a minimum, people are expected to behave peacefully towards other people, not abusing them or injuring them in any way. A person might fall short of being friendly or warm, but as a minimum, society (and the law) expects them to keep the peace with others.

3. Valuing: Right action. The term "right action" is meant to capture the idea of people, as a minimum, being respectful towards society and other people. It embraces the common concepts of fairness, justice and responsibility. If we think of the conduct that is expected of people when they appear in court, that gives us a clue as the general disposition that society expects all people to show towards itself and to other people. Beyond legal contexts, right action is a basic, threshold expectation of people to become part of particular groups – for example, it would be difficult to imagine someone being recruited for a job if they were offensive towards the potential employer.

4. Energy/spirit: Love. Love may seem a bit strong as a minimum, compliance requirement. How could this be? It is indeed a social expectation, however, in this sense: if you are walking down the street and you come across someone who is injured, it is expected that you will make reasonable efforts to assist them. This is not love in the sense of personal feelings or refined awareness, but in the sense of a practical act that helps a fellow human in need.

5. Identity/psyche: Insight. This dimension is not really an active part of compliance values, which are primarily concerned with actions that affect others rather than personal development. This dimension becomes active as the person grows and develops and countenances the aspirational aspect of the values.

Figure 3.1 shows the five dimensions of the person and it seeks to indicate some of the relationships between the dimensions. For example, cognition and emotion are shown on the left and right respectively to mirror the two sides of the brain.

Figure 3.1: The person as a five-dimensional model

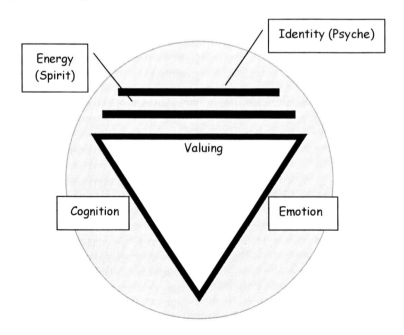

Values are shown as a horizontal bar that completes the foundation of the person, interacting with both cognition and emotion. Above this, the two bars represent energy (spirit) and identity as the culmination and outworking of the development of the three basic dimensions.

The overlaps between competency and ethical values occur for two reasons:

- it is quite broadly accepted across all societies that people *should* develop their given talents, their given areas of strength, which is to say there is an ethical obligation applied to the development of competency, and
- in order to act ethically, people have to develop skills, for example, skills at analysing situations in order to know what is fair, or skills at relating to people in order to be respectful or compassionate.

Table 3.4: Core human values expanded

Dimension of the person	Core value	Sub-values
Cognition	Truth	Honesty, integrity, reason, curiosity, trustworthiness, authenticity, reliability
Emotions	Peace	Dignity, humility, caring, cheerfulness, hope, politeness, discipline, harmony
Valuing	Right action	Fairness, justice, responsibility, non-violence, moderation, honour, courage, duty, respect
Energy/spirit	Love	Compassion, friendship, patience, enthusiasm, sincerity, kindness, tolerance, fun, sense of community
Identity/psyche	Insight	Appreciation, awareness, being, meaning, purpose, consideration, forgiveness, equality, beauty, wisdom

Values and valuing

One question that this model of the person and core human values might suggest is why it contains within itself a dimension called "valuing", when in fact every dimension has a core value attached to it. The reason for this was suggested in the account given above of the evolution of management theory over the last two decades of the 20th century.

The valuing dimension is where values are explicitly acknowledged as a discrete dimension of human functioning. One of the persistent streams of thought during the 20th century was that there are no such things as values, and the management role, for example, could be carried out in a value-free way. The view was that it is just a matter of analysing facts intelligently and making decisions.

Opposed to this stance were the management researchers who considered that relationships between people were an important factor in the success of business. They championed the human, or emotional, dimension as a modifier to the rationalists' one-dimensional approach. This was a battle fought over many years, as rationalists tended to regard the emotional dimension as an unfortunate, complicating factor for managers, and only present at all due to people's weakness.

This battle took place in a business environment (in the West) that was reasonably monolithic with respect to values. Values did not rate much thought simply because everyone made the same assumptions about values – they all swam in the same water, so there wasn't much need to comment on the water. Towards the end of the 20th century, there was increasing interaction between different cultures. This was the catalyst for a couple of realisations.

The first realisation was that there were discrete concepts called values, and societies could differ in the values they held (or in effect, the meaning and priority they gave to various values) – certainly when the values were translated into norms. The cross-cultural experience precipitated a search for what was basic and common in societies' expectations of people as members of groups, organisations and society – in other words, what constituted general agreement about right conduct. The values that came to the fore were the values concerned with respect, fairness, justice and responsibility.

The second realisation was that persons had a dimension which was concerned with a function called valuing. This process of valuing was distinct from either rationality or emotionality. Values could not be reduced to emotions, much as some philosophers tried to argue otherwise.

In valuing experience, humans denote things and conduct as good or bad, desirable or undesirable, right or wrong. Their values are robust and not confined to specific objects or situations. They are committed very strongly to them, regardless of the presence or absence of punishments or rewards. Although their formation has much to do with social mechanisms (eg church, school, family), they are held personally and individually. Values embody choices about how to behave towards others. Some acts are required and others forbidden.

Doug Lennick and Fred Kiel in their book *Moral Intelligence* (2008, p. xxxi), came to the same conclusion: "*Moral intelligence* is 'the mental capacity to determine how universal principles should be applied to our values, goals and actions'. In the simplest terms, *moral intelligence* is the ability to differentiate right from wrong as defined by universal principles." They hypothesised that "there was something more basic than emotional intelligence skills – a kind of moral compass".

With all of these thoughts in the open, it then became apparent that the desired or required qualities that people applied to cognition and emotions were in fact values. Honesty and integrity, for example, are not simply inherent properties of cognition, or part of the mastery of cognition. They are ethical values, denoting certain cognitive behaviour to be good and right, and contrary behaviour to be wrong.

Ethics, then, may be understood in terms of values, and those values can be structured in terms of a model of the person. The result is that we acquire a framework for making sense of all the dimensions of a person, as a prelude for addressing two practical consequences: (1) how people develop in their understanding of ethics, and (2) how people apply ethical values in their various activities. We are interested as well in activities that occur in organisations – how ethics applies in this context, and how ethics can be fostered collectively.

The next chapter takes up the question of the development of ethical values at a personal level, offering the Values Evolution Model as a tool for understanding the transitions that people undergo during their lives.

4

The development of personal ethics

The idea that we can talk about three different levels of ethics suggests that there may be a developmental pathway through these levels. Perhaps people start out with a focus on complying with social norms and rules and then become more concerned about others through the exercise of sympathy. And perhaps this concern further develops into a deep appreciation of others and a commitment to mutual development of potential. This chapter will explore the subject of how a person's understanding and practice of ethics develops.

To know that people have different perceptions of ethics, we have only to look at the different kinds of reasons they give for not carrying out actions they regard as unethical. Their reasons point to a variety of understandings of ethical standards.

Suppose a worker in a computer warehouse has the opportunity to take a piece of equipment. It has been superseded, and it probably would not be missed. Why might the worker decide not to take it? Consider the following possible reasons, and the ethical standards that these reasons might indicate.

Ch. 4 | The development of personal ethics

The worker's reasons	The ideas underlying the reasons
I might get caught, and get into trouble.	Fear of the possibility of detection and punishment.
I should ask a manager if I can have one.	Deference, and obedience, to authority.
I wouldn't like it if someone took something that belonged to me.	Based on empathy – being able to see the situation with roles reversed. This reason also evokes the Golden Rule – do unto others as you would have them do unto you.
I would get a bad name among my colleagues.	Concern for their reputation among other people.
I am not the kind of person who steals.	Focus on how the person regards him/herself, suggesting a strong sense of identity and self-esteem.
It is against the company's policies.	Concern for social/organisational rules.
The company might retaliate by removing our discounts on any hardware.	Concern for punishment, but in the context of the effect on all workers, not just self.
Stealing is a sin against God.	Appeal to authority – religious/spiritual authority.
My conscience would haunt me.	Personal focus – role of conscience.
It's just wrong.	Either a pointer to one of the above reasons or an indicator of clarity about values and personal identity.

Some of these reasons might co-exist, but generally we would expect one or a few of these reasons to predominate for a given person at a given time in their life. The question we need to address is, what theories or models are there that describe the development of ethical understanding and practice? But we also need to tackle the prior question of whether there is any socially shared basis for ethics. One of the most common objections to any discussion of ethics is that ethics are subjective: people have their own views and there is no objective basis for ethics.

Values as the common ground of ethics

To some extent we have already indicated that societies do share ethical values. The model of the social process of establishing ethics described in Chapter 2 posits a process wherein societies (and cultures and organisations) do reach agreement on many issues – the movement from Zone 2 to Zone 3 in Figure 2.3. This is not just theoretical agreement on abstract values, but practical agreements about specific types of behaviour.

The existence of laws and other types of rules demonstrates the reality of social consensus in the realm of ethics. There are laws against stealing and killing. There are laws directed at ensuring that people do not harm others, even carelessly or inadvertently – vehicular speed limits are a simple example. Moreover, the fact that laws are continually being introduced or reviewed indicates that this social process of clarifying and establishing ethical values and standards is alive and ongoing.

However, people still make the claim that ethics is relative and subjective. What are they saying? Is there a serious question about the existence of common ethical values at the personal or workplace level? We have already acknowledged that the law is a crude instrument for defining the links between ethical values and specific behaviours.

The argument that ethics is relative asserts that groups of people may have defined what is moral, but different groups have different standards, and there is no ground for saying that one group is right and the other wrong. This view gained support during the 20th century as a result of the explorations of anthropologists in different parts of the world. One of these anthropologists, Ruth Benedict, said, "We recognise that morality differs in every society, and is a convenient form for socially approved habits" (Benedict, 1934).

Ethical subjectivity applies relativity at the individual level, asserting that all moral statements are expressions of a person's own feelings or opinions. There are no objective standards for morals. I may believe that my feelings and beliefs are prescriptive for myself, but I cannot apply them to other people, nor can they apply their standards to me. Alternatively, I may simply conclude that all moral statements are meaningless.

There have been advocates for ethical relativity and subjectivity going a long way back in history. Jean-Jacques Rousseau promoted a subjective ethics in the 18th century, saying "What I feel is right is right. What I feel is wrong is wrong" (quoted by Judith Boss, 1998, p 81). But criticism of subjectivism is no less long-lived. Socrates asserted in the 5th century BC that "a system of morality which is based on relative emotional values is a mere illusion, a thoroughly vulgar conception which has nothing sound in it and nothing true" (quoted by Judith Boss, 1998, p 98).

Judith Boss (1998) gives an analysis of the arguments for and against ethical relativity and subjectivism. She maintains that the existence of moral disagreements does not force the conclusion that there are no universal moral standards. She also argues that we do pass judgement on our feelings and actions, and in doing so, we acknowledge that there is something operative for us outside of our own feelings. This is our moral sense.

What we can also say, based on the social process we described in the previous chapter, is that perhaps it is misguided to speak about objective standards. The fact of the social process indicates that ethics in societies is about reaching agreement. In Chapter 3 we saw that human societies around the world, in widely different cultures, reach a high level of consensus about the values that are most important to human social existence.

Another factor that needs to be highlighted also concerns the term "moral standards". This term probably leads us into difficulty because it conflates two concepts – values and standards, where the latter refers to specific prescriptions for behaviour. For example, integrity is a human value that is common to all cultures. It is a quality that is valued in people, it is something that is valued in itself and not merely as a means to further ends (although it is granted that there are also instrumental arguments for integrity – it contributes to the functioning of societies).

However, how this value is translated into standards, or rules for behaviour, often differs between societies (or sub-cultures or organisations). One of the central reasons for this is that the same action can have a different meaning in different social contexts. For example, a man might attend a funeral without wearing a tie. For him it is a matter of his personal integrity; it is his own, long-held position on the absurdity of this item of dress. It is not intended as a mark of disrespect. But others at the funeral are outraged and take it as exactly that – a sign of disrespect to the deceased.

In presenting this example we foreshadow a discussion we will take up in a later chapter, which is that disagreements about the translation of values into behavioural standards invariably involve conflicts between different values (eg integrity and respect).

We proceed on the basis that values form a reasonable ground for talking about how ethics develop in persons. Our concept of ethical development includes the idea that in developing, persons acquire a broader understanding of values and how they interact and apply in daily life.

Views of moral development

A great many thinkers have proposed theories about the moral development of persons and conducted research to find support for their theories. The starting point for this quest is the observation that people give different kinds of justifications for their choices and behaviour, as we noted above, and they also seem to differ in their motivations. We will present a brief account of some of these theories and an account of what we label the Values Evolution Model .

The Values Evolution Model is an illuminating framework for making sense of the differences between people's perceptions of morality. It is useful, too, because its scope is not confined to children and young adults, where many of the theories of moral development devote most of their attention. One aspect of this account that deserves particular treatment is how people shift from one stage to the next. This will be examined, looking at the factors that influence evolutionary shifts and, at times, regression.

Theories of moral development have been proposed within the framework of major psychological theories about human development in general, and child development in particular. Freud's (1930/1961) psychoanalytical theory saw the individual person in three co-existing modes – as a pre-rational organism, as an ego which exercised rationality, and as a self which had an identity as a member of society. Development was a process of the individual (as organism) coming to terms with the existence of others and the consequent strictures of society.

Development, on Freud's account, was a struggle and a compromise. The psychoanalytical model gave emphasis to the role of genetic predispositions and environmental factors in the individual's arena of activity. His account generated arguments about determinism and the scope of the individual's free will. Some critics argued for greater emphasis on the free will and choice of the individual. William Kraft (1992), for example, said that the self plays the major role in the development of virtue. The self (that is, the conscious, choosing self, not the unconscious forces of the id and ego) creates and then pursues an ideal of the highest expression of humanity, consisting of good, wholeness, love and intimate bonds, and unity with others.

Behaviourist models of the person, proposed by B.F. Skinner (1971) and others, like the psychoanalytic model, served to give strong emphasis to the impact of the environment on individual morality. External factors such as conditioning, punishment and reward were the primary explanatory vehicles for behaviour offered by behaviourism.

Social learning theorists such as Albert Bandura (1977) focused attention on how moral behaviour is fostered through the individual's experience of emotions such as guilt and shame. Bandura worked largely in the area of child development. He emphasised the importance of role modelling and imitation as the way individuals learn what behaviour is approved and what is prohibited. Social factors in learning include vicarious experiences, the impact of shame and punishment, and rewards and gratification. Through these means, individuals learn such things as how to resist temptation and how to be non-aggressive.

The social learning perspective sees moral development as primarily a matter of socialising a person into an existing social milieu. While acceding that the kinds of mechanisms Bandura examined do seem to operate in social contexts, some critics have argued that social learning theory has to be balanced by a consideration of self-efficacy. An individual's moral development, they maintain, is fostered through the actions they undertake, through the accomplishment of tasks and projects, verbal persuasion and the experience of emotional states.

A key component of the individual's development, according to William Hoffman (in Knowles & McLean, 1992), is empathy. He argues that growth in moral understanding is an outcome of the individual's struggles between egoistic need and emerging empathy for others. He says that the growth of empathy can be encouraged by:

- fostering and allowing the person's direct experience of emotions, and not repressing emotions;
- calling attention to the feelings of people who are hurting or suffering;

- enacting roles where the feelings of others are played out;
- giving affection; and
- modelling altruistic behaviour.

Cognitive psychologists have exercised a major influence on the way moral development is seen. Piaget's (1932; 1964) views on cognitive development in the child led to Lawrence Kohlberg's conceptualisation of six stages of moral development. Kohlberg's account is described and discussed below.

The cognitive perspective gives emphasis to cognitive reasoning in moral decisions. Other approaches are more interested in emotions and motivations. Erikson, for example, depicted the growth of a person into adulthood through several stages, and the key to growth at each stage was the resolution of conflicts between particular opposing emotions and values.

These discussions will lead onto the Values Evolution Model, which can be seen as subsuming and extending the above approaches to moral development.

The cognitive approach to moral development

Kohlberg's (1984) six stages of moral development are grouped into three levels, each of two stages. Prior to these levels, a person would be pre-moral. They would not make any judgements in terms of rules or authority, but solely in terms of what they can do and what they want to do (or avoid).

Level 1, the pre-conventional level. The person assesses situations from a concrete, individual perspective. Right and wrong are recognised, but they are determined by the material consequences of acts – punishments and rewards. The guiding principle is to avoid punishment and satisfy one's needs.

Level 2, the conventional level. The person can view situations as a member of social groups and society, and their objective is to maintain social relations and order. The person can identify with the group and shows conformity and loyalty to it.

Level 3, the post-conventional level. The person reasons and makes judgements on the basis of moral principles as a human being, not just as a member of a particular society or group.

The six stages are as follows.

Pre-conventional, Stage 1: Punishment and obedience. Fear of punishment is the primary motive for action, leading to submission to authority.

Pre-conventional, Stage 2: Egoistic needs. Satisfying one's own needs is the driver. Others' needs are considered only if there is some reciprocal benefit to be gained.

Conventional, Stage 3: "Good" behaviour. The person seeks to please and help others, win approval, "be nice", conform to peer and group stereotypes and norms.

Conventional, Stage 4: Law and order orientation. The person respects authority and social rules, maintains the existing social order, does their duty.

Post-conventional, Stage 5: Social contract. The person adheres to standards that have been agreed by society. They appeal to social consensus and majority rule as long as basic rights are preserved. Personal values may be relative.

Post-conventional, Stage 6: Conscience and universal principles. Reasoning at this level is autonomous, based on self-chosen ethical principles such as justice and equality which are universal.

Kohlberg's theory is based on the assumption that humans have an intrinsic potential and drive to grow from lower to higher stages of moral reasoning. Each stage involves a structurally different way of operating. People move through the stages in a fixed progression. The stages apply across cultures. Gains in moral development tend to be retained, although people often draw from several stages simultaneously.

Movement from one stage to the next occurs as people experience cognitive or social disequilibrium with their current stage. This may occur when a crisis occurs that they cannot resolve satisfactorily at the current stage of thinking. Transition from one stage to the next is more than a question of increased knowledge; it represents a new way of thinking.

Higher stages of moral reasoning have been correlated with other aspects of moral behaviour and personal development scales such as ego development, self-esteem and mental health. Kohlberg's research found that the majority of people operate at the conventional level of moral reasoning, and very few people operate at Stages 5 or 6.

Criticisms of the cognitive approach

Kohlberg's moral development theory has been explored in a large number of studies since it was first formulated in the 1960s. It has also been subjected to a variety of criticisms (Boss, 1998; Sprinthal, Sprinthal & Oja, 1994). Two areas that have been examined extensively are gender differences and cross-cultural validity.

Carol Gilligan (1982) argued that the Kohlberg formulation of morality was biased towards males, emphasising justice as the peak moral value. She maintained that females were more concerned with care issues than with justice issues, and that the major moral growth issue for females was about addressing dependence and self-sacrifice.

In later studies, Gilligan and others found that both the justice and the care perspectives are present in most people's thinking, although individuals tend to emphasise one more than the other (Boss, 1998). Gilligan also found that the accounts children gave of why they shared things with other children did not always fit Kohlberg's schema. Some children reported doing so in order to avoid punishment or to get something in return, as one would expect from Kohlberg, but many children gave responses that indicated they shared out of a sense of empathy for the other children. It would seem that any adequate account of moral development must include emotions and motivation as well as reasoning.

The cross-cultural perspective questioned whether Kohlberg's research had an inherent western bias. Much of the evidence about progression through stages appears to hold up under this examination. The core issue of the cultural debate is about whether there are universal values that override particular cultural perspectives.

The research of Hofstede (1984) highlights this issue. One of the characteristics identified in his extensive cross-cultural research was the difference between cultures on the individualism/collectivism dimension. Western, particularly American, culture emphasises individualism, whereas most Asian cultures emphasise collectivism. To what extent is it appropriate to define the highest level of moral reasoning in individualistic terms? The Values Evolution Model explores this issue further.

One of the limitations of Kohlberg's research is that it focuses only on moral reasoning. If our concern is with moral conduct, then we must address the relationship between reasoning and behaviour. James Rest (in Boss, 1998) identified four components of moral behaviour:

1. Moral sensitivity – awareness of a situation as having moral relevance, and being aware of and empathic towards others.

2. Moral judgement – exercise of critical reasoning, and valuing behaviour as good or bad, the aspect addressed by Kohlberg.

3. Moral motivation – commitment to making moral decisions and acting morally.

4. Moral character – putting moral decisions into action, consistently, in accord with a self-perception of high moral character, exercising courage, perseverance and strength of conviction. This is also known as development of virtue.

Rest's perspective opens the way to consider approaches to personal ethics that focus on emotions and attitudes.

Emotion and moral development

"Sympathy is the chief source of moral distinctions", according to the 18th century Scottish philosopher, David Hume (in Singer, 1994). Hume's point was that purposeful action requires the functions of reason, but the objectives of human action are ultimately based in the emotions. Or, we might appeal to Aristotle's explanation of actions in general – our actions are moved by thought "wedded" to desire.

The Dalai Lama's definition of ethics in Chapter 1, which bases ethics in its effects for our own and other people's happiness, also reminds us of the necessary link between emotion on the one hand and moral choices and actions on the other.

In Kohlberg's moral development theory, the progression we see in terms of emotions is:

- At Level 1 – fear of punishment and hope of pleasure and reward;
- At Level 2 – emotions related to dutifulness, conformity and loyalty; and
- At Level 3 – transcending of the above emotions by abstract, principle-centred reasoning.

If we were to take a broader look at all the emotions that might impinge on morality, what would be in the list? We would want to include the emotions that Kohlberg identified as above, and we would want to include the emotions of sympathy, empathy and compassion. Drawing on the social learning theorists as well, we can compile the following list.

Anxiety and fear of punishment. These emotions operate at childhood level in relation to immediate threats in the child's environment, including parents and siblings. In later years they relate to other agencies that can impact on the child (or adult), such as peer groups, school, teachers, police, sporting groups etc.

Hope of pleasure and reward. Similarly, these emotions operate first in childhood as possibilities contained in the surroundings, especially associated with parents. Later they extend to other avenues such as friends and authority figures.

Shame. Shame arises as the result of a violation of social norms, whether deliberately or accidentally. It is an emotion associated with being other-directed, ie dependent on approval from others. Shame results in feeling inadequate, embarrassed and humiliated in front of others (family, friends, peers). Shame is seen as a central element in social learning and behaviourist accounts of moral development.

Guilt. Guilt is distinguishable from shame. Guilt arises as an internal feeling of having violated a moral norm. It demands that we accept moral responsibility for our actions, that we make reparations to those we have injured, and that we change ourselves if necessary to prevent a repeat of the action. Guilt is similarly seen as a central element in social learning and behaviourist accounts of moral development.

Pride, security in belonging. These are the emotions linked with people at the conventional level of moral development in Kohlberg's theory. Their emotional equilibrium is mediated by their sense of belonging to and being accepted by the institutions in their lives, including their family, school, church, peer group or sports group.

Anger and indignation. Anger in this context is linked to moral outrage. This sentiment develops early in children, as evidenced by their anger when they feel they have been treated unfairly. At this stage it is related to a keen sense of the importance of rules, as in Kohlberg's conventional level. Later in life, moral outrage can be understood in terms of more developed concepts of ethics, including attitudes about injustice at the societal level.

Sympathy, empathy, love and compassion. These terms are not identical, but they all indicate recognition and appreciation of the needs of other people, their feelings, and their inherent value. They are the drivers for altruism. At a conceptual level, these emotions are consistent with Kohlberg's post-conventional level, but as we have indicated, they are not highlighted sufficiently in his model. The attitudinal model presented below seeks to acknowledge the importance of empathy and altruism in moral maturity.

Joy in helping others. Psychologists refer to the feeling of "helper's high", a joyful emotion which is generated by having helped another person. The reality of this emotion has long been recognised. Plato said we behave justly not only because it is the right thing to do but because of the positive effect it has on us. Again, the Dalai Lama's definition of ethics embodies the idea that doing good for others cheers our soul. However, as Boss (1998) observes, this is not to say that the primary reason we do good is because it makes us feel good. There is more to it than that.

This description of the emotions that are relevant to moral action should make it clear that emotions have a role to play in this area as well as cognition. Some writers have offered an approach to moral development that focuses on attitudes rather than cognition, and we shall explore this approach now.

Attitudes and moral development

The popularity of Kohlberg's cognitive theory of moral development has pushed other approaches into the wings over the last 30 years. Prior to 1970 a considerable amount of research was conducted into attitudes as the vehicle for understanding moral development.

Attitudes are an attractive way of looking at moral development because they focus attention on the intersection between three components – cognition, emotions and the influence of the social context. Moreover, attitudes are accepted as one of the key antecedents of behaviour (Fishbein & Ajzen, 1975).

An attitude is defined by Myers (2001, p 90) as "a favourable or unfavourable evaluative reaction toward something or someone, exhibited in one's beliefs, feelings or intended behaviour". Attitudes are learned; they are relatively enduring orientations but they can be modified. They relate to specific objects, situations, people or types of behaviour. William

Kay (1968) argued that morality can be considered as a series of stages in development where each stage is characterised by a dominant attitude.

In discussing the authoritarian stage that children go through, Kay says that the stage is dominated by a positive (we could say, dependent) attitude toward authority figures. Development through different stages consists of one dominant attitude being displaced by another. The major stages described by Kay (following Peck & Havighurt and other researchers of the 1960s) are:

- **Prudential.** Self-interest dominates. The person acts to avoid punishment or hurt; there is no concern for others. Personal needs/interests dictate behaviour, manipulating others if necessary.

- **Authority-focused.** Deference to authority. The person obeys rules and complies with leaders' expectations, fulfils their duty.

- **Social-focused.** Acting to achieve approval from others (family, colleagues, friends). Peer pressure maintains adherence to social norms. Rules are understood now as being worthy of respect because they uphold society.

- **Personal.** Moral maturity, characterised by the building of a personal ethic which displays reasoning about universal ethical values as well as societal rules, and incorporates the role of conscience.

It will be noted that the first three stages reveal the same succession as in Kohlberg's theory. Kay's model begins with the child's direct concerns about punishment and reward, as does Kohlberg's. Kay's following two stages correspond with Kohlerg's conventional level. What differs is how the mature stage of morality, the stage of the personal ethic, is defined.

The personal ethic level is the level of moral maturity according to Kay. It consists of an emerging complex of attitudes, with four main features:

1. **Rationality** – ability to attend to the "hard facts" of situations, to see the probable consequences of actions, to apply knowledge and beliefs and to see the applicability of moral principles.

2. **Altruism (concern for others)** – ability to attend to the feelings of others and to treat other people as ends in themselves, not as means to one's own ends.

3. **Responsibility (accountability)** – acceptance of one's part as a moral agent in the situation, with the ability to affect outcomes.
4. **Autonomy (moral independence)** – recognition of moral principles as separate from social norms and mores, and readiness to act in terms of those principles.

Figure 4.1 below shows the developmental pathway through moral attitudes proposed by Kay. As the four features indicate, the model of moral development through attitudes gives weight to emotions as well as cognition. The validity of this approach has been strengthened in recent years by research into the functioning of the brain, and by the explosion of interest in emotional intelligence based on the works of Daniel Goleman (1998) and others.

Figure 4.1: Moral development through attitudes

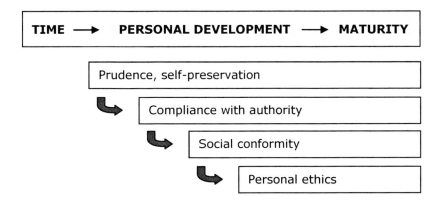

Emotions, reasoning and ethics

What is the relationship between cognition and emotions (affect)? Some writers argue that the two domains overlap. Barbara Martin (1989) supports this view, maintaining that cognitive skills can be pre-requisites to affective skills, and vice versa. Recent research on the brain makes a much stronger connection between the two domains than this account suggests. The research (Carter, 1998; Claxton, 1994; McCrone, 1993) indicates that thoughts and emotions are inseparable from each other.

The account of emotion that has been formulated based on this research maintains that there are two aspects of emotions:

- "raw" perceptions and feelings, which are immediate and have a biological basis (in oneself and others) – eg precipitated by the experience of pain, or by seeing others in pain or in imminent danger; and

- enculturated feelings, which are strongly reliant on language and social learning – eg the complex feelings generated by receiving a Christmas card from a friend to whom you had forgotten to send a card.

Between these two camps there is an "inner voice" which constantly commentates on the person's situation (not to be confused with traditional concepts of a conscience).

The culture-based feelings require cognition, and include feelings like pride, loyalty and guilt. McCrone (1993, p 251) says "each emotion is a learned body of ideas wrapped around a relatively small kernel of sensation". They are related closely to attitudes and values. One of the views about the role of the inner voice is that it somehow mediates traffic between the cultural and biological spheres, through the person's sense of purpose and meaning.

If we apply these findings to moral development, we can appreciate that the approach based on attitudes gives due weight to both cognition and feelings. As the definition of attitudes given above shows, feelings towards a particular situation are an integral part of attitudes.

What we can do with this new appreciation of the interaction of cognition and feelings is to explore further the process of transitioning from one stage of moral development to the next. We introduce this issue below as a prelude to a more detailed treatment. At this point we should also reflect on the model of ethics that was presented earlier. We described ethics, as it is applied in common parlance, as operating at three levels:

- Ethics as law, rules, and right/wrong or good/bad judgements;
- Ethics as quality of relationships and concern for others; and
- Ethics as deeper identity and fulfilment of ideals.

Is the conception of moral development that we have formulated in our current discussion compatible with the three-level account?

Referring to Kay's attitudinal model above, we can say firstly that the initial level, Prudence, is not generally descriptive of children once they have reached school. Kohlberg's findings on Pre-conventional reasoning were similar. Children have, by then, graduated to conceptions of rule-keeping and the desire to please. Hence we are left with the three levels in Kay's model of Authority-focused, Social-group-focused and Personal Ethics.

The three levels of ethics we described in the previous chapter thus align broadly with the three levels of attitudes:

- Authority-focused attitudes correspond to our description of a concern with rules, laws and right/wrong judgements. (In the three-level account, this is intended as a broad category, including the younger child's person-centred perception of authority through to the older person's wider understanding of rules as society's boundaries.)

- Social group-focused attitudes correspond to our description of a concern for the quality of relationships. (Again, the scope of this category ranges from the younger person's eagerness to please and belong, through to the mature person's appreciation of the value of human relationships.)

- Personal Ethics correspond to our conception of realising one's identity through clarity of values, consistency of conduct and development towards ideals.

Moral growth – transitions

Looking at moral growth is in some ways problematic. Most of the research on moral development has focused on children and the steps they take in their passage to adulthood. So we might think that its findings would not be very useful for adults to consider. Then there is the rather pessimistic finding of Kohlberg's that most adults do not move beyond conventionalism. This is to say that most people never truly make ethical judgements – instead, they rely on the established rules of society and what other people think.

To make things worse, research that was carried out in the 1920s by Hartshorne and May (Sprinthal, Sprinthal & Oja, 1994) found that the moral behaviour of people was highly conditioned by context. People who cheat in one situation may or may not cheat in a different situation. This would suggest that moral character is a creature of myth. However, the reality may not be as stark as Hartshorne and May suggested. Kohlberg's investigations of the conduct of people who operated at higher levels of moral reasoning did find significant consistency in conduct across contexts.

Another finding from Kohlberg's theory also indicates that there is the possibility that adults grow in ethical understanding. Young adults in moral development education programs have been found to develop their ethical reasoning even more than adolescents or children (Trevino & Nelson, 1995).

The views of William Kay provide a starting point for finding out what precipitates moral growth. Kay's perspective was that of educator, so his concern was with what parents and teachers could do to foster moral growth in children. Despite this focus, Kay makes two recommendations that seem applicable to adults and work contexts:

- the most effective assistance is that which corresponds to the person's current level of development – "readiness for moral growth" is related to the person's current and next stages of moral attitude; and
- since attitudes form the basis of a person's level of moral functioning, the appropriate interventions are those which engage and challenge current attitudes.

The factors that are involved in moral growth will thus draw on what is known about attitudes. According to Fishbein and Ajzen (1975), the factors include beliefs that people hold about the issue, which includes their knowledge. Also included are "subjective norms", which are what the person believes other people would think about them performing the action in question – and this in turn will be influenced by how much weight the person gives to other people's views.

The earlier discussion did give some indications, too, about how transitions occur. A shift can occur when a person encounters a crisis that they are unable to resolve at their current level of reasoning.

The person's level of cognitive reasoning is also a factor. In child development this is an obvious factor, as children evolve from concrete to abstract reasoning largely in accordance with their age. However, it is also the case in adults that study, experience and education contribute to their continuing cognitive development.

We have acknowledged the importance of the social context to the level of moral reasoning. This factor operates by reinforcing the standard of morality that prevails in the group (the norms), adding its own weight to individual moral machinations. The group norms extend to the type of reasoning that is applied to issues and what categories are used to interpret situations.

This chapter has treated the issue of making transitions to more integrated levels of moral reasoning and conduct only briefly. The next chapter opens up the question of how to describe these different levels of understanding of the world and of ethics. The chapter will then examine how individual persons (adults) evolve from one level to another.

5

The Values Evolution Model

We have looked at the different understandings of moral thinking that people have, drawing on the literature on the moral development of children. Given that our interest is in adults, particularly as they work in organisations, we wish to turn to literature that is more focused on adults, and combine this exploration with our understanding of values.

The terrain of values development in adults has been extensively explored in the decades since the 1970s, and we can link it to our focus on ethics. The first observation we can make about values is that values do not cluster in an individual at random. There are definite patterns to the combinations of values that people hold at a given time.

It was Rokeach (1973, p 5) who made this discovery, in his studies of American values. He employed the concept of a value system to describe it, defining a value system as "an enduring organisation of beliefs concerning preferable modes of conduct or end-states of existence along a continuum of relative importance". Individuals and organisations organise and prioritise their values in particular ways, forming values hierarchies. The purpose of these values hierarchies is to enable people to make choices when values conflict with each other.

Brian Hall's work on values (1986, 2003) extends the idea of value systems. He maintains that the values to which people subscribe rest on a particular set of beliefs and assumptions about the world. He identified seven different world views. The world views are made up of how individuals perceive the world, how they perceive themselves functioning in the world and what human needs they seek to satisfy. This approach to understanding values has been furthered by other researchers, particularly the Australian researchers Paul Chippendale and Clare Colins (2002).

A world view provides the person with a model of reality, which leads to the adoption of corresponding values. This framework is termed here the **Values Evolution Model**. The seven world views are described below. Movement through the world views represents an expansion of a person's understanding of reality through four phases, characterised respectively by: surviving, belonging, self-initiating and inter-depending.

Under each world view there are values relating to goals and modes of conduct that characterise the person. These value sets actually undergo a transition within each world view, so the person begins to take on some of the characteristics of the next world view in the framework. So, for example, in the descriptions below, Security is a second stage of the first world view, but at the same time it constitutes the first stage of the next world view.

World view 1: The world is alien and threatening.

"People are out to get what they can for themselves. It is survival of the fittest. You can't trust anyone. Look after Number One."

The primary goal under this world view is self-preservation, but there is also a sense of wonder and awe about life. The primary values relating to the mode of conduct are safety and survival.

The second stage of this world view focuses on the goal of security – interest in one's physical comfort and security. Modes of conduct are governed by sensory pleasure and property/economics.

World view 2: Family and friends are my refuge in an uncaring world.

"It is an uncaring and impersonal world, but you will be alright if you have a loyal family and work group and you follow the rules."

The goal of security continues under this world view, along with concern for economics and pleasure. To this is added the goals of family and belonging, and self-worth. Modes of conduct that govern behaviour are tradition, duty, control, belonging (being liked), care and nurture, social prestige and competence/expertise with tools and technology.

World view 3: The world is a problem with which I can cope through education, work and participation in institutions.

"The world is a difficult place, but if you learn, work hard and do the right thing by the organisation and your family, you'll do well."

The goals of family and belonging and self-worth continue under this world view, together with the modes of conduct that accompany them. To them is added the goal of confidence in one's skills and abilities to perform work productively. Complementing the work goal are the goals of play and deference. Play refers to the ability to balance work with recreation, amusement and leisure. Deference includes participation in formal religion (membership of a church and acceptance of a structured doctrine of beliefs), as well as acceptance of social traditions (eg in Australia, beliefs and customs relating to Anzac Day).

The modes of conduct associated with these goals include: focus on achievement, competency with administrative/organisational skills, patriotism and institutional loyalties, education, obedience to laws and fulfilment of civic duties.

World view 4: Institutions are not absolute, and individuals have to find their own meaning.

"The world is uncertain and organisations are not always right, so I have to work things out for myself."

The values relating to confidence in work and commitment to institutions still hold sway, but there is a new awareness of oneself as an individual with one's own perspective and contribution to make. The emerging goals are about self-actualisation and service.

Approval by institutions remains important, but the person's modes of conduct are now influenced by: expressiveness and freedom, autonomy, search for one's place in the scheme of things, well-being and health, empathy and generosity. Confidence in one's right to be respected for one's own thoughts, feelings, words and actions is growing. Some tensions are also emerging – the law, instead of being viewed solely as a literal and obligatory duty, is beginning to be seen as a set of underlying principles about how I should behave; a guide.

World view 5: The world is a project in which I am a collaborator.

"I can work with others to make a difference to the world, using my talents to help create a better quality of life."

The goals that emerged in the previous world view now form the foundation of a sense of personal vocation. To this is added the concept of a New Order, the focus of which is new forms of organisation that develop and dignify persons. Justice, beauty, contemplation and insight are all accompanying and supporting goals for this world view.

The modes of conduct that pertain to these goals are: research to increase knowledge (which is valued for its own sake), organisational development (aimed at both quality of life for organisational members and socially worthwhile corporate purposes), community-building and intimacy (regular deep sharing with other people), combined with detachment and ethical accountability.

World view 6: The world is a system that will work best when people mutually support each other.

"The world is a complex, interdependent system where responsibility and cooperation create synergies that benefit us all."

The concept of the New Order takes further shape here. This is not an illusion that the world is somehow a "green and pleasant land". It fully recognises the presence of ugliness and injustice and the obstacles many people face to be safe and acquire basic necessities. But this world view draws from the chaos perspective, asserting that everything is inter-related, and responsible action for good can make a significant impact. The emerging goal here is wisdom, defined as knowledge of what is true and right combined with just judgement as to what is appropriate action.

The modes of conduct that operate under this world view relate to explicit actions to foster a better world, such as speaking to others and explaining and advocating about human and environmental issues. Community with others is also a characteristic of this world view. Relationships among such communities of interest are characterised by simplicity, intensity, richness and mutual empowerment.

World view 7: The world is a mystery for which we (together) must care.

"A universal, communal and global perspective is required if we are to enliven the environment and create a harmonious world where technology is convivial."

This world view is the most expansive expression of values. It moves from the level of wisdom to the vision of communion between all people. Under this world view, the possibility lies for an existence where the physical world is encountered from an ecological perspective – beauty and harmony are fostered through appropriate (convivial) technology. The human domain is founded in an understanding of mutual interdependence, so that persons and communities are respected and nurtured from their current phase of consciousness.

World views and ethical values

The view of ethics that was presented earlier is that there are ethical values which correspond to the five dimensions of the person. This gives us a universally applicable ethical standard. However, we also recognised that people differ in their perception and understanding of the world and their place in it. People consequently view the ethical values somewhat differently. It is this area that we wish to explore now, through the seven world views just described.

Table 5.1 describes the dominant themes in a person's ethics under each of the world views.

Table 5.1: World views and ethical priorities

World view	Ethical priorities
World view 1: The world is alien and threatening.	Choices are based on self-interest. The person seeks to survive in an alien world by being practical and realistic.
World view 2: Family and friends are my refuge in an uncaring world.	Ethical choices are based on fairness, duty, respect and obedience to authority. Loyalty to and care for friends and family determine choices.

World view 3: The world is a problem with which I can cope through education, work and participation in institutions.	Ethical choices are based on rules of law and respect for institutions.
World view 4: Institutions are not absolute, and individuals have to find their own meaning.	Ethical choices are based on informed awareness of social justice. There is a heightened awareness of unjust actions by organisations, especially those of which one is a member.
World view 5: The world is a project in which I am a collaborator.	Ethical choices are based on a consciously chosen, personally meaningful, core set of values. Rules are respected but not treated as absolute. Peers bind themselves through shared priority values (which may be implicit or explicit).
World view 6: The world is a system that will work best when people mutually support each other.	Ethical choices are based on dedication to human dignity and rights, understood on a global and local level.
World view 7: The world is a mystery for which we (together) must care.	Ethical choices are based on a profound understanding of the needs and possibilities of all people and the world.

What follows from the Values Evolution Model is that people will, as a matter of fact, differ in how they perceive the five dimensions of the person, that is, the five dimensions of ethics. Is this an unsatisfactory conclusion? Is it simply another way of saying that all ethics is relative?

We cannot argue with the fact that people have different perceptions and understandings. We have to ask instead, what is our concern with this? Does it mean there is one standard for one person and another standard for another? To address this, we have to go back to the distinction we made between compliance-based ethics and aspirational ethics.

Compliance is the issue when we act as agents of society, institutions and organisations. Compliance sets the minimum standard for participation in – and enjoyment of the benefits of – association and belonging. Aspirational ethics involve a different set of motivations. In the latter case, we are concerned with what we desire (for the social entity) rather than what we need as a minimum.

In practice, we accept the differences that exist between people's personal ethical standards. We can observe this in "small" things and in situations where action could be regarded as optional. Suppose there is a jacket left in a public place. It is nice. It fits you. And it has no identification in it. You have a number of choices – you can leave it there (best not to get involved), you can take it to the police station (too much trouble; pointless?), you can put a sign up nearby with your mobile phone number on it, saying you have the jacket (risky, uncertain), you can take the jacket and give it to a charity (at least someone needy will benefit) or you can claim the jacket and take it home.

This simple case can generate much discussion about the ethics of each course of action. For our purposes, what is interesting is the different ethical perceptions and motivations that could lie behind each option. In none of the scenarios has the person committed a crime, and each option can be given some kind of justification. Moreover, if we thought about all the people we know in the organisation where we work, we could imagine every option being selected by someone. Indeed, the same person might select different options depending on the particular circumstances and their personal situation at the time – perhaps they were hurrying to get to an important meeting, for example.

The message is that ethical choices are complex and we cannot easily specify standard rules of behaviour at an intimate level. At the level of organisations, institutions and societies, rules and policies have to be concrete and clear, and the primary concern has to be confined to compliance – minimum standards. If a higher level of behaviour is desired, this becomes a question of developing shared norms through social and personal dynamics. Behaviour then begins to move towards aspirational motivations.

Shared norms in groups, and policies in organisations, actually operate to extend compliance beyond strict ("black letter") law. Norms are more detailed and complex, and more often intrude into a person's motivations, than laws. What the world views show us, as did William Kay's model of developing moral attitudes, is that people move from obedience to rules towards acceptance of social groups' mores, on their way to establishing a personal ethics.

Organisations (employers) thus have an important role to play in clarifying and maintaining ethical standards because, perhaps for most people in the organisation, the organisation's norms (that is, their actual practices, not so much their policies) play a large part in defining ethics. Employees are subject to the organisational environment for significant portions of their weekly lives, and they easily become "institutionalised". They struggle to offset the power of organisational ethics with the influence of other institutions, sources and experiences. This discussion will be continued in later chapters.

We were discussing whether the Values Evolution Model forces the conclusion that ethics is relative. The conclusion has to be that rather than being relative, ethics are often contested. From the perspective of society as a structure, the objective has to be establishing minimum standards for compliance. It is a social development task to engage at more intimate levels to clarify values and explore motivations. The Values Evolution Model illuminates the fact that people may have very different perceptions about situations and the meaning of actions. But once we enter this domain, we are in the territory of what is desirable rather than what institutions require compliance with as a minimum.

Exploring core human values and world views

If people who subscribe to particular world views have their own perspectives on ethics, it would now be useful to look at the five dimensions of the person under each world view. This will give us a much finer sense of how people's perceptions and motivations differ. Once this is clearer, it will then be helpful to examine how people make the transition from one world view to another.

Each of the world views is examined below, taking the five dimensions of the person in each case and describing how the person with that world view tends to see ethics.

World view 1: *The world is alien and threatening. Choices are based on self-interest. The person seeks to survive in an alien world by being practical and realistic.*

TRUTH. The truth (eg honesty, integrity, trustworthiness) is treated expediently. Whatever serves the person's survival ends is what is said and done.

PEACE. Values directed towards peace (eg caring, cheerfulness, politeness, dignity) are treated expediently.

RIGHT ACTION. Right action (eg duty, respect, fairness, responsibility) is regarded with expediency.

LOVE. Values exemplifying love (eg friendship, sincerity, patience) are regarded with expediency.

INSIGHT. Not applicable.

World view 2: *Family and friends are my refuge in an uncaring world. Ethical choices are based on fairness, duty, respect and obedience to authority. Loyalty to and care for friends and family determine choices.*

TRUTH. The truth is treated selectively, that is, whatever serves the interests of self, family and friends is what is said and done.

PEACE. Values directed towards peace are similarly employed selectively.

RIGHT ACTION. Right action extends only to the select group of family and friends.

LOVE. Values exemplifying love extend only to the select group of family and friends.

INSIGHT. Not applicable.

World view 3: *The world is a problem with which I can cope through education, work and participation in institutions. Ethical choices are based on rules of law and respect for institutions.*

TRUTH. The truth is honoured but is filtered through the institutional perspectives that constitute the person's reference groups. The understanding of truth tends to be literal.

PEACE. Values directed towards peace are fulfilled in a way that is consistent with the person's commitment to family, authority and institutions.

RIGHT ACTION. Right action is pursued passionately in the context of family, institutions and accepted authorities.

LOVE. Love is exercised as an aspect of belonging to and being part of family, organisations and institutions. It is conditioned by fears about the world, which may intrude into the person's close circle of friends and colleagues.

INSIGHT. The meaning of reality is understood in terms of social structures, institutions and traditions.

World view 4: *Institutions are not absolute, and individuals have to find their own meaning. Ethical choices are based on informed awareness of social justice. There is a heightened awareness of unjust actions by organisations, especially those of which one is a member.*

TRUTH. The truth is pursued in a principled way rather than in an acquiescent or doctrinaire way, and this may lead to some conflicts between the person's viewpoint and the institution's.

PEACE. Values directed towards peace are incorporated into enlarged personal goals, in tension at times with other principles, eg when injustice occurs.

RIGHT ACTION. Right action is pursued passionately, but from a more independent perspective than as an uncritical representative of an organisation.

LOVE. Love is exercised through the recognition of others as individuals and there is a blossoming of compassion and tolerance.

INSIGHT. Awareness is seen as personal, unshackled from institutional perspectives, although this may be accompanied by trepidation.

World view 5: *The world is a project in which I am a collaborator. Ethical choices are based on a consciously chosen, personally meaningful, core set of values. Rules are respected but not treated as absolute. Peers bind themselves through shared priority values (which may be implicit or explicit).*

TRUTH. Truth and reality are seen from an expanded perspective, as holistic, incorporating many different dynamics, eg social, political.

PEACE. The person pursues peace as a way of exemplifying the better world they are trying to create.

RIGHT ACTION. Right action is pursued as the foundation and pre-requisite of human creativity and joy.

LOVE. Love is exercised out of a sense of the connections between people and the possibilities for community across social and political divides.

INSIGHT. Insight begins to assume priority, informed by an appreciation of the world and by the integration of the value-dimensions of truth, peace, right action and love.

World view 6: *The world is a system that will work best when people mutually support each other. Ethical choices are based on dedication to human dignity and rights, understood on a global and local level.*

TRUTH. Truth merges with peace and love. Until now they have been seen as separate and sometimes in apparent tension with each other.

PEACE. The person has a deeper understanding of how peace and all the other values serve the world purpose.

RIGHT ACTION. The person has a deeper understanding of how right action serves the world purpose.

LOVE. A greater sense of unity is conveyed to others. The person imparts to them an understanding of inter-connectedness, the need of individuals and communities for each other.

INSIGHT. Forgiveness, compassion, equality and wisdom come to the fore as the systemic nature of reality becomes clearer.

Ch. 5 | The Values Evolution Model

World view 7: *The world is a mystery for which we (together) must care. Ethical choices are based on a profound understanding of the needs and possibilities of all people and the world.*

TRUTH. Truth is seen from an inner perspective, where external (material) reality is seen as the expression of inner truth.

PEACE. Peaceful action proceeds from insight and a sense of oneness.

RIGHT ACTION. Right action is superseded by insight and oneness.

LOVE. Love expressed is palpable and transforming.

INSIGHT. The place of everyone and everything in the overall scheme of things infuses all perceptions and actions. "Humanity's natural state is bliss."

Reflecting on the world views perspective

The latter world views are exalted, and perhaps disturbingly so. Few people would claim to exhibit that level of development. Nevertheless, if we are to posit a framework that maps the full extent of possibility, including the highest aspirations, then we must endeavour to describe these latter views. Even if they seem far removed from our current state, they stand as desirable ideals.

As might be expected, the research that Brian Hall and his colleagues carried out discovered very few people who fell into the sixth or seventh world views. There are a few famous and outstanding individuals in the 20th century that would commonly be regarded as inhabiting world view 7 – Mahatma Gandhi, Mother Theresa and the Dalai Lama would be among those few.

Similarly, Kohlberg did not find many people who operated at the highest stage of moral reasoning. He discovered that most adults operated at the fourth and fifth of his six stages. At these stages, the persuasive influences for people are rules and laws and social conventions. However, we have also observed that Kohlberg considered it to be productive to take steps to foster ethical reasoning among individuals and groups.

As to the first world view, this could be described as a "pre-ethical" stage. Ethics, on the definition of Schweitzer that we have adopted, is about good behaviour and concern for others. The person described by the first world view is solely engaged in self-preservation and security. They have no concern for anyone else, except insofar as others serve the person's own survival.

The next three world views see an expansion of awareness and consideration to include others, so in this sense ethics can be said to have emerged. However, we would also want to observe that the ethical orientation is external – it is triggered by external agents, not internal principles. The external agents are organisations, authorities and the opinions of social groups. The person acting from these world views operates to ensure that they are not punished or excluded from participation in social entities, from which they derive their meaning.

It is from world view 5 onwards that ethics becomes a consciously chosen basis for action and judgement. The person now begins to evaluate their beliefs and values in contradistinction to the social groups and institutions of which they are part. They question the basis of traditions and rules and see the importance of context to ethical decisions.

We will now take a closer look at what prompts people to make transitions from one world view to another, and hence a transition in the values that are important to them. These "world views" are, of course, convenient categories rather than tightly constructed boxes into which people fall neatly. Life is rather messier than our ideas about it. People may also move to an expanded world view in a sporadic way, retreating and advancing as circumstances and their will and attention interplay.

Transitions in personal values and world views

We have made some broad assertions already about the general direction of changes in ethical values and about what factors are at work to generate change. The seven world views that form the foundation for the Values Evolution Model illustrate the progressive expansion of ethical values posited earlier, namely:

- ethics is first of all seen as a matter of rules and laws (in world views 1-3);
- ethics then comes to be seen as a matter of relationships – other people are respected and treated fairly and decently (in world views 2 onwards); and
- ethics subsequently comes to be seen as a reflection of ideals and the realisation of deep identity (in world views 5 onwards).

It was also said that ethics arise out of the tensions people feel in seeking to engage with the world. Under each world view, people have a relatively stable configuration of values that accord with their beliefs about the world. However, it is never entirely stable, because of the tension between self-orientation (because of doubt, fears and consequent egotism and selfishness) and the counter-balancing outward-looking forces (the desires for growth, expression, harmony and interaction).

A person who has a particular world view has reached some equilibrium between these forces. Their world view corresponds with a set of values which are their primary focus; it is these values to which they devote most of their energy and which they seek to fulfil. The values associated with the previous world view are their foundation values – the person is essentially satisfied that these values have been fulfilled, or are continuing to be fulfilled, without special effort on their part.

If the person's situation changes dramatically, and the foundation values become threatened, then the person may revert to the previous world view. This is not necessarily so, however, because the situation may trigger a change in perception and understanding that leads to an expansion of the person's perspective instead – a transition to a greater world view.

Ordinarily, the next world view is latently available to the person – it constitutes a set of vision values about how the future could be. These are motivating values that draw the person forward. As the person acts to see the focus values fulfilled, the next world view starts to take shape and expand their understanding of the world.

The three types of values that act upon a person at any one time (Colins & Chippendale, 2002), therefore, are:

- **foundation values** – those values that under normal circumstances are already fulfilled in the person's life
- **focus values** – the values that currently engage the person's attention and energy
- **vision values** – the values that loom at the fringe of the person's attention as more expansive ideals.

Movement towards a more expanded world view may be uncertain and gradual, or it may be sudden and dramatic. Facts that "do not compute" with one's current set of beliefs may at first be discounted, as "examples that prove the rule". A second form of change is where change is incremental, so the world view gradually shifts. The person is changing, but they might not see themselves as having changed significantly until some time later. Over time they can see that their perceptions and motivations have shifted considerably from what they used to be.

There is also a form of change where the person has a sudden switch from one view to another. For example, a person joins a sect and rejects the world. In this case, the person simply abandons one world view and replaces it with another. There is no attempt to assimilate change, or compare the old and the new. Often this type of change falls apart after a while, because there are just as many questions left unanswered as there were beforehand. For this reason, this type of change is often called a pendulum shift.

A stable shift to another world view requires that the old knowledge be reviewed and integrated into the larger view. This is sometimes called a paradigm shift. This type of change recognises that the former view was partially right, but incomplete. This perspective also recognises that the new paradigm is probably also incomplete! This is to say that at a certain point it becomes clear to the person that their perceptions of the world are not absolute, and the growth towards understanding is a continuing journey.

The skills required to live out values

For a person to make a transition from one world view to another, they also need to have a corresponding set of skills that enables them to function and cope within that world. There are several kinds of skills that are needed to actively pursue a given set of values. What are these skills?

In one sense, the skills are specific to each world view. They are the skills that enable the person to act towards fulfilling their focus values, and the skills they have acquired in bringing their foundation values to fruition. A person who lives out of world view 3 has acquired the general skills of education and the specific work skills needed to fulfil their organisational role. They have established a sense of identity as a competent, functioning member of the organisation and they are able to interact with other people in this capacity.

However, there are four types of skills that recur in each world view, so at each stage the person has to reinvent those skills (Hall, 1986). They are: instrumental, interpersonal, imaginal and systemic skills. The need for these skills indicates that the transition to another world view, or the evolution of values from one set to another, depends on the growth and practice of these skills. It can also be said that awareness of the skills is useful in fostering their development.

The four types of skills are described below.

Instrumental skills

Instrumental skills are the skills and knowledge required to fulfil roles, either social roles generally or specific occupational roles. They will differ from society to society, but they will be commonly understood within given social contexts. In work organisations, instrumental skills include what are variously known as generic skills, employability skills or foundational skills. A certain reading level, numeric skills, general knowledge, personal organisation, use of ordinary technology such as a telephone, and time management are some of the skills expected, along with ability to use common tools (eg broom, screwdriver).

Without this basic knowledge and skills a person is unable to live at, say, the third world view where the focus value is to carry out a useful role as a member of an institution. Instrumental skills also include more specialised occupational or professional knowledge and skills.

Interpersonal skills

Interpersonal skills are skills that enable the person to manage their emotions, communicate and interact with other people, and establish and maintain relationships. These skills are first learned through family and school relationships.

A lack of these skills would stunt a person's possibilities to connect with the world and expand their perception of its possibilities. Even at world view 1 there are communication and interaction skills that are required in order to fulfil basic personal needs. Development of deeper relationships is likewise dependent on the improvement of interpersonal skills. The fulfilment of values related to advocating social justice goals in organisations rests on the person being able to interact with a wider range of people – managers as well as workers, customers as well as other stakeholders with whom the organisation deals.

Interpersonal skills also develop because the person with the more expansive world views will interact with a wider range of people for a wider range of motivations. In contrast, a person whose main focus is their family and friends will have more limited types of interactions.

Imaginal skills

Imaginal skills draw together the emotions, cognitive thought and fantasy to produce ideas. The task of imaginal skills is to process information from the senses, integrate it and explore solutions to problems. Imaginal skills are responsible for generating new ideas and creatively evaluating data that seems unconnected.

Imaginal skills underlie other skills. For example, they come into play when we interact with other people as much as when we are faced with a technical problem. The development of empathy with other people is essentially an imaginal skill, but it underpins effective interpersonal skills.

Imaginal skills can be cultivated or repressed, but such as they are they contribute to a person's fulfilment of their focus values under all the world views.

Systemic skills

Systemic skills look beyond particular parts to the functioning of a whole. These are the skills that recognise how things work together and how parts are inter-related, as opposed to awareness of component parts only. These skills concern awareness of the impact of dynamic processes and of the function of feedback.

There are different types of systems and there are natural properties of systems. According to Alistair Mant (1997), there are two types of systems. One is mechanical, where component parts can be removed and reassembled, or assembled in different ways, without damaging the capacity of the system to function. The other is organic, where parts are interrelated in such a way that removal of parts affects the whole. The possession of systemic skills includes the judgement to distinguish between these two types of systems.

There are various properties of systems that go beyond instrumental and interpersonal skills. The essence of systems thinking (see Senge, 1992) is to be able to see beyond immediate, linear cause and effect, to see processes of change and to be aware of such factors in systems as lags between actions and their effects. The ability to monitor systems and respond to them through feedback is also central – feedback can serve to reinforce effects or to counter-balance them.

Integration and transformation

Hall (1986) argues that people become ready to transform their current world view when they have, through experience and learning, not only developed the instrumental, interpersonal and imaginal skills applicable to their current world view, but they have integrated these through systemic skills. This integration includes self-awareness of one's skills, how they fit together and also, what one's limitations are. The person develops a sense of the wholeness of themselves and their world.

In terms of instrumental skills, a person becomes aware of what they can do and through observation of others, what they cannot do or can do only poorly. In terms of interpersonal skills, a person becomes aware of what they can achieve comfortably or with effort in the midst of the uncertainty of interacting with other people – such as entering into conversations with people they do not know, or asserting a point of view, expressing a feeling or making a request. In terms of imaginal skills, a person becomes aware of their own experiences in addressing problems, making decisions and pursuing optimism.

Systemic skills, at any particular point along the evolution of world views and values, enable the person to balance their efforts and attain emotional poise, and to discover values that give their life meaning. This continual questing leads to periodic shifts in perception of the world and motivations – hence the transformation of values. At every stage, the consolidation of focus values and the movement towards vision values is characterised by the submission of the ego to the larger vision. Some writers talk about the shrinking of the self (the ego-self) or of self-transcendence. The definition of ethics that was adopted earlier from Schweitzer fits well with this idea; Schweitzer saw the essence of ethics as being the selfless serving of others.

Sharing ethical standards

If people subscribe to different perceptions of the world and to different values and motivations, the question returns again: is there any meaningful sense in which we can discuss or share ethical standards? The five core human values claimed to give us a basis for sharing ethical standards, but now it seems that people's perceptions and experiences can be all but mutually exclusive.

There are several reasons why the picture is not as gloomy as this. The first reason is that as people move from one world view to another, they are moving into an enlarged understanding of the world, so they can comprehend the perceptions and motivations of the previous world views. As the diagram of William Kay's model of developing moral attitudes (Figure 4.1) showed, we bring along with us our earlier experiences of motivation, and circumstances can bring these to the fore again.

This indicates that people who work out of a particular world view can comprehend the perceptions and motivations of people working out of earlier world views. We should note, though, that a person who has moved beyond a particular world view may have an antagonistic or evangelical attitude towards people operating out of a world view they formerly held. This was discussed above in terms of the different ways in which people experience changes in perceptions and values.

The most important reason why people are able to converse and engage with one another about values, however, is that most people are in fact engaged with values in the same sense. According to Hall and Chippendale, most adults operate out of the world views 3, 4 or 5. The implication is that most people are dealing with common sets of values; the difference, for the most part, is that for some people they will be foundation values, while for others they will be focus values or vision values.

This realisation makes it easier to understand why people argue about values. When, for example, a person operating out of world view 3 talks about the importance of truth, they are inclined towards the versions of truth purveyed by the institutions to which they are loyal. A person who subscribes to world view 4 may have a more challenging, doubting approach to truth. The flashpoint in the argument is not just about what is true, however; it is the clash between the conflicting values of truth and loyalty. The difficulty is that it may not be clear to either party that that is the source of their differences.

Another aspect of the "do we share ethical standards?" conundrum is that the standard of behaviour demanded may be common, even though the reasoning and motivations for the behaviour may differ. This was illustrated by the example at the beginning of Chapter 4, where a wide range of reasons was given for not taking the hardware item from the computer warehouse where the person worked. One person's reason might be fear of punishment or deference to authority, while another person's reasoning might be an internalised, principled commitment to honesty.

A wide range of behaviour is covered by either laws or social mores. The effect is that the behaviour is either prohibited (stealing property) or required (helping an injured person), regardless of personal motivation. Recalling Verne Henderson's model of the development of shared social agreements about ethics (Chapter 2), we have to say that society determines many boundaries for ethical standards – and the primary focus of that social discourse is behaviour rather than motivations.

Insofar as motivations are included in the discussion of shared ethical standards in society, the result is a formulaic model of the "good citizen" and how that model citizen's motivations are described. We could say the common expectation is that people will operate, minimally, out of world view 3, and optimally out of world views 4 or 5. Accordingly, the corresponding motivations are imposed on everyone as social role expectations, regardless of personal perspectives or feelings. This being so, people who are self-obsessed or absorbed only in their own survival and success are forced to behave in accordance with the agreed social behaviour.

Nevertheless, the power of social expectations to expand the world views and values of individuals is limited. As Verne Henderson's model also illustrates, there is ample scope in work and living for people to engage in legal but unethical conduct. The effect of the social discourse about values is more to provide a common language about values than to achieve adherence to them. The common language often serves, contrarily, to mask the perceptual and motivational differences between people.

The existence of social models for ethical conduct can also substitute for personal reflection about one's "real values". As long as a shared model of the "good citizen" exists and is constantly reinforced by the organs of social discourse (speeches and comments by leaders, news media, television programs, movies, songs), it is easy for people to believe that they fulfil that social model. People may therefore be only minimally aware of their personal values (ie their values as lived rather than as espoused) or their underlying world view.

Evolution through world views and value sets goes hand in hand with growth in awareness of yourself, your values (espoused and lived), and your skills (the four types of skills described above). Growth in awareness has an impact on the five dimensions of the person and leads to enhancement of skills. The person develops the perception, the clarity and the emotional robustness to address life – consistently – from a new and expanded perspective.

The next two chapters will explore in more detail the way individuals can function ethically in organisational contexts, based on the meaning we have given in this chapter to the idea of functioning ethically. Chapter 8 will deal with the task of the leader – those who have power and position to influence and structure the environment and culture of organisations.

PART B   Workers and managers at work

Part B explores how our working lives can be strengthened and enriched through the ideas presented in Part A. The five-dimensional model of the person, the core human values and the Values Evolution Model combine to enable us to understand behaviour in the workplace and how to foster positive ethical conduct.

Applying the core human values in our work, whether we are managers or not, gives us a basis from which to evaluate conduct and a means of elevating behaviour from a compliance focus to the pursuit of higher values.

6

Working ethically in organisations

Many of the books on business ethics are pitched primarily at people who are in positions of power in organisations. There is certainly a need for books of that sort, but at the same time they are of scant comfort to the many people who are not in positions of power. These are the people who do not make the rules or the business plans, but who are expected to carry them out. On a regular basis they face the problem of witnessing behaviour they think is unethical and wondering if they should speak up about it, and the problem of being directed to do things they consider to be unethical. Can any useful counsel be offered about working ethically in situations where one does not have power?

One preliminary observation is worth making, to put the plight of the non-managerial worker into perspective. It is not uncommon for business ethics researchers to discover the same sentiment among business leaders. The CEO whose company engages in questionable business practices will often lament that they too feel powerless. They may be in charge of thousands of employees, but they say they are ruled by the shareholders, the board of directors, the stock market, or the practices of competitors. If they tried to take a more ethical stance, the business would fail or they would be driven out of their job.

The business leader's dilemmas will be addressed later in the book. The message we can take from their predicament for our present purposes is this: if they can fool themselves into thinking they are powerless, then perhaps that is true of workers too. Perhaps there are indeed things that workers can do to assert the importance of ethical behaviour, to act more in harmony with their personal values, and to foster better ethical ideals in organisational behaviour.

The previous chapters described a framework where people may derive their ethics from very different views of the world. We also described a sociological perspective where societies and organisations have an ongoing dialogue about values, but where they also reach a certain level of agreement about how to judge behaviour. Workers in organisations are therefore faced with two levels of concern:

- the various people they interact with (managers and other workers) may have different personal ethical standards and motivations, and

- organisations have operational cultures that hold a certain amount of sway over people's individual predilections – there are organisational ethical norms which dominate discourse and actions.

The question of ethics and organisational cultures will be examined from the leader's perspective in a later chapter. The issue here is that workers operate within the pressures and persuasiveness of this environment. Recognising this context, the first question that workers need to answer is: do I make a distinction between my own standards, what other people do and what the organisation does? Workers often face the difficulty of seeing others operate in what they think are unethical ways, and wondering how to deal with this. The second question is, what do you do when managers require you to do things you think are unethical?

The chapter will look at these two questions and what scope there is for the worker to act as an ethical agent in the organisation. The parameters of the worker's role will be defined as they give rise to duties and obligations to the organisation. The worker's response to this situation takes place in three layers. Much behaviour in organisations is routine and does not involve explicit decision-making; decision-making is subsumed in scripts and habits. That is the first layer.

The second layer consists of the web of relationships in the organisation. Workers are an active part of this web, forming their own relationships and being affected by relationships with all manner of people across the organisation, including co-workers and managers.

These two layers will be discussed in this chapter. The third layer will be discussed in the following chapter. The third layer is the area of decision-making, traditionally treated as the central issue for workers concerned to work ethically. How workers make decisions, and how they incorporate ethical concerns into their decision-making processes, is indeed important, but the situation would be misconceived if the significance of the other two layers of action was not acknowledged too.

Ethical standards for self and others

As the questions above indicate, there are lots of issues that need to be clarified before you can make intelligent decisions about ethics, even when you are "just" the worker, with (notionally) no power to dictate to or influence others. The question about your standards for your own behaviour versus your standards for other people's behaviour is an important one, and one that is often ignored in ethics books.

When should you speak up or take action on another person's actions that you think are unethical? There is a large class of behaviour where you might have your own standards but you recognise that you have no right to apply this standard to other people. However, there are some actions where you would consider you ought to intervene in some way. It may be that you think future repetitions of the action should be prevented, or it could be something more serious, where you think that this instance of the person's conduct should be punished.

The distinction we intuitively apply is related to the three-layered pyramid of ethics consisting of law, relationships and identity. We discussed earlier that ethics begins with what is defined as right and wrong by law; the next level of ethics consists of matters that pertain to good-quality relationships; while the highest level of ethics is about aspiring to be the best one can be and all that one can be.

The movement through the levels is a movement from compliance to aspiration. The rule we intuitively apply when monitoring other people's behaviour (in situations where we have no authority over them) is the inverse of this pyramid. If an action is a crime, then we feel obliged to report it. If it is about poor versus good-quality relationships, then we feel varying degrees of compulsion to speak up about the matter. When it comes to a person not fulfilling their personal potential we would not consider we had any right to speak up, unless we had some specific role in relation to them, such as a career counsellor or mentor.

In situations where the action breaks the law, the moral imperatives involved are generally about either harm or unfairness. Two good examples are work safety and equal opportunity, which are both regulated by laws which apply to most organisations in most countries. The nexus between law and the moral imperatives of harm and unfairness is indicated by the fact that when we see such conduct we look to see if there is a law we can use to upbraid the person responsible. Within an organisation we would first look to its policies.

An illustration of how the inverse pyramid applies to evaluating others' behaviour is the issue of drinking during work hours. Suppose a group of workers regularly drinks alcohol at lunchtime.

In one situation, the workers work in a call centre. The effect of drinking at lunchtime is that they are less attentive to customers in the afternoon, and sometimes careless in dealing with administrative details. As a fellow worker, you may disapprove of this laxity; nevertheless, no law is broken and no one is harmed.

In a second situation, the workers operate heavy machinery. Not only can this expensive equipment be damaged as a result of the workers' carelessness, there is a real risk of someone getting seriously injured. This risk is reflected in safety laws that prohibit workers from operating the machinery while under the influence of alcohol.

Thus, in the second situation, the rules you apply to other workers are the same as you apply to yourself, because both the law and potential risk to people's physical safety are involved. Similarly, if a person is being harassed at work and is too intimidated to speak up about it, the existence of equal opportunity laws and the harm to a person's safety and well-being indicate that you should take some action to address the matter.

When the action is not so much a breach of legal compliance but more a matter of the quality of relationships, the imperative to censure the behaviour is more diffused. This question has to be seen in the context of the society's culture. In most countries today there are accepted notions of personal choice, freedom and difference which take much human behaviour and interaction out of the realm of legal strictures. Similarly at a social level, people's behaviour is not as subject to rigid mores, because people either belong to different churches or to no church at all, and were schooled in different types of schools.

But the most important aspect of responding to other people's actions that impact on the quality of relationships is that ethical development depends on personal choice, not compliance. So, to a certain extent you can force people to obey the law, but you cannot force them to act ethically in a more elevated sense. Rudolf Steiner (1982, p 68) makes this point in relation to children's education: "We may be able to enslave the child with commands, but we can never foster the moral life which must spring forth from the depths of the soul. This we can only do if, apart from commanding or forbidding, we can arouse in the child a fine feeling for good and bad, beautiful and ugly, true and false."

If this is true of a relationship where authority is involved, as with the teacher/parent and the child, then it is even truer of the worker who is not in a position of authority over others. One cannot compel others to comply with one's own personal ethic, and nor would that be productive. The situation calls for methods of influence rather than coercion.

There are other factors at play here too, namely meaning and context. We may think a person's action is unkind or untruthful but fail to see the meaning of the action from that person's perspective. Similarly we may fail to see the entire context in which they acted. This is one strong reason for not judging others. Meaning and context will be discussed further below.

A problem still remains – we may accept that our rules for our own conduct differ from the rules we will apply to other people. However, the big question that individuals regularly face in organisations is how to respond when managers and company norms demand that they do something they think is unethical. Workers also face the arguments that managers give for these actions. We need to examine this more closely.

Tales of managerial denial of ethics

Promises to customers are one of the hot spots for individual ethical dilemmas, For example, "Yes, we can have that to you by next week". Suppose a salesperson and his manager are meeting with an important client. The manager wants to be sure of the sale, so she makes the promise. The salesperson knows there is no way that delivery can happen by next week; the manager does not know this, but she doesn't ask the salesperson and is only interested in getting the client's commitment. Possibly the manager thinks she can motivate the production people to rise to the challenge, and that will work.

In this situation, when the salesperson suggests that the promise was unethical, the manager responds that maybe the salesperson is just not tough enough to be in the industry. Some of the salesperson's friends agree with both statements – yes, it was unethical, but yes, that is the nature of business, and perhaps he should look for a job in the public service, or as a teacher. In the next chapter, we will discuss the different ways in which workers can respond to concerns about their organisation's ethical conduct. Here, we want to discuss the situation of the worker faced with what they see as a demand to act in ways they consider to be unethical.

We need to dig into the "toughness" argument and see what drives it. What is the payoff for the manager? She wants to win the client's business, shut competitors out, and achieve revenue that exceeds budget. This is an enterprise that she sees as difficult, and one where she may have to resort to risky manoeuvres, tricks and aggression to achieve the goal. But she is ambitious and willing to try almost anything. For her, ethics are off the radar – the closest she gets to ethics is when they manifest as threats; more particularly, when they manifest as legal threats *and* there is a high risk of being caught.

There are two kinds of beliefs that underlie the conduct of people like this manager. The first belief is what we described in the early stages of the Values Evolution Model: the world is a hostile place and security and victory have to be obtained by whatever means possible, by force if necessary. The second belief acknowledges that business could be done in a more ethical way, and success on that basis would be possible, but it takes too much effort and is less certain, so blunt methods are used instead.

So, when pressed, people like the manager above take refuge in beliefs, and the question becomes, are those beliefs true or not? For the worker faced with these arguments, the choices are unpalatable. The manager's way of operating is founded in deep beliefs which may not even be conscious or articulated, and those beliefs are accompanied with deep fears about security and failure. The worker first has to examine their own beliefs and test the truthfulness of the manager's assertions. Avoidance and denial, married to authority and power, are a formidable opponent.

The two following stories, related by the fibre asbestos, illustrate the potency of denial and avoidance in driving corporate decisions and behaviour into unethical territory. The stories concern the behaviour of corporations and their leaders, but we shall use the stories to illustrate the arguments that leaders and managers often make, as a prelude to addressing the situation from the worker's perspective.

The Manville Corporation in the USA and James Hardie Industries in Australia both engaged in systematic denial of the dangers of asbestos over long periods of time (Haigh, 2006; Peacock, 2009; Weiss, 1994). The first indications that asbestos caused cancer and asbestosis had come to Manville as long ago as the 1930s. Manville's managers actively suppressed this information for decades, and its medical staff even concealed workers' own illness from them. In one of the many trials over workers' claims for compensation, a Manville lawyer said the company decided that keeping employees working until they died would save them a lot of money (Paine, 2003; Weiss, 1994).

Manville filed for bankruptcy in 1982, facing claims of US$2 billion. It was, at the time, the largest US industrial corporation ever to file for bankruptcy. The Australian asbestos-manufacturing company, James Hardie Industries, faced a similar situation from the 1990s onwards, with mounting workers compensation claims by workers. The same pattern of management conduct appears to have prevailed. Evidence has surfaced to show that managers knew decades earlier of the dangers of asbestos, and they suppressed this information. By 2004, a total of 27,000 Australians had died of asbestos cancers (Hills, 2004), and as many again are predicted to die by 2020.

Despite the earlier example of Manville to observe, James Hardie (which shifted its corporate headquarters from Australia to The Netherlands in 2003) sought to disown any responsibility for the people who attracted asbestos-related diseases. Its narrow legal analysis was that all asbestos manufacture was carried out by two of its subsidiary companies, and it could legitimately allow them to lapse into liquidation if the cost of claims became too high. Aware that this would not be acceptable to the community, it set up a trust fund to handle claims, the Medical Research and Compensation Foundation. However, the funds it handed to the trust fell far short of its own calculations of likely claims – the trust would have run out of funds within a couple of years.

An inquiry by the New South Wales Government (the Jackson Inquiry) concluded that the real figure for claims could reliably be assessed at around AU$2.25 billion, not the AU$293 million originally placed in the trust fund (Sexton & Stephens, 2004). Even so, James Hardie remains a very profitable company, and can afford to pay the costs of asbestos victims' claims.

The more difficult decision was that facing Manville, namely, to provide for the costs of claims *even if* it meant that the company would cease to exist. At a much earlier stage they should have asked, should we stop manufacturing asbestos products, even if that means we may, or will, go out of business? And this is essentially the same question facing managers and workers regularly at the micro level – should we do X or refrain from doing X even if it costs us business?

The comparisons between Manville and James Hardie are even more interesting when we look at the behaviour of particular managers in each company. The New South Wales Government Inquiry observed that there was a "culture of denial" in James Hardie. This was the same comment made in proceedings against Manville.

Ethics or survival?

In contrast to the prevailing ethos, one of the managers at Manville strived to tackle the asbestos issue. Bill Sells had commenced work there as a young man during the 1970s, when large numbers of workers began to manifest asbestos-related diseases. Sells spent much of his time visiting them in hospital and was strongly affected by that experience. He emerged as a vigorous advocate for product stewardship, the idea that companies have a responsibility for the effects of their products, extending through the entire stream of commerce (Paine, 2003).

In contrast, despite the fact that by 2004 the number of claimants had grown to hundreds, the new chairperson of James Hardie in 2004, Meredith Hellicar (who had been a Board member since 1992) had not met an asbestos victim until some of them attended a company shareholders' meeting following the Jackson Inquiry. She offered an apology to the victims for their distress.

Despite this, the company's Chief Executive Officer, who was responsible for statements to the stock market in 2001 maintaining that the trust fund being set up was fully funded for future claims, remained absent from Australia during and following the inquiry. The inquiry criticised his conduct severely, even suggesting that he may have breached the corporations law in his statements to the stock market. Subsequently, the

Ch. 6 | Working ethically in organisations

CEO was reassigned to another role in the corporation in the USA, a safe distance from accountability.

The message that comes through these stories is that the defence of protecting corporate success and survival should always be questioned. Sometimes it is just a way that people fend off issues they do not want to face – perhaps the manager who felt the need to make the rash promise to the customer does not want to tackle the harder task of working out how to do business ethically. In Chapter 8 we will look at the argument that doing business ethically is also the pathway to sustainable success.

Sometimes, the ethics of the situation indicate that the business should do the right thing even if it means that the company may die. Asbestos is a good example to illustrate this message, because it was not as if the instigators of the mining and manufacture of asbestos products initially knew that it was dangerous. Asbestos was seen for a long time as the miracle fibre of the 20th century, and it was used in house cladding, roofing, brake linings, insulation and water pipes. If it is assumed that the company leaders of the time were ethical and had good intentions towards their workers and customers, then the knowledge that asbestos was an insidious killer should have stopped them in their tracks.

By mid-2005, James Hardie had agreed in principle to fund compensation for asbestos victims over the next four decades. Its business, three-quarters of which is now in the USA in fibre cement (non-asbestos) home cladding products, is performing well. Australian governments are still pondering proposals to introduce tougher laws for corporations to prevent a replay of the James Hardie affair. The New South Wales Attorney-General, Bob Debus, commented, "I cannot understand that directors and managers should assume it's appropriate for a company to behave in a profoundly anti-social way in order that they may maximise profits to shareholders".

A well-known example that shows it is possible for a company to act in a socially responsible manner in the face of a threat to its viability is Johnson & Johnson (Paine, 2003). In 1982 (ironically, the same year Manville filed for bankruptcy), seven people in the USA mysteriously died and the link between them was Tylenol, a market-leading pain reliever made by Johnson & Johnson. It was subsequently learned that the product had been subjected to tampering, and the tablets contained cyanide.

The product held 40% of market share for pain relievers and it was a major portion of the company's profit. Despite this, without hesitation, Johnson

& Johnson took the product off the market and undertook costly measures to ensure the safety of consumers, accumulating losses of over US$100 million. The significant aspect of this story is CEO James Burke's explanation for the company's decision. He said, "I think the answer comes down to the value system." The decision was not conditional on whether the company could afford it, or whether it would recover. It was simply not prepared for its products to put customers' lives in danger.

Johnson & Johnson's managers did, in fact, have a strong belief that doing what is right works. And the product subsequently more than recovered its position in the market, when Tylenol was reissued in new tamper-proof packaging. This is a reassuring story for ethical conduct. What we need to do is translate this message into the context of the individual worker up against an authority that is unwilling to see things ethically. Our immediate concern is what a worker can do to carry out their own work ethically, even if the working environment is not conducive to it.

Returning to the salesperson's predicament, we can at least say that he does not have to operate in the same way as his manager. In his own contacts with customers, he can restrict his promises to those he can keep, and he can demonstrate honesty in all his dealings. He can focus on the other factors which make his company an attractive supplier compared with the competition. He can do his homework with the production people before he sets up a sale to ensure that delivery is possible in the time frame promised. He can put in extra effort to follow up on sales, and build up trust between himself and the customer by keeping communication regular and clear.

The essence of this course of action for the salesperson is that he operates out of a belief in ethical values, and he models this for others. Remembering that people's values evolve through a process of seeing their vision values come to life and their focus values fulfilled (Chapter 5), he seeks to provide a positive role model. The dedicated effort towards bringing his own values to life brings energy and intelligence to bear upon his goals, and this fosters success.

With regard to company instructions to workers to do things that are clearly wrong, such as telling lies to customers in order to hook them on a purchase, the range of options for action described later in this chapter needs to be explored. But there is another important aspect of the worker's situation that needs to be discussed prior to that – the impact of roles on ethics.

The worker's role and its impact on ethics

The Values Evolution Model declares that people have different understandings of ethics depending on their value set. If they have adopted world view 3, then the organisation is an important focus for them. Their view of ethics is wrapped up in views of loyalty and acceptance of the organisation as a promulgator and arbiter of rules. Their strong tendency is not to question the organisation's conduct. An employee who operates out of a different world view will see the ethics of the situation differently. A person who sees the world under world view 4 or 5 will apply a greater scrutiny to organisational policies and actions.

However, layered over the employee's world view is society's consensus about right and wrong, and the laws that give expression to this consensus. These two factors provide a further set of influences on individual employees when they face situations of conflict between society's consensual ethics, the law, and organisational policies and practices. The law and socially agreed ethical standards insist that our duties as human beings and members of society come before organisational demands. However, the ethical demands of society are generally less specific than company practices, more distant and less subject to accountability.

Moreover, the employer pays the worker's wages, so workers are directly dependent on the employer for their livelihood. This factor may be more or less important to the worker according to the vagaries of the job market and the worker's economic circumstances, but it holds some weight as an immediate, conditioning factor on the worker's freedom to choose.

The tensions between the pressure to carry out one's duties unquestioningly and the pressure to apply an independent ethical standard to one's actions as an employee is to some extent mediated by legal factors. The employment relationship is regulated by the law in many ways:

- the employment relationship is a legal relationship and as such is regulated by common law precedents and contract law;
- industrial laws and tribunals regulate the employment relationship, providing a recourse for both employees and employers to resolve many kinds of disputes;
- other types of laws, along with associated government bodies and tribunals, regulate more specific aspects of employment, such as

- occupational health and safety, discrimination and harassment, and privacy; and

- whistleblower protection laws in the USA and Australia extend legal regulation to some types of employment-related activities, in particular, the reporting by employees of suspected unlawful activities by their employer or its officers.

The existence of these laws is the dynamic outcome of ongoing debate in society about the respective rights and duties of employers and employees. The laws are not a substitute for debate about the ethics of employee and employer actions, but a contemporary expression of society's judgement on employer-employee incidents and situations that have occurred to date. The flavour of the laws varies from country to country according to the particular events that have occurred in each place.

As an example, the Sarbannes-Oxley laws on whistleblower protection in the USA were framed as a response to the spate of bankruptcies around 2001 (Enron and others) which involved large-scale, fraudulent corporate practices. Australia's experience was with HIH (the insurance company) and a number of other companies, but the laws created were part of the ongoing Corporate Law and Economic Reform Program (CLERP). The laws in both the USA and Australia created a scheme whereby employees could report wrongdoing with impunity, but the US laws go further in specifying how organisations go about establishing their own whistleblowing programs.

The whistleblower protection schemes are of interest here because they assume a context where both employers' and employees' general rights, duties and responsibilities are defined. These can be described in terms of broad principles that apply across countries, even though the specific legal cases and legislation which support these principles differ from country to country. The duties are set out below. This description is not intended to be a treatise on employment law, but a sufficient summary of the legal framework in order to explain the context in which employees make their ethical decisions.

Employer duties and obligations

The starting point for employers is that they are deemed by the law to have a "managerial prerogative" to run their businesses as they see fit. The task that legislators address is to determine what boundaries to place on this prerogative. As was noted earlier, the twin purposes of law in the area of employment, insofar as it deigns to intrude on the employer's business, are to protect employees from harm and to ensure fairness. The employers' duties towards employees, as prescribed by the various laws referred to above, generally include:

- to pay wages or salary in accordance with the contract of employment and any industrial instruments (awards, workplace agreements etc) that apply;
- not to reduce the employee's pay rate, status or classification;
- not to increase the employee's workload and responsibilities unreasonably or without consultation;
- to ensure the employee's health and safety (physical, but also extending to psychological harm, eg through bullying or harassment);
- to ensure the employee is not subject to discrimination in any aspect of employment (recruitment, promotion, conditions and pay) on the basis of non-job-related attributes such as race, sex, religion or age;
- to act with reasonableness and fairness;
- to ensure confidentiality of information about the employee; and
- to act fairly and reasonably in situations relating to job security (eg consulting with employees about redundancies, compensating employees for redundancy etc).

Even over the last two decades the above duties of employers have shifted. For example, job security was considered to be a general duty of employers until the 1980s. Now the employer's duty is generally understood to extend only as far as acting reasonably and fairly when redundancies occur. Tribunals will also examine whether redundancies are legitimate. If they are a sham intended to fulfil other employer agendas, then tribunals will not accept them. In one Australian case, a mining company made its entire, unionised and award-based workforce redundant and then sought to rehire a smaller number of workers on individual contracts. The tribunal which heard the subsequent dispute refused to allow the redundancies to stand.

Nevertheless, the ground has shifted away from the view that employers have an obligation to provide security of employment to their employees.

Many employers have moved towards a more contingent workforce, and in Australia in 2008, 28% of people in employment were part-time, while 25% were employed on a casual basis (ABS, 2008). Australia ranks high among world economies in terms of the level of contingent work, even higher than the USA. Contingent work represents a shift of balance between companies and governments when it comes to responsibility for the employment and income of the population. Corporations seem to have overthrown the idea that they have a duty to provide employment for people in the areas in which they operate.

This shift affects the ethical context of employees' and employers' responsibilities, because it changes the conception of mutual duties. Just as the employer's duty to provide job security is much more attenuated than it was 20 years ago, so the employee's concomitant duty to be loyal to the employer has to be seen as diminished.

The other aspect of the shift towards the contingent workforce is that it potentially lessens even further the power that such workers have to question what they are asked to do. If they do not do what the employer wants, they may not get work. This argument is complex, however, because the countervailing factor is that demographic trends are causing workers to be in shorter supply – the ageing population and the expected increase in retirements of skilled workers over the next few years suggest that workers, whether contingent or not, may be looking towards an increase in power that would give them leverage to insist on higher ethical standards.

Duties and obligations of employees

Just as the employer's starting point is the managerial prerogative, the starting point for employees is the historic idea of the servant-master relationship. Historically, the servant was owned by the master and the master virtually had free rein in directing and controlling the servant, even to the extent of beating them if they displeased them in any way. The current construction of the employer-employee relationship is derived from this history of a stark imbalance of power. The relationship nowadays owes more to contract law, with the employee being seen as a free agent who contracts with an employer for the supply of their skills and labour in exchange for specified remuneration and conditions.

This framework carries a number of implications for the employer-employee relationship, as follows:

- employees, in accepting a particular job, hold out that they have the competencies to carry out that job; in conjunction with this, they accept a duty to apply those skills in the job and to do so with reasonable care and effort;
- employees have a duty to obey "the reasonable and lawful directions of the employer";
- employees have a duty to act in good faith – this duty means that they will look after their employer's interests, they will cooperate with the employer and they will not carry on their own business while on the employer's time;
- employees have a duty to be honest with the employer, eg they will not steal the employer's goods or money, or deal with the employer's equipment dishonestly or use it for their own purposes;
- employees will preserve the confidentiality of the organisation's information and not use it to compete with the employer or assist a competitor;
- employees agree that works created or inventions made as an employee belong to the employer;
- employees will abide by any agreements made as part of their contract – this could, for example, relate to moral rights or restraints of trade following termination of employment.

Employee duties and ethics

Each of the employer and employee duties described above is supported by a long history of legislation and/or case law in Australia, the USA, the United Kingdom and other Western countries. This implies an existing wealth, or weight, of precedents on which to base a discussion of how workers can work ethically in organisations. However, the situation is not so determinative; society's standards change and particular legal cases tend to apply to specific jurisdictions or types of applicants. The issue of job security illustrates well how legal rulings have shifted along with the economic environment of society.

Moreover, as was pointed out in an earlier chapter, many of the issues that confront workers are not neat, legal/illegal questions. Most often, quandaries fall into the category of "legal, but, is it ethical?". The criterion of "lawful but reasonable" commands does little to help the employee clarify ethical issues. And people in organisations have particular roles to perform, so the scope of expectation is narrow, and geared towards the organisation's interests. For all of these reasons, there is a strong tendency for employees to accept their organisational role unquestioningly.

Even people who have a profession – to which they supposedly make a commitment above their organisational affiliation – tend to favour the organisation's interests over their professional judgement. Engineering offers many examples. The Challenger space shuttle explosion, for example, that killed the seven people onboard seconds after its takeoff in January 1986, was a situation where engineers knew about problems that could lead to an explosion, but did not speak up.

Roles may also contain conflicting demands. Call centre operators, for example, have to try and conclude calls quickly. On the other hand, they have to be polite, meet customers' requests and find answers to their questions. Performance targets are usually based on the more easily assessable criterion, that is, number of calls concluded, and bonuses may be riding on the attainment of these targets. Added to this, many call centres monitor workers' performance electronically, and the pressure of this surveillance on the worker can be quite intense.

Note too, that in this call centre example, the behaviour that is difficult to monitor is the behaviour related to customer satisfaction. The temptation for the worker is to use whatever tactics they can think of to get the customer off the line. Transferring the customer to someone else is one tactic, saying that a product/service/person isn't available (that is, lying) is another.

Maurice Schweitzer from Wharton Business School and two colleagues (Schweitzer, Ordonez & Douma, 2004) conducted some experiments to examine the impact of goals and rewards on ethical behaviour. Their first observation was that all the studies they looked at only talked about the benefits of goal-setting and rewards. In the experiments they conducted they found that people were more likely to cheat when they were falling just short of reaching a goal, there was a reward involved, and there was a low likelihood of being detected.

The problem in work situations is that the factors that are really important to the success of the business tend to be the qualitative ones like customer satisfaction, not the quantitative ones like number of calls completed. And the qualitative goals are harder to monitor or measure. From our perspective of the ethics of the worker, where we take the broad view that ethics includes good relationships as well as compliance with rules, there is an exquisite tension in trying to be ethical in a work situation like the call centre.

From the perspective of the organisation, the system of monitoring the crude, quantitative goals and rewarding the attainment of those goals (especially where base rates of pay are low) is destined to encourage unethical behaviour. Schweitzer concluded that cheating was very likely where the reward was high when a target was reached, but zero until that point. He gave the example of a car sales business where the reward for selling 30 cars in a given period was a trip to Hawaii, but selling 29 cars was not rewarded at all.

As far as the worker is concerned, this discussion yields the conclusion that the work environment can make it difficult to operate on an ethical basis, especially when the worker's performance is treated competitively against other workers. To take the call centre environment again, if a customer rings up about an insurance claim and they are in a very emotional or confused state, the pressure to conclude calls quickly discourages any inclination to be compassionate. If the worker does take the extra time to calm the caller and guide them gently through the business they have to transact, they are not rewarded for building customer satisfaction; they are punished by the company's system of rewards for spending the time with the customer.

The demands on employees in their work roles can lead to situations where they do things at work that they would never do at home or among their friends. Their standards of conduct in the two spheres are totally separate and at odds with each other. Workers may lie to customers, cheat on performance measures, divert work that is their responsibility to other employees, and yet go home and be a model of virtue with their families and friends.

Much of this problem, we have indicated, lies with the structure of the situation. Company systems, managerial and peer pressures can militate against ethical behaviour, and can lead to employees narrowing their conception of ethics in two ways:

- ethics is narrowed so that it is viewed as just a matter of compliance with rules rather than the broader, aspirational view that includes treating other people decently; and
- ethical responsibility is handed over to the organisation – employees narrow their vision to merely carrying out their specific job role, without regard to the ethical impacts of the organisation's activities as a whole.

Scripts

Despite the imbalance of power in the work environment – workers are dependent by definition and generally in fact, and workplaces are not democracies – integrity at work can begin with an understanding of the dynamics of the situation. Workers are subject to a context that operates in three layers – (1) scripts and routines, (2) relationships, and (3) decision-making.

By scripts, we mean the normal, taken-for-granted routines that people follow regularly without question. Decision-making does not consume the greater part of daily work in organisations. Rather, people carry out tasks and address situations by calling on set patterns of behaviour. These patterns form out of organisational culture, policies and operating procedures. We will discuss the importance of scripts and relationships before turning to decision-making.

Linda Trevino and Katherine Nelson (1995) define scripts as "cognitive frameworks that guide human thought and action. Information processing is made much more efficient because a cognitive script allows the individual to call on an established behaviour pattern and act automatically without contemplating every case in great detail." Given that we deal with huge amounts of information every day, scripts are a valuable asset. They simplify our experience and allow us to concentrate on what is new and challenging, the situations that require real decision-making energy.

However, the danger of scripts is that we screen out a lot of information as we look for the familiar pattern. In looking for the pattern that generates a comfortable script, we may miss the clues that this particular situation is different. We may also act unethically without ever giving it much thought.

This concept is best explored by observing yourself in the workplace for a week. Work at identifying your routine actions and decisions, and try to "unpack" the scripts you use to handle these situations. What assumptions are you making about persons, situations, background factors etc? Could this lead you to treat someone unfairly or unkindly, or do something that is unethical? What could you change about the way you process these situations?

Dennis Gioia, a management writer who had a profound experience of being involved in a corporation's unethical behaviour, drew the following lessons from the experience about the dangers of script processing: "because scripts are context-bound and organisations are potent contexts, be aware of how strongly, yet how subtly, your job role and your organisational culture affect the ways you interpret and make sense of information (and thus affect the ways you develop the scripts that will guide you in unguarded moments)" (in Trevino & Nelson, 1995).

The last comment of Gioia's is significant, namely, the reference to "unguarded moments". His point is that sometimes, circumstances require a swift but ethically-charged decision that will have far-reaching consequences for yourself or your organisation. There is little time to ponder, so what governs your choice at that moment is important.

There is something of a paradox here. On one hand, you want to be alert to the uniqueness of the situation, so that you do not do the wrong thing because you acted automatically, according to a script, and were blind to an ethically significant factor in the particular situation. On the other hand, you want to ensure that your scripts incorporate ethical principles so that you can rely on them to steer you through the many situations that do in fact fall within the bounds envisaged by those scripts.

This idea has much in common with Stephen Covey's idea of habits, as in *The Seven Habits of Highly Effective People* (1990). An example of how this manifests is in the response of the management at Johnson & Johnson during the Tylenol crisis, referred to above. If they had not had well-established habits based on ethical conduct, their response was more likely to have been confused, indecisive, defensive and evasive. A similar point is made by Lennick and Kiel in *Moral intelligence* (2008).

Relationships

The second layer is relationships – the quality of decision-making is conditioned by the quality of relationships in organisations, and even from a non-managerial position, a worker can exercise influence through the relationships they develop with their peers and managers. To go back to our definition of ethics – the essence of ethics is how we learn to go beyond ourselves and consider the well-being of others, of society and the world as a whole.

Relationships with other people are both the outcome of our efforts to live out ethical values and the means by which we do so. But there is a critical difference between relationships in a community context and relationships in a business and organisational context. The latter type of relationships are goal-driven, and on some accounts at least, this is at odds with ethics.

Business and organisational life consists of a series of transactions, where it can be argued that relationships are often not necessary at all, and are at best only secondary. An example is getting on a bus and buying a ticket from the driver. We do not ask each other about our families, and seldom even comment on the weather. There may be ten people in the queue behind me, who will get very annoyed if we do, and the bus has a timetable to keep. This is the scenario that seems to undermine the idea that relationships are important in business. If ethics advocates are going to argue for relationships, it suggests that ethics is irrelevant in business life.

The moral theory that is most problematic in this regard is that of Immanuel Kant. His moral theory was founded on the concept of duty. In one formulation of that duty, he said "Act so that you treat humanity, whether in your own person or in that of another, always as an end and never as a means only" (Kant, 1994, p 279). While Kant's formulation accommodates situations like the bus ticket purchase (ie don't forget that the bus driver is human), it has to be said that the balance of many organisational interactions leans heavily towards the transactional rather than the relational. In addition, the rhetoric of goals, efficiency and effectiveness that conditions much of organisational life increases the emphasis on the transactional focus.

The perception of the importance of relationships in organisations is, however, changing. It was noted in an earlier chapter that knowledge has increased in importance in recent decades as the basis for commerce, in contrast to a reliance on physical capital and resources. This realisation initially fuelled a focus on technical systems for managing information.

However, more recently, understanding about the significant factors in fostering a knowledge-based organisation has evolved. Now, the emphasis is far more on the importance of tacit knowledge and the building of communities of practice (Nonaka and Takeuchi, 1995; Bassi & McMurrer, 2004). Suddenly, relationships are seen to be important to business outcomes.

In parallel with this evolution, the discourse about emotional intelligence has likewise thrown the focus onto the importance of relationships to the business success of organisations. Daniel Goleman (1998) and others have argued that cognitive and analytical skills are necessary but insufficient for effectiveness, both for managers and workers. The emotional intelligence that is required is the set of skills to manage one's emotions so that one can build good relationships with others.

In the emotional intelligence literature, relationships are considered in the business context. Unlike Kant, with his emphasis on people as ends in themselves, with the corollary of relationships existing for their own sake, Goleman deals with relationships that do have ulterior purposes. The perspective of Goleman's work is essentially pragmatic – as a matter of fact, the people who have most success in business are the people who can cultivate relationships.

We may think that Kant's dichotomy between viewing people instrumentally and viewing them as ends in themselves is more radical than need be. If we consider the bus driver, when we greet her civilly and offer her the right money, we are endeavouring to treat her considerately and are to that extent acknowledging her humanity within the confines of our transaction. There is no contradiction between this and transacting our business. The two levels co-exist.

Nevertheless, we might also think that the literature on emotional intelligence ignores the ethical import of relationships or, perhaps, glides over it. When we say a person establishes effective relationships, our orientation is towards organisational and personal success objectives. This is fine as long as the situation does not present a conflict between my ends and your ends, but it does not illuminate how we should resolve situations where there is a conflict between the two.

To look at this matter more closely, let us take some of the descriptions Goleman gives of the elements of social competence. These fall into two groups – those concerning empathy (awareness) and those concerning social skills. The former seem unproblematic from an ethical perspective. Empathy and awareness are in fact the foundations of ethical development.

The social skills, however, are a two-edged sword. Goleman identifies eight elements:

- **Influence** – wielding effective tactics for persuasion
- **Communication** – listening openly and sending convincing messages
- **Conflict management** – negotiating and resolving disagreements
- **Leadership** – inspiring and guiding individuals and groups
- **Building bonds** – nurturing instrumental relationships
- **Collaboration and cooperation** – working with others towards shared goals
- **Team capabilities** – creating group synergy in pursuing collective goals.

There is an assumed ethical base here, which shines through at certain points but is neither made explicit nor generally distinguished from the unethical use of these skills. For example, if one takes an ethical stance, then one can see how some of these attributes should tend to further the five core human values. Managing conflict, for example, furthers the ethical goal of peace. Collaboration furthers the ethical goal of love, and leadership may further the ethical goals of peace and right action.

However, if one imagines a less ethical person making use of this information to further selfish and unethical ends, then we would have to say that Goleman's account as presented, does not distinguish between the ethical and the unethical. A person may build bonds with other people, but with the sole intention of using those people for their own ends. A person may be good at influencing others but mislead or manipulate them. Emotional intelligence, then, may be valid (ie useful) but it is ethically neutral. It does not of itself embody values.

Kant would probably have agreed with this conclusion, given that the essence of his approach was that ethics cannot be reduced to anything else. It cannot be reduced to what is "rational" or what is emotionally "effective". The main problem with Kant's perspective was that he could not accept that reason and emotion coexist with ethics, and our motivations for actions are not "pure" but complex. Hence, we may develop genuine relationships with people, but we still conduct business with them whereby they perform functions for us, and presumably we do similarly for them.

The real art of conducting oneself ethically is not in keeping functional and non-functional relationships separate, but in knowing how to keep a healthy balance between the two aspects. The parameters of ethical relationships are provided by the core human values, and we recognise that there are some forms of conduct that may be effective in terms of emotional intelligence (eg persuasive, inspiring) but could be applied unethically.

Note we have said that good relationships are both an expression of ethics and an outcome of them. Good relationships are an expression of ethics because they are characterised by the core human values (truth, peace, right action, love and insight). But relating to others in this way results in the ongoing strengthening of relationships – this process is incorporated into the core human values themselves, as love and insight build the energy and uniqueness of relationships if the relationships are based on truth, peace and right action.

Can we apply these observations about relationships to the situation of workers in the organisation who are not in a position of power? Indeed we can, because none of these observations is dependent on the person having authority over others. Workers may establish relationships with their work colleagues, with managers and with other people across the organisation. In doing so, they are giving expression to their understandings, their values and their needs. The relationships they build may exhibit integrity, trust, respect and responsibility.

In fact, establishing relationships based on integrity and respect is the foundational step towards a more ethical organisation. Every such relationship creates a small zone of integrity and creates a small nudge of momentum towards a positive ethical climate.

In saying good relationships are based on the core human values, we need to add a further comment about how this relates to the functional/non-functional distinction in relationships. In organisations, most relationships are functional, whatever else they may be. It follows that values relating to competency are factors in these relationships – the competency/ethics distinction that Rokeach made.

Given the business pressures on organisations, it is to be expected that organisations will emphasise competencies, and spend time defining and fostering them. The work of Goleman constitutes a wake-up call that the nature of business has changed, and there is now a business aspect to relationships. So it is understandable that emotions have been drawn in and incorporated into the discourse of competencies.

We have also discussed at length the concept of roles in organisations, and how the expectations of workers are comprehensively defined both by law and business imperatives. But what we also identified in that discussion was that ethics calls us to recognise other employees as humans first. This is the real struggle for people in organisations. "Keeping the balance" between functional and non-functional relationships is perhaps not doing sufficient justice to what the core human values are asking for.

The identity/psyche dimension of the core human values makes the aim explicit – it is simply to be aware of others and to appreciate their humanity. It is the only one of the five values that is not connected to any immediate actions or worldly (business) projects. So, at their highest point the core human values are saying we need to see beyond the closed shop that organisations tend to become – it is perfectly natural for organisations to only see their own purposes.

What we have labelled "insight" – appreciating the humanity of others – is what needs to inform our relationships. In forming and maintaining relationships in organisations we need to be clear about what we are doing. In many relationships, both parties see quite clearly what the functional aspect is and both are quite happy to operate on a predominantly functional level. The problem arises when one party is proceeding on different assumptions to the other. This is when people get hurt and feel abused.

Hence the reason that integrity is given so much emphasis in relationships. To call upon Stephen Covey again, he asserts that personal integrity comes before the establishment of strong relationships with other people. In *Principle-Centered Leadership* (1992) he defines four levels of effectiveness, starting at the centre with the personal quality of trustworthiness and working outwards through the interpersonal, managerial and organisational levels. Goleman, too, includes trustworthiness in his list of the self-management competencies that precede social competence.

Perhaps we need to remind ourselves at this point that the endeavour to live ethically in organisations is not necessarily a recipe for worldly success. "The duties we owe to ourselves", as Kant put it, "do not depend on the relation of the action to the ends of happiness. If they did, they would depend on our inclinations and so be governed by rules of prudence" (Kant, 1963, pp 120-121).

What the works of Goleman, Covey and others do assure us, however, is that there is some sense in which it is worthwhile to be ethical. Although he does not devote much discussion to the concept, Covey talks about the "abundance principle" that sits behind principle-centred living – the belief that there is enough for all out there, and that acting ethically is the foundation for personal security, wisdom, guidance and power. He talks about win/win approaches to conflicts in organisations. The belief that win/win outcomes are possible in relationships with people accords with the more evolved world views that we discussed in Chapter 5.

Relationships, then, are the second arena of action for workers in organisations seeking to work in an ethical way. Given relationships and the scripts and routines that influence much of the worker's conduct, the third area, to be explored in the next chapter, is decision-making.

7

Making decisions ethically

This chapter deals with how to bring ethical principles to the decision-making process. It is intended for workers in organisations as guidance for their own conduct. Nevertheless, it also informs the next chapter, which speaks to managers about how they can foster ethics in their organisation. Encouraging an understanding of decision-making processes from an ethical perspective is part of what managers need to do to foster ethics.

To put the work of this chapter in context, decision-making is one aspect of people's behaviour. The previous chapter discussed other aspects of people's behaviour – the scripts which guide many of their daily actions and the culture of which those scripts are a part. We observed that scripts serve the function of simplifying work when the environment is complex but many actions are repetitive or fall into a class. However, scripts often operate to remove actions from ethical scrutiny, because in using a script, the person applies the assumption that the actions are part of a class which satisfies their (and the organisation's) ethical rules.

The decision-making model we develop will provide a process for working through the types of ethical issues that workers face. It will address questions such as:

- How do I identify the ethical aspects of work situations?
- How do I analyse and evaluate work situations in terms of ethics?
- How do I make decisions about what actions to take when I face ethical dilemmas?
- What do I do when I am faced with conflicts between values?

General propositions about ethical decision-making

There are a number of general propositions we can make about ethical decision-making before we proceed to develop a model. Hence, the first proposition of this chapter is that ethically responsible behaviour requires ongoing awareness that all actions are open to ethical scrutiny, even actions that seem to satisfy rules that we accept as aligning with our values. Ethical awareness is a continuous and expanding quality, and actions that we may have accepted routinely for long periods may come to be seen as deficient in ways that we have not previously recognised.

This is part of the tension of being human, where on the one hand we have to find ways of acting that allow us to be at peace with ourselves, but on the other hand we have to retain a "divine discontent" (in GK Chesterton's phrase) with our current level of achievement. This tension underlies everything that is said in this chapter.

The second proposition of this chapter is that an ethical decision-making model should be an integral part of all decision-making, not something that exists in isolation from other decision-making processes and models. It was not uncommon for textbooks on management up until the 1990s to have one chapter on managerial decision-making and a separate chapter on ethics. The ethics chapter often had its own decision-making model. This was an unfortunate situation, especially as it probably reflected common managerial thinking and practice. Ethics was seen as something special or problematic that cropped up from time to time, not as something that was part and parcel of everyday work and management practice. In these circumstances, when would the ethical decision-making model ever get used?

The third proposition is that ethical decision-making reflects back on our personal values, and this observation raises another common weakness of decision-making models. Often, decision-making models consist of a description of a process but not much of substance about the criteria for making the decision.

A rational process for making a decision can be described in quite generic terms. First one would gather information, then one would analyse it and consider and weigh options before deciding on a course of action. This is uncontroversial but not specific enough to be really helpful. The fact that this is commonly understood is indicated by our shared amusement with the following lines from Lewis Carroll's *Alice in Wonderland*:

> "Now for the evidence," said the King, "and then the sentence."
> "No!" said the Queen, "first the sentence, and then the evidence!"

The criteria for ethical decision-making are the heart of the process and the source of the real difficulties with making ethical decisions. In this chapter we will look at how values are applied in the decision-making process, and in particular, the thinking that takes place around conflicts between values. This will be linked back to the Values Evolution Model, with its challenging notion that people hold different sets of beliefs about the world and are persuaded to action by different values.

So far we have inferred that decision-making is a rational process that requires a step-by-step model. That is certainly the message one would get from a review of management or ethics texts. However, the model we have developed of the person sees cognition and rationality as one of only five dimensions of the person. The description we have presented sees rationality as one influence on behaviour, while emotions are another, with values playing a judging/evaluating role in between.

The fourth proposition of this chapter is that much decision-making in everyday organisational life is better characterised as intuitive and holistic rather than objective and methodical (Klein, 1999). Moreover, this is not a criticism – this is the way that experts seem to operate in making rapid but effective decisions in complex, stressful situations. There are qualities in this kind of decision-making that should be cultivated rather than eliminated. We need to discuss how this view of decision-making, which appears to be diametrically opposed to the rationalist view, can be reconciled with it.

A fifth proposition concerns the nature of ethical dilemmas: not every problem that is presented as an ethical dilemma is an ethical dilemma. In some cases, the truth is that the person knows what the right and wrong courses of action are; it is just that the risks and costs of doing the right thing are high. In Kant's terminology, this is a conflict between ethics and prudence, not a conundrum about what is right.

Consider this example. You work in a call centre selling a product that costs $500. Your job is to call people on a list and convince them to buy the product. It is difficult, and the response rate is very low, but then you realise that if you can just get them to the point where they are half-interested, you can send them the goods on approval, together with an invoice. You reason that many of them will buy the product because they then feel obliged to. Another factor is that they have to bear the cost of sending the product back. This tactic works long enough for you to book some good "sales" figures and earn a bonus.

Is this situation an ethical dilemma? No. Quite simply, the practice is illegal; it is in breach of trade practices law. It is also clearly unethical. The dilemma is about prudential factors only – do I risk not reaching my sales target by acting ethically, and go against the group's practices or the boss's directions?

However, there is a lot that can usefully be said about these kinds of situations. Harking back to the fourth proposition above, we noted that decision-making can involve intuitive thought processes. We should also see that ethical decision-making can involve exploring the complexities of situations and looking for innovative solutions rather than impaling ourselves on stark choices. Some writers refer to "moral imagination" (Johnson, 1993; Werhane, 1999) but it is more a case of applying our ordinary imagination to ethical dilemmas (Badaracco, 2002).

Finally, a sixth proposition is that decisions are of no value unless action ensues as a result. Decisions have to be implemented. This proposition also harks back to the fourth proposition, because the idea of an intuitive or expert model of decision-making is that situations are dealt with by actors who are immersed in the context and draw their judgements from there, not dispassionate, objective gatherers of data who sit apart from the fray.

> **SUMMARY: SIX PROPOSITIONS ON DECISION-MAKING**
> 1. All situations are subject to ethical scrutiny, even routine ones where we tend to operate from a script.
> 2. Ethics must be an integrated part of all decision-making, not just to some that we deem to be ethically problematic.
> 3. An ethical decision-making model consists of both a process and a set of criteria for decisions, and the criteria are based on values.
> 4. Much decision-making is intuitive and expert-like rather than objective, detached and step-based, and it may involve imagination and innovation.
> 5. Ethical dilemmas are about conflicts between ethical values, not about ethical choices that are difficult because high personal risks are involved.
> 6. Decisions alone are not sufficient. Decisions have to be implemented.

Types of decisions

Above, we referred to being attentive to whether a given situation is a routine, unproblematic one or whether it raises ethical questions that we should examine. How we classify situations also concerns the actions we choose to take in response. Having satisfied ourselves about the ethical import of a situation, we then have a choice about how to deal with it. We could confine ourselves to the particular situation we are facing, or we could decide that it has broader implications and our response should be at a wider level.

In organisations, actions are described hierarchically as operational, tactical or strategic. If we respond to a situation at an operational level, then we make a decision on the single instance. This might or might not be ethical. We might be making an exception to a rule for compassionate reasons or for corrupt reasons. Or we might deal with a situation as an exception because that is easier than dealing with the broader policy issue.

If we decide that there is a broader strategy or organisational policy that needs to be challenged, then we have to consider the ethical arguments in favour of that, and we have to take account of the proportionality of our response – for example, is the change justified by what it will cost? These

Ch. 7 | Making decisions ethically

questions will be discussed as we develop a model of ethical decision-making.

Perceptions: defining the situation

There is a great deal of truth in the saying that the way you define a situation determines the way you will respond to it. That puts it perhaps too strongly, but the intent of the saying is to emphasise just how much our perceptions affect our choices, or at the least, the scope of our choices. This reminds us again that to a hammer, everything looks like a nail.

In Chapter 5 we described how people under each of the seven world views regard the five core human values. So, for example, a person who subscribes to world view 3 looks at peace in terms of how it affects the stability of the institutions they rely on, starting with their family and extending to other institutions which are important to them, particularly their employer. Right action is understood in terms of, for example, their employer's company policies, and adherence to them. In other words, ethics is in fact defined by the need to preserve the institutions.

We know from the many public stories about whistleblowers, just how hard it is for them to gain a hearing from anyone, much less a willingness to consider the possibility that the organisation is doing wrong. World view 3 makes it easier to understand why this is. People who subscribe to this world view actually define ethics in terms of institutions; they rely on them as the source of stability in their lives. Questioning them is tantamount to questioning God or objective reality, and accusations made by whistleblowers are therefore extremely difficult to believe.

If this is how the world is understood, then every situation will be seen as a manifestation of that view. Thus, when an employee says that the organisation is doing wrong and covering it up, it is the employee who is questioned, not the organisation. The common experience of whistleblowers is to be accused of being mentally unstable, angry about something in their private life, they are looking for a diversion or revenge, or they are over-scrupulous and unrealistic.

We all share the knowledge from whistleblower stories that have been recounted in the public domain that it can take years and incredible persistence for whistleblowers to convince anyone that what they are saying is true, and that organisations have been doing wrong. The movie, *Erin Brokovitch*, is one example. The asbestos episodes in the USA and

Australia are another. It is not just people in authority who are sceptical and dismissive of the unpleasant message – more importantly, other people, ordinary employees who are colleagues, disbelieve and reject the possibility too.

This knowledge gives us some idea how strong world views and perceptions are. People are very strongly inclined to interpret what they see or hear through the filter of their beliefs about the world and how it operates. If something is to challenge this framework, the evidence has to be both powerful and persuasively presented.

What effect does this have on the consideration of ethics in decision-making? At an individual level, it means that we have to continually question whether our perception embraces the universal ethical values – the core human values of truth, peace, right action, love and insight – or whether our perception has been skewed by our world view (the way we think things are, or the way we fear things are). This struggle with our own world view will be explored further in Chapter 9.

A poignant example of how beliefs (world views) affect choices is given by a case that came before the Scottish Courts in 2000 ("Unholy orders", SBS, 2004). The case was brought against a nun by people who had been residents of an orphanage run by Catholic nuns in Aberdeen in the period from the 1930s through to the 1960s. The complainants described their treatment as young children in the orphanage, a gruelling experience that lasted throughout their childhood, with all manner of emotional cruelty and in many cases, physical beatings on a daily basis.

Yet the defence of the nun was that she believed that she had to beat the devil out of the children. She said that her practices were accepted at the time. Children were beaten savagely for wetting their beds, for not going to sleep when they should, and for any kind of disobedience. Today this type of conduct towards children is condemned, and the nun's argument on the basis of her beliefs about the devil is rejected. We should also note that the argument based on beliefs is complicated by social factors – the nun on trial also said she was only young and she was doing what she was told.

Despite the fact that beliefs about proper treatment of children and about the devil may have changed, there is a message in this sad story that remains true – that people's views about what actions are ethical or necessary are framed by our beliefs. And the area where this truth can be seen most clearly today is in the conduct of supervisors and managers.

We have argued that one important aspect of ethical behaviour concerns relationships. Workers should be treated with dignity and respect by their managers. But the issue of workplace bullying is on the rise. Why? Because in the current work environment, many managers are under pressure from their own bosses, and lack the emotional intelligence to process this conflict properly, so they retreat to the belief that they have to exert power over their workers in order to attain goals. Hence, workers are deliberately subject to humiliation, impossible workloads and conflicting demands. This situation is driven by the managers' beliefs, that are based on their lack of readiness for leadership, and their consequent fears.

Howard Gardner, Mihaly Csikszentmihalyi and William Damon stressed the importance of this perspective in *Good Work* (2001). They used the expression "one's construal of the situation". The ethical decision an individual makes, they maintained, will be significantly different according to the kinds of beliefs they have about themselves and their place in the world. A person's self-confidence, optimism and commitment to retaining control over their own life will lead them to adopt a robust stance when ethical issues arise.

The writers conclude: "All of us need to take stock of our own situations, weigh the various alternatives in light of our own values and goals, and make decisions that are optimal under the circumstances and that we can live with in the long run" (p 13).

The second aspect of perception and our definition of the situation is that life as a worker or a manager in an organisation is complex and fast, and ethics are often buried underneath this frenetic activity. Our scripts, which we discussed in the previous chapter, also make it harder to bring the ethical aspects of situations to the surface, because we routinely work on the assumption that the ethical questions have been settled through organisational policies, protocols and practices.

Researchers have investigated this phenomenon, and refer to it as lack of moral awareness or ethical sensitivity (Trevino & Nelson, 1995; Trevino & Brown, 2004). Awareness of the moral aspects of a situation is influenced by the moral intensity of the issue, which is a product of two factors:

- **risk of consequences** – how likely is it that the action will produce harmful consequences, and what would the extent of those consequences be?
- **social consensus** – do most people have the same ethical view about the situation and do they hold this view strongly? Note that this factor is linked to the fact that many people subscribe to world views that make conformity with the social group important.

There is another factor at play in awareness of the ethical aspects of situations, and this is, the extent to which ethics is part of people's language and discourse. Management is often very adept at excluding ethics from discourse in their organisation. In the health sphere, the term "negative patient outcomes" has come into use by administrators seeking to anaesthetise people from the consciousness of the human consequences of failed medical treatments. Don Watson (2004) claims it has even been used to refer to the death of a person.

In one egregious case of management double-talk known to the author, a corporate decision to transfer a function overseas and to make about 70 people redundant as a result, was described by senior executives in their communications to employees as a "project", an "initiative" and a "transition". The words "redundancy" or "job loss" were not used at all, and when the initial announcement was made, some staff did not realise that this was what the "project" entailed.

The biggest clue was the statement that the transition would involve the "reallocation of resources" to the overseas country. Later communications said staff had been advised of the "change" and they were described as "impacted". At the same time, the executives asserted defensively that they had communicated "openly and honestly about the project".

This kind of deceptive obfuscation is apparent every day in the media, and Scott Adams, with his Dilbert cartoon, has made a good living lampooning such use of language. The point to be made here is that bringing ethical language into the discourse of organisations has been found to positively influence moral awareness (Butterfield, Trevino & Weaver, 2000). This is clearly a responsibility of management. For the non-managerial worker, the goal may be furthered through the astute asking of questions that raise the ethical aspects of decisions.

The definition of the situation, then, is the foundation for ethical decision-making, so we need to approach it with our eyes open and our minds alert. The following qualities need to be fostered:

1. Be thorough and comprehensive in observing the situation and collecting information rather than coming to a hasty conclusion based on a narrow slice of phenomena – an incident or a comment.

2. Look for underlying causes and explanations rather than looking at the situation superficially.

3. Question whether your world view, biases and preferences are blinding you to important aspects of the situation.

The decision-making process

In *The Fifth Discipline* (1992), Peter Senge talks about two types of thinking. The first is divergent thinking, which people employ when they are in the exploration phase of problem-solving. In this phase, people think expansively and generate a range of different possible solutions. The other type of thinking is convergent, which is used when people have to analyse these possibilities critically, subject them to scrutiny and narrow them down so as to make choices. Both types of thinking are necessary.

In the same way, we believe that there are different types of decision-making situations, and two types of processes are required. The first fits a rational framework which follows logical steps. The second is the intuitive, embedded-in-context approach characteristic of experts in "live" situations.

The rational decision-making process will be described first. This approach is appropriate when a person, or a company, has to make a policy or strategy decision. There may be many factors that have to be weighed, and many facts and perspectives that have to be gathered and considered. Consequences and their likelihood may have to be calculated or estimated.

In this type of situation it would simply be irresponsible not to operate rationally. An intuitive "best guess" would be an abdication of responsibility. Recall that when we defined ethics earlier in this book, we included rationality as a pre-condition of ethical conduct.

Although we call this first decision-making model "rational", it does not exclude emotional or ethical factors. To make this clear, we will refer to this model as the Integral Decision-making Model. The model is rational in the sense that it follows a methodical process, but the material with which it deals incorporates all the five dimensions of the person – cognitive, emotional, values, energy and identity.

The model is also called the Integral Model because it unites the generic decision-making process and the ethical decision-making process. The model draws on the findings of management education, with the intention that it be applied to any management or workplace situation, not just those that are identified as ethically intense. This has to be so in order to avoid the trap of having a separate model that is only brought out when someone deems the situation to be about ethics. Hence, if necessary, at the appropriate stages in the model, the usual range of management techniques and theories can be used to elucidate aspects of the problem.

Integral Decision-making Model

STEPS	ACTIONS
Step 1 Formulate the problem.	Gather facts. Some facts may be clear, others may be uncertain and require assumptions and estimates to be made. (NB Decision-makers often ignore facts!) Be aware of how perceptions influence which facts are observed and how the problem is defined. Investigate causes, looking beneath the surface of what seems obvious. This may require attention to people's actions and motivations as well as physical and system events.
Step 2 Define a goal, or solution.	At this stage, emphasise goals rather than identifying rules to follow. Goals should be expressed in terms of ideal solutions, not limited by pessimistic assessments. Part of the process of decision-making is exploring the limits of the possible.
Step 3 Identify relevant stakeholders.	To an extent this occurs in steps 1 and 2, but the integral decision-making model ensures that the impact of decisions on all stakeholders is considered. These may include: workers, managers, customers or clients, suppliers, the broader public and community,

Ch. 7 | Making decisions ethically

	governments, trade unions and the physical environment.
Step 4 Identify decision criteria.	Consider what criteria are relevant. This must go beyond profit and loss, and extend to human ends. Aspects to consider include: • long-term financial consequences • impacts on specific stakeholders (see Step 3); • legal obligations, extending to codes of practice, complaints-based legislation (eg EEO), and the spirit of the law • person's or organisation's image and reputation • reactions of people, eg attitudes of customers, fellow workers and managers, including social norms and cultural factors • human (moral) values that are important to the person or organisation • impact on the physical environment.
Step 5 Decide importance of each criterion.	Some criteria are quantifiable, others are not. Questions of value cannot be avoided by reducing all the elements of the situation to what can be enumerated – quantify what you can, but include non-quantifiable factors in the consideration. Decide what importance you will assign to each criterion. Make it clear and explicit where you are making value judgements.
Step 6 Develop options.	Think creatively about what options are possible. Anticipate all relevant consequences of each. Look for solutions that can generate the "greatest good". Try to accommodate all stakeholders, but (1) respect your (or the organisation's) purposes and (2) do not "sell out" human values.
Step 7 Analyse options.	Alternative options are assessed against the decision criteria, quantifying only where it is appropriate to do so. The consequences identified include financial, physical and human resources, political (within organisation and externally), social and ethical. Any assumptions made are identified and re-

	examined – assumptions about both facts and values.
Step 8 Select option.	Unless an optimal solution that satisfies all criteria is obvious, the options should each be reviewed. What weaknesses are there in the analysis? Can the alternatives be combined or modified? Creativity should still be at work here. Repeat the above steps as necessary before reaching a final decision. Select the option which: (1) satisfies the human values filter, and (2) gives the maximum benefit overall, considering the whole spectrum of factors and their effects.
Step 9 Implement the decision.	Commit to the decision, communicate it to the relevant stakeholders as necessary, and proceed to implement it.
Step 10 Evaluate the decision.	At a pre-determined time, assess the results of the decision in terms of the original criteria, covering ethical as well as financial and production aspects.

As with any tool, this model proves its value as you use it, applying it to different types of problems and personalising it to your own style. The model takes you through the decision-making process step by step, but it is also a checklist. In practice, people find that in addressing step 1, for example, they already cover some of the issues in steps 2 and 3. In this case, steps 2 and 3 serve to ensure that you have covered all the issues adequately.

The model provides a process, but it does not embody an ethical perspective. If you are unclear about your ethical point of view, the model, of itself, will not make your ethical perspective any clearer. At steps 4 and 5, the model requires you to bring your ethical criteria into play. The notes given above in describing the steps provide an indicator of what ethical criteria to consider, but more needs to be said about this aspect.

Figure 7.1 illustrates what we wish to assert – that in many situations we need a model to help us to work through a problem in logical steps, but at the same time we cannot rely on a process model to supply, or take care of, the ethical issues the situation raises. The crux of ethical decision-making is to determine how to express our highest ethical values in ethically intense (and generally complex) situations. We need to address the issue of ethical criteria for decision-making in more detail.

Figure 7.1: The decision-making context

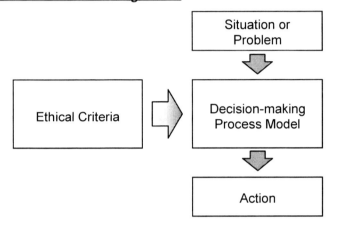

Ethical criteria: values

Many ethical decision-making models focus on the process and underplay the central issue, which is how we determine what is ethical, or what action will further the highest human values in a situation. Some models contain an appeal to all the classical approaches of moral philosophy and some give a list of rules of thumb to apply.

The dilemma in devising a set of guidelines for ethical decision-making is to reconcile the need to create a model that is usable, ie not too complex, with the need to acknowledge the complexity and intensity of many ethical dilemmas. Mary Guy (1990), a writer on business ethics, accompanies her decision-making model with a short set of guidelines:

- Consider the well-being of all stakeholders.
- Think as a member of the community, not just from the individual or organisational perspective.
- Obey, but do not depend solely upon the law.
- Ask, "What sort of person would do such a thing?"

- Respect the customs of others, but not at the expense of your own ethics.

The Ethics Resource Center in the USA (2004) offers a model which uses the acronym PLUS as the tool to identify the relevant ethical criteria. PLUS is described as the ethics filter, where the letters stand for:

- **P = Policies.** Is my proposed action consistent with organisational policies, procedures and guidelines?
- **L = Legal.** Is my proposed action acceptable under applicable laws and regulations?
- **U = Universal.** Does my proposed action conform to the universal principles and values my organisation has adopted?
- **S = Self.** Does my proposed action satisfy my personal definition of right, good and fair?

The model provides additional assistance by supplying an account of the basic universal principles, using another acronym – EPIC. The universal principles it identifies are: Empathy, Patience, Integrity and Courage.

Manuel Velasquez and others (Markkula Center for Applied Ethics, 2004) present a framework for ethical decision-making which incorporates discussion of different ethics theories, such as utilitarianism, virtues and human rights. They leave readers to make up their own minds about which of these theories they find persuasive.

Efforts to formulate ethical criteria to inform the ethical decision-making process have to recognise the following factors:

- If the ethical criteria simply consist of a number of ethics theories, it suggests that one can treat ethics theories as a kind of smorgasbord, from which one chooses a justification to suit the occasion.
- We have to go further than ethical criteria – we also have to address what to do when one principle happens to conflict with another, and how to make a decision when there does not seem to be any "right thing to do".
- These efforts would be clearer if we distinguished between ethical principles (or values) and psychological factors. For example, empathy, courage or the opinions of others may well affect our

decision-making processes, but they are psychological factors, not the ethical principles which should form the basis of our decision. We should be clear about the nature of these influences.

One important implication from these factors is that the decision we feel obliged to make may not be what we think is a satisfactory solution. In the world of moral philosophy, this is the problem of "dirty hands" (Grace & Cohen, 1995). One of the writers who has explored the difficulty of making decisions that achieve morally satisfactory outcomes is Joseph Badaracco (2002).

Badaracco says (p 11) that sometimes, "simple-looking problems turn out to be treacherous and complicated. This is why quiet leaders move carefully, put together contingency plans, and watch their backs." He describes our common moral problems as being messy and ambiguous. The course that he prescribes is, as he says, unorthodox, but what it does reinforce is that we have not finished discussing ethical decision-making until we have looked at the psychological aspects, and we shall do this below.

The criteria that can be applied as part of the decision-making process are those that were developed in the previous chapter. We have noted that one's world view and its embodied values has a major influence on our perceptions, so that we start the decision-making process with built-in biases and we need to be aware of these. As we proceed to gather information and analyse it, we need to consider the question of what our role is with respect to other people. Is it appropriate to apply our personal ethical standards to others' conduct? Is the conduct of people in the situation violating shared community standards – laws, regulations, company policies?

The next guideline was the three-levelled pyramid, where the bottom layer was laws and regulations, the second layer was conduct related to the quality of relationships and the third layer was issues related to the fulfilment of personal/collective potential (identity). Ascending through this pyramid involves moving from a primary concern with compliance to a primary concern with ethical aspiration. Again, our ethical decisions must be weighed in accordance with whether we are determining our own conduct or how to respond to the conduct of others.

Lastly, we discussed how the five core human values provide a universal ground for evaluating conduct. People may indeed have different perceptions of the world and this affects their understanding and interpretation of the values, but the core human values present the best prospect for reaching agreement about good and bad, right and wrong. The five core human values were expanded in Table 3.4 and this gives a comprehensive guide to apply to problematic situations.

Conflicts between values

In the account that the Ethics Resource Center gives of ethical decision-making, emphasis is given to the need to consider as many alternatives as possible. It uses the following scenario to illustrate the point:

> *Your company owns an office building. Tenants are complaining that there is always a long delay in getting an elevator during the rush hour. What do you do?*

The "obvious" solution is to install more elevators. But there are in fact many other ways to address this problem. Other possibilities include assigning banks of elevators to particular floors so they are used more efficiently; making the elevators faster; encouraging employees to use the stairs. In the real version of this problem, the owners piped music into the waiting areas, and complaints stopped – waiting became relaxing instead of a frustration.

The moral is simply that it is easy to get trapped into thinking there are only two choices and both may be decidedly unappealing. As in the scenario above, the choice could have been seen as either putting up with continued complaints or going to the huge expense of installing more elevators. Judgement is always required. Sometimes a course of action that we are being pressured into is clearly unethical and we have only one ethical option, one which seems dangerous or costly. But most times, our response to a situation will benefit from innovative thinking that generates different (ethical) alternatives.

The situation which is probably familiar to everyone is the conflict between "truth" and emotional support (ie love) that commonly occurs in appraising performance. School teachers know this dilemma well, especially when they are upbraided by politicians who claim that educational standards are falling. But the dilemma is exactly the same in the workplace in performance appraisals. What kind of feedback does the teacher or manager give to students/employees?

Ch. 7 | Making decisions ethically

A manager might have an employee whose performance is not as high as they would wish; perhaps the employee is too slow, or they are not as attentive to customers as the manager thinks they should be. But the manager also knows that the employee is trying, and senses that if the employee received harsh feedback, they would be hurt and their performance would deteriorate rather than improve. So the manager decides that love is more important than truth in this situation.

What is exquisite about this situation is that we know the answer lies, not in choosing one over the other, but in improving one's skills as a teacher or manager. The ideal is when the teacher/manager can give both the encouragement that is essential to the student/employee and the clarity that is required about performance standards.

We have probably all known teachers or managers who have been able to do this well, inspiring outstanding performance in their class or team. The lesson is that as long as threshold levels of ability are present, high performance is more a function of the spirit engendered by the leader than of the raw intellectual prowess of individuals. The conflict between love and truth that afflicts performance appraisals is thus resolved through improved leadership and communication skills.

The further point that needs to be made about this is that the teacher or manager only improves their skills in this area once they (a) see that it is a possibility, and (b) they become deeply committed to realising that possibility – just as Edison persevered through thousands of failures to find the right material to make a light bulb work.

Recall that in Chapter 5 we looked at how people evolve their world view through the development and exercise of various skills. Conflicts between values may be an indicator of the kinds of skills that we need to develop, rather than being an inherent feature of a situation. Then again, in making an ethical decision about a particular situation, one has to do so on the basis of the skills one currently possesses. This thought alludes to the discussion that will be taken up below, about an approach to decision-making that emphasises expertise and intuition.

Conflicts between values, however, are an inherent feature of human situations. An American writer, Donald Wolfe, says of this: "Every human system, from individual to society, is guided by multiple needs and values and thus has a stake in a multitude of conditions and possibilities. The measure of integrity, therefore, is not just how well one succeeds in pursuit of a single value but also how well one manages the complex of values that are inevitably interdependent in action, if not in conception" (in Srivastva, 1988, p 143).

Weighing the criteria

In the Integral Decision-making Model, at step 5, one must decide the importance of each criterion. Those who have a preference for numbers are often seen at this point advocating that we assign varying weights to the different criteria. Tempting though this may be, it is difficult to see how such an exercise can give more than arbitrary certainty. Similarly, applying the tools of cost/benefit analysis leads to the perversion or neglect of ethical concerns.

Paine (2003) cites a number of US cases where inappropriate quantification of "values" resulted in corporations persisting in conduct that was eventually deemed by the public to be manifestly unethical. One example was the Ford motor company's conduct in relation to the Pinto car model in the 1970s. The car's flaw was its tendency to explode after even minor impacts from behind, such as another car running into it at low speed. The fuel tank would rupture and ignite.

The deaths of a number of people did not persuade the company to recall the vehicles to fix the problem. The company's actions were based on calculations that a human life was worth about US$200,000. It reasoned that the cost of the recall was greater than its estimates of the cost of lost lives and injuries. It was not until a jury awarded damages against the company of US$125 million that the company decided to recall the cars and fix them (by the insertion of a safety valve that cost US$11).

Paine makes the point that the blind spot in Ford's analysis was that the value placed on a human life related to accidental death (by indiscriminate forces somewhere on the planet), not to a death caused by a known fault in the company's product, a fault that had been known for several years. The issue of responsibility is evaded by this analysis. More generally, Paine concludes (p 222): "For all its aura of objectivity and precision, cost-benefit analysis is highly vulnerable to distortions and biases that cloud the moral issues".

There is a stronger point to be made as well. In assigning weights to the various criteria, one makes the unconscious assumption that there are no criteria that are binding. But there are situations where one would want to

Ch. 7 | Making decisions ethically

say, "This is not negotiable. It does not matter that there are some benefits, this action is just wrong."

A simple example is appointing the boss's son/daughter to a position they are not qualified for. There may be strong arguments in favour of this action – it will help your career; it will save on recruitment expenses; and at the least the decision could be rationalised – they will probably learn how to do the job well enough. But a cost-benefit analysis is not the appropriate way to decide the ethics of the action. The action is wrong in principle, and we should treat that principle as not negotiable.

Hence, in deciding the importance of various criteria, we should be aware that some criteria will act in different ways to others. Some will act as threshold criteria (yes/no), while others will need to be considered (weighed up) in relation to each other.

Even so, many ethical dilemmas are messy and there is no self-evident pathway through the situation. We will now look at a scenario where the decision taken was not, to use Badaracco's language, heroic, but it served the purpose in the best way the manager knew how.

Applying the integral model

The example we will use to illustrate the integral model is the case of a general manager of an organisation that runs a children's accommodation service. The service is for children with severe intellectual disabilities, ranging in age from four to sixteen years. The manager, who commenced only recently, has been informed by the house manager that she suspects a staff member of sexual abusing the oldest child in the home, a girl who is sixteen. However, the child has limited communication abilities, and it would be extremely difficult to prove the abuse. It is also not possible to monitor all of the staff member's actions at work.

The manager learns that the staff member is being paid at a much higher pay rate than other staff, and the manager can justify cutting their pay rate. The manager hopes that this decision will cause the staff member to resign. The pay cut is communicated to the staff member, and the staff member says it is unacceptable and resigns. No industrial action results from this action.

We will examine this scenario in more detail using the Integral Decision-Making Model.

Integral decision-making model

Step 1. Formulate the problem.

The following facts clarify the situation further. The house manager has communicated to the general manager her uneasiness with the staff member (a middle-aged man). She wonders if sexual misconduct of some kind is occurring. Staff members have personal care responsibilities with the children, who are in need of a high level of support. It would be difficult to exclude this man from some personal care duties without inferring that there was a suspicion about him.

The particular child has no speech, is severely epileptic and is on a variety of medications. The house manager reports that it would probably be difficult to discern from her behaviour whether she was being interfered with and was under stress. Similarly, it would be difficult to obtain a report from any of the other children.

Both the house manager and the male staff member have been working at the residence for over 12 months. The general manager, from conversation with the man, finds him slightly strange, but knows he has no real basis for drawing any conclusions about abuse. The house manager reports that no accusations have been made by other staff, although some of them say they "do not really understand him".

The man is paid on a different award to the house manager, a decision that was made by the previous general manager, and one that is manifestly unfair. The general manager thus also has to consider whether the house manager is motivated by dissatisfaction over the pay rates. It could also be that all the other staff are female, and the house manager does not like having to work with a male staff member.

It is also the case that the man and his wife, who is also a staff member, work their shifts together, and do not share shifts with other staff.

Step 2. Define a goal, or solution.

An ideal solution would be if the child could somehow communicate the truth, or if a discreet investigation could conclusively prove whether or not the man was guilty. Appropriate action could then be taken. The pay issue could be dealt with separately, and an equitable solution negotiated.

Step 3. Identify relevant stakeholders.

The key stakeholders in this situation are:

Ch. 7 | Making decisions ethically

- the child;
- the male staff member;
- the other staff and the other children (who are all younger);
- the house manager and the general manager;
- the organisation and the local community.

Step 4. Identify decision criteria.

The decision criteria should be understood as arising out of both the general manager's prevailing values and his role in the organisation. So, for him, the most important criterion is the well-being of the child, to reclaim or protect her from physical and emotional violation and distress. The next criterion is the protection of the other children.

Finding the truth is itself a criterion of high importance.

Procedural justice for the staff member suspected is another criterion. Allied with this is regard for the staff member's reputation, ensuring that nothing becomes public where nothing is proven.

Pay equity and payroll budgets are other, albeit minor, criteria in the resolution of this situation.

The reputation of the service, the other staff and the organisation are also considerations for the general manager.

A further consideration is the risk management issue – if the organisation should face a law suit, from either the child's parents or the male staff member.

The service could also lose its funding and community support if a sexual abuse scandal became public.

Step 5. Decide importance of each criterion.

The criteria above have been listed in the order of importance the general manager assigned them. What was the justification for this ordering?

The general manager reasons that there is a double-barrelled reason for placing the child's well-being first. Protecting a vulnerable person in an organisation from harm at the hands of another person in a position of power is enough reason in itself. But this is also the core mission of the service, to care for these children.

Hence, the general manager is appealing to the value called respect for human dignity, or love for persons as ends in themselves.

Truth is another value engaged by this situation. So too is fairness and justice.

Financial issues and reputation are given lower priority, but it is part of the general manager's responsibility to look after these aspects too.

There is no quantitative way of determining this ordering. The weight of each factor will differ in each case. The only factor that would affect decision-making in this situation is if the organisation had a standard procedure for dealing with such accusations or suspicions.

Step 6. Develop options.

There are many possible courses of action here. Some of the possibilities are described below. A course of action could involve several of these in combination:

- Do nothing. There is no proof or evidence of misconduct, nor even of distress by the child.
- Ask staff to observe. However, there is little opportunity for this, given that the man and his wife work their shifts together and separately from other staff.
- Perhaps the teacher at school could be asked to track behaviour, and the general manager could cross-check this with the man's rostered days on.
- Conduct a work history check and police check on the man. Privacy issue: what right does the organisation have to do this, and does it require the man's knowledge and permission? (Note that when this situation occurred, there were no laws requiring police checks to be carried out for people who work with children.)
- Consult an expert for their opinion on action.
- Confront the man with the accusation.
- Obtain medical advice on whether the child has been molested.

Ch. 7 | Making decisions ethically

- Introduce policy changes generally that try to reduce the possibility of staff members being in situations with the children where misconduct can occur.

Step 7. Analyse options.

Most of the above courses of action in themselves raise moral issues. For example, asking staff to spy on another staff member is both risky and morally questionable. Introducing policy changes may be advisable but it does not address the immediate issue of the child's situation.

Assume for this exercise that the courses of action that were both possible and deemed to be ethical were carried out. For example, the police check did not turn up anything. The observations of the child's behaviour by teachers at school (who were not told anything about the reason) did not contribute any useful information.

Step 8. Select option.

The decision taken by the manager was to inform the man that a pay reduction was to be effected, and the reasons given referred to appropriate industrial awards. Why did the general manager select this course of action?

The course of action was regarded as a first attempt to establish the safety of the child. If it did not work, other changes would be instituted which would make it more difficult for the man to offend, if he were in fact guilty. The decision to reduce the man's pay was not unjust in itself. The pay inequity was real.

However, the key reason for the decision was that it was considered to be intolerable to have the child in a situation where it was not even possible for the managers to satisfy themselves that no sexual misconduct was occurring against the child.

The next policy change envisaged was for all staff to work on alternating rosters so that the man would work with people other than his wife. This was advisable in any case, and was effected after the man left. The rationale for the policy change was that no one should be in a position where their conduct was not open to scrutiny by others.

The decision involved a judgement call by the general manager about the motivation of the house manager. He judged that she would not make up a story about the man because of discontent about pay.

Step 9. Implement the decision.

The letter to the man about pay rates resulted in the man (and his wife) leaving the organisation immediately. This meant that the man left with his reputation intact. Was this acceptable? What if the man was an offender and he found employment in another children's residence? This was a tricky aspect of the outcome. If a future employer had contacted the general manager for a reference, what would he say?

Step 10. Evaluate the decision.

An evaluation of this decision was made in terms of how to avoid a similar situation arising. Policy changes were made about how work and shifts were structured, to try and ensure, as far as possible, that staff were accountable for their conduct towards the children at all times. Policies were also instituted about what procedure would be followed if an accusation was made against a staff member or if an incident which suggested unacceptable conduct by a staff member occurred.

The unsatisfactory nature of the strategy was acknowledged. It was fortuitous that the pay issue had arisen at the same time as the concern about the possible misconduct. And it was possible that the man, although unbeknownst to the man himself, had been treated unfairly. To cite Joseph Badaracco (1997, p 6) once more: managers' problems "typically involve choices between two or more courses of action, each of which is a complicated bundle of ethical responsibilities, personal commitments, moral hazards, and practical pressures and constraints".

The psychological aspects of decision-making

It was suggested earlier that we would think more clearly about decision-making if we distinguished between ethical values and psychological factors. Courage, for example, is certainly necessary if a person is to act ethically, given that acting ethically often puts a person under pressure from other people, both colleagues and people with power and authority. But courage is something that comes into play when we have already decided, on other grounds, that a particular course of action is what ethics requires of us. So we want to enlarge our picture of the decision-making context, as in Figure 7.2.

Figure 7.2: The enlarged decision-making context

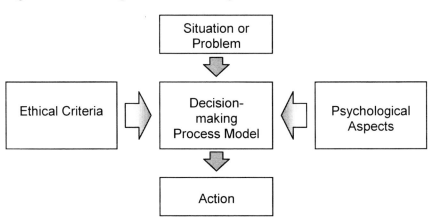

The significance of psychological factors in ethical decision-making is that people may recognise the necessity of rational thought processes and ethical principles, but in fact they are heavily influenced by emotional factors and other people. If the prevailing world view of a person is structured through loyalties to family, organisations and institutions, then regardless of the abstract conclusions of moral arguments, what other people think will matter to them.

Kohlberg, in his model of moral development, concluded that most people did not reason in terms of abstract principles, but in terms of social affiliations. One philosopher (Goldman, 1993, p 341) put it this way: "Ordinary moral thinking may consist more in comparing contemplated activities with stored exemplars of good and bad behaviour than with the formulation and deduction of consequences from abstract principles."

Mark Johnson (1993), in exploring the concept of moral imagination, maintained that learning through stories and other people is not confined to certain classes of people, but is true of all people. He observes that people who care about their moral self-development turn, not to philosophical texts on moral theory, but rather to fiction. Stories about people are an important vehicle for learning, as Johnson says (p 196), "about what it is to be human, about the contingencies of life, about the kinds of lives we most want to lead, and about what is involved in trying to lead such lives".

This is the way that minds work. Just as young children learn behaviours by absorbing what their parents and siblings do and later imitating it, so is this mode of learning still strong in adults. Even when a person can arrive at an ethical decision by following a chain of reasoning, the commitment to carry that out in action is strengthened by having a mental model of an admired person doing likewise.

It is not merely glib for so many writers to emphasise the importance of leadership to the performance and conduct of organisations, and there is good evidence that a large part of the influence of leaders lies in role modelling. Kouzes and Posner (1996) assert that the first rule of leadership is, if you can't believe the messenger, you won't believe the message. Dave Ulrich (1996, p 215) quotes Mahatma Gandhi, who said, "my life is its own message.....You must watch my life, how I live, eat, sit, talk, behave in general. The sum total of all those is my religion". Stephen Covey (1992) describes a "pyramid of influence" for leaders, where the foundation of the leader's influence is the model they present for their followers.

Identifying admirable role models, then, may be an important part of developing one's abilities to make ethical decisions. This is not a substitute for reasoning, but recognition that we are energised by the outstanding moral achievements of others. Our five-dimensional model of the person tells us that people have an energy dimension as well as a cognitive dimension.

Many of the guidelines that are contained in various ethical decision-making models are alluding to this psychological aspect. As we have indicated, it is not surprising that a lot of these guidelines concern relationships with other people. For example:

- Consult with other people before making a decision – discuss with a colleague, a mentor etc.

- Ask yourself: would I be happy for my mother, manager, spouse, or mentor to know my decision?

- Ask yourself: would I be happy to read about my decision in the newspaper?

Some of the guidelines also refer to the personal qualities that are illustrated by the decision:

- Does the decision accord with my personal values?

- Is this what a wise and virtuous person would do?
- What are my motives?

As we have seen above, however, the decision we conclude is necessary may involve compromises with some principles, and the best decision we can see may still be accompanied by complex motives. In the story above and in some of the stories that Badaracco (2002) tells, the person cannot make a public justification of their action, so the comfort that one has been wise and virtuous is not confirmed by anyone. It is best, therefore, that we realise and accept that sometimes this is what an ethical action will require of us.

Similarly, the qualities of courage, patience, benevolence, wisdom and the like are needed to follow through on ethical decisions. In making a decision, we need to take into account whether we have the strength to do that. And in this, we should be careful about our assumptions. The "heroic" act of challenging a person's or organisation's actions may not be the wisest or most effective course. We need to question ourselves continually – Are we giving vent to personal anger that is sourced in other events? Do we have "martyr syndrome"? Are we guilty of trying to take the moral high ground?

In the situations examined above it has been appropriate to apply the decision-making model, because the situations were complex ones where some time needed to be taken to weigh various options and manoeuvre towards a solution (imperfect though it was). We indicated earlier that there is another approach to decision-making as well, one where actions are taken rapidly, in the midst of time-pressured situations. We asserted that skill in this type of decision-making is also required. We now turn to the intuitive decision-making approach.

The intuitive approach to decision-making

The label "intuitive approach" is intended to capture what happens when an "expert" operates in an intense, ambiguous and possibly dangerous situation, and needs to make instant judgements about what to do. Many of the decisions we have to make in the workplace are not made in a leisurely fashion, but in the moment, and we have to commit to immediate action and accept the consequences. This applies to ethically charged situations as well as those that test our competence.

Badaracco (1997) advises that we should be ready to play for more time when other people or situational factors are pressuring us to make an unpalatable decision. But sometimes that is not possible. The Tylenol crisis that hit Johnson & Johnson in 1982 required an immediate response. We are interested here in how ethical decisions are made under these circumstances.

It is interesting to examine the work of Gary Klein (1999) on the decision-making processes used by a variety of experts in stressful situations. Can we apply any of that understanding to ethical decision-making? There are two aspects that may be helpful: (1) the qualities displayed by experts, and (2) the processes that are employed by experts.

Klein conducted extensive field studies of the behaviour of competent, experienced people in a wide variety of occupations. His subjects included fire fighters, nurses, naval officers in combat and airline pilots. He concluded that there were a number of qualities exhibited by experts that were not exhibited by novices.

Experts see things that novices do not see or are not aware of. They pick up patterns in a situation. They see anomalies; they have a rich bank of experience that enables them to posit expectancies for a situation, so they detect when these expectancies have been violated. Their observational skills are highly refined; they can pick up differences that are too small for novices to detect. They have a strong awareness of the overall situation, and of how things work. They project into the past and the future to understand the flow of events – what happened to bring events to their current point, and what is now likely to happen? Allied with this, they are alert to opportunities to fulfil their purpose and are ready to improvise. But despite their skills, experts are also aware of their limitations.

The idea of applying the concept of expertise to the area of ethical behaviour may give rise to a feeling of unease, so we should discuss this issue to clarify what we hope to obtain from this exercise. We may be uneasy about the idea of an "ethical expert" because we feel that everyone is subject to ethics in the same way. Ethics is not an occupational choice, like being a fire fighter.

It also irks us to think of someone being an ethical expert because it suggests that, without this alleged expertise, we cannot be as ethical as the expert is. We would like to think that, in any given situation, as long as we chose to, we could be as fair, as honest and as principled as anyone else.

Ch. 7 | Making decisions ethically

We would assert that being ethical is about making a moral choice, not about a special realm of knowledge and skill, or competence.

Let us accept this distinction in language. In the ordinary sense in which people use the words, expertise is about competence, as distinct from ethics. We argued earlier that it is important to make this distinction and here we are merely maintaining it. However, is there something to be learned from Klein's account of the qualities of experts that we can apply to ethical decision-making?

We may have an aversion to the idea of ethical experts, but the process of making decisions can be complex and difficult. It is conceivable that a person can improve their skills and knowledge in making decisions (and in acting upon them). This is what we argued when discussing how to resolve conflicts of values, using the examples of managers appraising their employees and teachers appraising their students.

The language that has been used to refer to this development of skills and understanding in ethical conduct is the Greeks' notion of the virtuous person. In Aristotle and in Plato, virtue is cultivated by effort and practice. The concept of virtue is associated for them with excellence, perfection and effectiveness. A virtuous person fulfils their purpose well, just as a "virtuous" knife is one that cuts well. We understand that virtue needs to be developed, hence we may look to the generic idea of expertise to see what it suggests for the development of virtue.

The key is effectiveness. An expert has a deep understanding of the forces at work in a situation and is alert to their presence, so is able to act with effectiveness. A novice would not do as well. This is simply to indicate, uncontroversially, one hopes, that the study of the ethical aspects of situations is likely to improve the effectiveness of our ethical decision-making in the future.

However, there is a sting in this conclusion. It indicates that it is not enough to have good intentions; if your decision is going to be ethical and foster well-being (ie the compliance and the constructive aspects of ethics), then you must understand what is happening and what the likely outcome of your action will be. The work of the expert in understanding people and situations is thus likewise the work of the person who would be ethical.

One of the aspects that Klein highlights is that experts mull over critical events afterwards. The fire fighter might run through the same fire episode many times, from different angles, and examine each decision to see if the situation could have been handled better, and whether any clues were missed. The knowledge is added to their store of experience, to be drawn on in future events. Given that we understand ethics to be about the broader human endeavour rather than simple conformity to rules, the person who would be ethical needs to give the same attention to reviewing critical ethical events.

Klein's account of the decision-making processes that experts use is at odds with the essentially rationalist account of decision-making given earlier in this chapter. In his research, Klein started by looking for evidence that the experts followed a rationalist model – gathering data, proposing options and weighing each against given criteria. Yet he found that the experts did not spend time weighing options.

What the experts did was pattern matching – they had the ability to see if a situation matched a prototype, and if so, they acted according to a given set of actions. At the same time, they were alert to signs that the current event did not match the pattern. The allied process was mental simulation. Experts could play out a set of actions in their mind to decide whether they were feasible and effective.

Klein calls this intuitive approach the **recognition-primed decision model**. Experts firstly observe the situation to see if it fits a prototype, and can do so even for situations that novices would find non-routine. If a situation is seen as "typical", then the expert calls on a set of expectancies for that kind of situation. They look for relevant clues, establish feasible goals and embark on routine actions. Their ability to mentally simulate the outcomes of those actions enables them to adapt to non-typical aspects of the situation.

In situations that are outside their experience, experts will take time to diagnose, and will draw on their bank of experiences to find parallels. They will look for features that match previous events, transferring ideas across contexts to find a way of achieving a result. In time-pressured situations, they do not spend time weighing up options against each other. If the first option is judged to meet the purpose, it is used. If it does not meet the purpose, it is rejected and the next one examined.

With this model in mind, let us return to the Tylenol incident and the actions of the Johnson & Johnson executives. It was a situation where time was critical. Seven people had died in quick succession and it was not known how extensive the problem was. But, we might say, the expert's

Ch. 7 | Making decisions ethically

situation is different – they are quite clear about their goals and the constraints, whereas for Johnson & Johnson, it was the very goals that were in question.

Fire fighters go to a fire knowing that the goals are to save lives, keep the fire team itself safe, and stop the destruction of property. Nurses use their observational skills to determine when a premature baby has attracted an infection. The issues for these experts would seem to be more about competence than ethics. Their goals are well-established and not at issue. In contrast, it was the very goals that were in question for Johnson & Johnson.

Yet this observation gives us the clue for understanding why Johnson & Johnson was able to respond ethically in such a time-pressured situation. As we have noted earlier, its ethical principles and standards were clearly determined and consciously adhered to. Hence it was able, in the face of an unprecedented crisis, to act in the same way as the experts we have just described. Its goals (based on its values) were established, and although the situation was unique, it called for a particular course of action.

An analogous example from Klein is the story of the fire fighters who were in a house fighting what appeared to be a kitchen fire. But the fire was not responding to the hoses in the way it should have. Something was odd, and the commander felt his team was in danger. He immediately called them out of the house, and the floor collapsed seconds later. The source of the fire had been in the basement, not the kitchen. The commander's action was based on his unequivocal commitment to the safety of his men. He could not explain what was amiss at the time, but putting the fire out was secondary to protecting their lives.

Similarly, then, Johnson & Johnson was in business and its goal was to sell goods for profit, but it exhibited an unequivocal commitment to the safety of its customers by withdrawing Tylenol from sale. Just like the fire commander, at the time it did not know what the source of the problem was and it did not know what the effect of the decision would be on its business. Clarity about goals and values enabled the fire commander to act competently, and we would say, ethically, and in the same way, clarity about goals and values enabled Johnson & Johnson to act appropriately.

Through this account of intuitive decision-making we have suggested that people can build knowledge and skills in ethical decision-making. This is not only possible, it is important, because having the intention of being ethical will not prevent us from being naïve or wrong, and on occasion we may even achieve the opposite of what we want, or what we perceive that ethics requires.

Reconciling the integral model and the intuitive approach

There remains the question of how these two seemingly different approaches to decision-making can be reconciled. We suggested earlier that time pressure may be the distinguishing characteristic – one uses the integral model where time allows and the intuitive model where time is precious. Generally this would mean that longer-term strategy and policy issues would be dealt with by eliciting and evaluating various options and refining them.

The problem with this rule is that sometimes matters of great strategic import in organisations can present with the urgency of a house fire, as the Tylenol incident shows. Nonetheless, the rule is generally applicable. Klein compared the two models and concluded that the following conditions lent themselves to the use of the recognition-primed decision-making model:

- greater time pressure
- people making the decision are experienced in the domain
- the conditions are dynamic
- the goals are ill-defined.

On the other hand, the conditions where the rational (integral) decision-making model would be preferred are where:

- the decision needs to be justified to others
- the views of different stakeholders need to be resolved
- the goal is to find the optimal solution rather than the first workable one
- the matters under consideration involve complex computations.

Klein's views were supported by analysis of various types of occupations. Design engineers, for example, resort to rational, comparative processes more than soldiers in battle command teams do. The engineers have more time to make decisions than soldiers do. Klein also found that novice fire-ground commanders resorted to rational processes more often than experienced commanders did. The novices found value in identifying options and weighing them up, while experts more often moved immediately to a course of action.

In the realm of ethical decision-making, the same could be expected to apply. Practice in identifying ethical issues should enable the rational evaluation of alternatives to be short-circuited in many cases. Practice should also enable better predictions about the outcomes of decisions.

The area where there is great potential for improvement in our ethical decision-making skills is in wrestling with ill-defined goals. Klein discusses how decision-making slides across into the territory of problem-solving. One of his observations is that the rational process of decision-making becomes difficult when goals are ill-defined. This is because the steps then do not always take place in the expected order. In natural problem-solving situations, the identification of goals is often not set in stone at the outset. The determination of goals may be affected by the steps of identifying options and evaluating them, because a given goal may be judged to be not feasible. Klein says (1999, p 146), to solve ill-defined problems "we have to clarify the goal even as we are trying to achieve it, rather than keeping the goal constant".

Under our view of ethics, our goals will often be much broader than adhering to a given law or rule. The goal may be to enhance a relationship, which is an ill-defined goal, like the goal of writing a good story. Views may differ about the quality of the outcome. The prospect for improving our ethical decision-making and problem-solving skills does not lie in rigid adherence to the rational models, because their virtue is in the analysis of given alternatives, not in the generation of new, breakthrough solutions.

The improvement of ethical decision-making skills lies in the key factors of:

- being clear about our core values and being committed to them
- being able to see the patterns in situations, so we can relate them to our existing store of experience
- being able to detect the forces at work in a situation so that we can mentally simulate what has happened and what will happen.

These factors will enable us to effectively use the two modes of thought that Senge talked about – divergent thinking where we seek to understand the situation and explore responses to it, and convergent thinking where we evaluate the results of our explorations.

Scaled responses to situations

Ethical decision-making generally deals with particular responses to particular situations, although we know that this merges eventually into the fields of relationships and organisational culture, as we saw in Chapter 6. Particular responses can range in scale from narrowly focused, tactful actions to broader, confronting actions. What is the scope of possibilities, and how do we decide what level of response is appropriate?

The assumption here is that the person involved is not in a position of power. Our concern to this point has been our decision-making processes as an employee. And the hope is that we work in organisations that are amenable to dealing with ethical issues in the ways described. But we may need to consider what our options are if our organisation is not so amenable to acting ethically. Then we may find ourselves affronted by the actions of the organisation or of its managers. How can we approach this issue?

Step 1: Understand. This step has already been noted – we need to understand the people and the situation. What are their motivations and payoffs?

Step 2: Determine who knows. Before acting, we need to know the nature of the situation. Are the unethical actions occurring with or without the knowledge and approval of others (especially higher managers) in the organisation?

Step 3: Determine perceptions. This step has also been noted, but here the focus is on finding out what the ethical perceptions of the key players are. The Values Evolution Model is the framework for articulating this. What are the values in conflict, and how would the key players see the conflict? Often it is clear enough what is driving a person who is engaging in unethical behaviour, but it may be more difficult to know what kind of reception you will get from senior managers if you inform them about it.

These steps are preliminary to considering what to do. Many writers have dwelt on this question and offered advice. Badaracco (1997) takes an unusual line, preferring strategic manoeuvring to grand gestures as a way of achieving good ends without attracting self-damage. Trevino and Nelson (1995) discuss the vicissitudes of whistleblowers, noting that being right seldom saves them from trauma.

Ch. 7 | Making decisions ethically

The general rule is to start modestly, either making a direct approach to the person involved or using the available channels, with a view to finding a resolution. Your actions should escalate systematically if these first moves do not produce a result. Yet there are no rules that can be offered with unreserved confidence. In some cases it might be fatal to your cause to say anything at all, or threatening to your job.

There are some situations where the consequences could be serious if you spoke up within an organisation. That much should be acknowledged. And depending on the nature of the issue, you may decide that you need to speak up regardless of your own position, or you may decide you cannot do that, and leave the job. What can we say about this type of dilemma?

This becomes a very personal decision, and a lot of factors can come into play. If you have a family, for example, they are affected. The experience of many whistleblowers is distressing, it can last for years and it can end all their career prospects. But, on any account of values, knowing that something is wrong gives a person some kind of responsibility to do something about it.

The thrust of the two models of ethical decision-making presented in this chapter is that we need to foster our moral imagination. We noted that when faced with ethical dilemmas, we often find it difficult to see past two stark choices. Of course we need to ensure that we do not avoid the dilemma, but we do need to devote our energy to thinking about how we can best utilise the people and resources in the situation to "combat the evil and foster the good". And in this we need to be conscious that different people in the situation may have very different perceptions of what the ethical issues are, so that attaining a common understanding of the situation is part of the challenge.

Having done our best to determine a course of action to address the dilemma, we then have to decide if we have the strength to carry it out. So that sometimes a person may decide there is too much stacked against them, and that leaving is the best thing to do. It may be the most principled thing to do. What goes into this decision? Are people being hurt?

We can remember the engineer at Ford who knew that the Pinto was likely to cause more deaths in car fires. He left, and he also spoke out about the issue. In other cases, the situation may be less dramatic. It may be that the company's selling methods are dishonest and you do not want to be associated with it. You find a new employer that does operate honestly.

In saying that this is a personal decision, in one sense we affirm that no one can tell us that we did the wrong thing, either by leaving or by taking on the whistleblower role. But we should not forget that the question we have to answer for ourselves is whether we took the easy way out. We think of people who took on epic tasks who never stopped to ask themselves whether they had the strength – they kept doing what they did because it had to be done.

So, this question about deciding what part we shall play in an unethical situation becomes a question of deep identity – who do I want to be?

8

Ethical leadership in organisations

Although this book is directed primarily at people who do not hold positions of power or authority in organisations, we observed earlier that even senior executives often perceive themselves to be lacking in the power to do what they think is "the right thing". Conversely, most people in organisations, even those in non-managerial positions, often have opportunities to lead or influence people, events and practices. At the least, everyone has some scope to lead by example, by acting as far as possible in an ethical and values-based way. Hence there is a place in this book for a chapter on leadership.

It is not the intention of this chapter to traverse the full scope of the concept of leadership. What we would like to do is present an account of how people can play a leadership role, regardless of what position they occupy in the organisation, to foster ethical conduct and core human values. As we define leadership in this chapter, people at any level in the organisation can exercise leadership and, by doing so, they can add a new dimension to the organisation's behaviour.

It is necessary, first of all, to say something about the context in which leadership is exercised in organisations. We can talk more usefully about what leaders do and how they exert influence if we understand how people see the purposes of organisations. As we shall see, some people advocate a very narrow, profit-focused view of organisational purpose, while at the other end of the spectrum some people argue that organisations have a significant role to play in the well-being of their communities and society.

The spectrum of perceptions about the purpose of organisations reflects the spectrum of world views we examined in earlier chapters. We will discuss the range of ways in which people see their organisation, and how this is a major conditioning influence on the role they see that leaders should play with respect to ethics and human values.

Regardless of the prevailing world view in an organisation, there are some common roles that organisations and their people typically expect of leaders, and these roles can be linked to the broad requirement of leaders that they maintain operations and facilitate change. These common expectations are described in the context of the current business environment, with its impact on the kinds of values needed to achieve business survival and success.

We can then explore how leaders can positively influence core human values in the organisation, within the constraints of business imperatives and limitations on resources. This discussion will take us back to the leader as a person and the question of how the core human values apply when other frameworks of meaning (economic competitiveness, images of success, psychological explanations of personal style, preoccupation with return on investment, to name a few) jostle for attention.

Views of the purposes of organisations

Ethical leadership in organisations is conditioned by the view that leaders hold about the purpose of the organisation. One way of examining the range of views that are held is to use the Values Evolution Model, applying it to organisations as we have done with persons. This is not to say that organisations fit neatly or consistently into these categories, just as persons do not; but it is to say that this is a powerful tool to help us understand the behaviour and beliefs manifested by organisations.

There are numerous precedents for applying a psychological perspective to the conduct of organisations. Petrick, Wagley and Von der Embse (2001) used Kohlberg's theory of moral development to describe the behaviour of organisations. Annamaria Garden (2000) used a psychological construct from interpersonal relations to explore the "mind" of the organisation. Gareth Morgan (1986) explored a number of metaphors for organisations, including organisations as organisms, brains, cultures, political systems and Freudian prisoners.

Our discussion will accept the premise that it makes some sort of sense to talk about the psychological characteristics of organisations. We simply take the view that we can observe the conduct of organisations from the outside and speak *as if* the organisation were a person. It is a useful construct – useful because these characteristics are a major influence on how individuals, especially leaders, act in the organisational context. Having described things from that perspective, we harbour no doubt that it is individuals who through their own contribution and their participation in collective acts that ultimately create the personality and character of the organisation.

Applying the Values Evolution Model to organisations, then, we obtain a description of seven different types of values orientation that organisational cultures manifest. These are summarised in Table 8.1. We will then amplify the descriptions and discuss the issues that this framework raises for ethical leadership.

Table 8.1: Organisations under the Values Evolution Model

World view	Organisational Perspective
World view 1: The world is alien and threatening.	Authoritarian/Survivalist Fear of extinction confines attention to financial survival and profit, driving a "win at all costs" mentality. The organisation is strictly hierarchical; leadership is harsh and authoritarian and does not tolerate challenge.
World view 2: Family and friends are my refuge in an uncaring world.	Paternal/Machiavellian Organisational gain guides actions. Structure is hierarchical and paternal; people play stereotypical roles. An "us and them" culture prevails and methods may be manipulative.
World view 3: The world is a problem with which I can cope through education, work and participation in institutions.	Orderly/Bureaucratic The organisation is characterised by orderly structure and tradition – management rather than leadership. Organisational members are loyal and there are established rules and norms of behaviour.

World view 4: Institutions are not absolute, and individuals have to find their own meaning.	Participative/Creative The organisation exhibits tension between desire for order and need for innovation and involvement of employees. It shows signs of transition, with individual participation being facilitated and values and goals being subjected to question.
World view 5: The world is a project in which I am a collaborator.	Collaborative/Excellence Teamwork, commitment and a quality focus characterise these organisations. Leaders encourage collaboration and networking, and values are explicit. Flexibility, innovation and a customer service focus are fostered.
World view 6: The world is a system that will work best when people mutually support each other.	Distributed leadership/Social well-being These organisations have developed their own vision of how they can serve the well-being of society. They work from an understanding of the systemic, interdependent nature of the world. Leadership is shared around the organisation as tasks require.
World view 7: The world is a mystery for which we (together) must care.	Global harmony/Virtual relations These organisations are focused on the highest ideals for humanity and the planet. They may consist of informal networks but may also employ complex technologies. They seek to exhibit the balance and wisdom that they foster in their environments.

The perspective operating through this spectrum is that organisations act as they do as a reflection of the prevailing values in the organisation. From this perspective there is not much to gain by arguing that any particular view of organisational purpose is the "right" one. World view 7 is clearly the highest ideal for organisational purpose; as explained in previous chapters, each world view is a more expansive view than its predecessor, and rests on a greater sense of understanding of the world and greater personal capability.

The question is: what is it feasible for a given organisation to strive for from its current state? The enterprise of improving an organisation ethically is analogous to the individual's challenge – to address the three levels of development described in Chapter 2: (1) legal compliance, (2) quality of relationships, and (3) realisation of identity. Organisations cannot, just as individuals cannot, simply decide they are going to apply world view 7 to their activities. A developmental pathway is necessary, because each world view implies a set of understandings and skills; they are not simply the result of a desire to be "good".

The implication which will be pursued in the latter part of this chapter is that ethical leadership has to be appropriate to the situation. Leaders have to take stock of the current perceptions and behaviour of the organisation and work to expand its understanding, beliefs and values. The discussion below of organisations that exemplify each of the seven world views will enable us to see what leaders have to work with to enhance core human values in their organisation.

1. Authoritarian/Survivalist

There is ample evidence of organisations that subscribe to this world view. Such organisations may be small or large, and new or long-established. This view carries its own rhetoric that justifies the necessity of their methods. The world is seen as difficult and dangerous, so harshness is demanded. These organisations have scant regard for the well-being of people affected by their actions, or the environment.

The struggle for survival often overshoots financial success to become a quest for domination. It is not sufficient for them to survive; they feel compelled to harm or eliminate others. McDonalds' founder, Ray Kroc, is accredited with the statement: "What do you do when your competitor is drowning? Get a live hose and stick it in his mouth."

It was noted in an earlier chapter that the values set that tends to establish the tone for public discourse in society is around world views 3 and 4. This means that organisations that in fact operate under world view 1 have to create a rhetoric that pays lip service to those other views. An organisation may have a code of ethics, it may have a policy of corporate social responsibility and it may even conduct some programs that suggest it is socially responsible, but the driving forces in the organisation come from a fear of failure and extinction. Thus hypocrisy is born.

In their analysis of the fall of Enron, Sims and Brinkmann (2003) describe how it established a façade of cultural artifacts like ethics codes, ethics officers and the like, while in practice creating a working environment where the bottom line was pursued without any reference to ethics.

Mining companies are frequently of this mindset. An example publicised by Oxfam is the impact of a copper mine on the local inhabitants of Marinduque Island in the Philippines. Placer Dome, in partnership with the then President of the Philippines, Ferdinand Marcos, began mining on the island in 1975. As part of its mining operations it dumped millions of tonnes of toxic waste into the surrounding sea, on which 20,000 people depended for their food and livelihood through fishing.

Twice, in 1993 and 1996, tonnes of toxic silt swept down the river from the mine and caused destruction. Two children were killed, homes were destroyed and farmlands were smothered. The government forced the mine to close after the second incident. The company failed to clean up its waste adequately, leaving the area in 2001. People on Marinduque continue to suffer health problems from contamination due to the mine, including skin problems, stomach disorders, dementia and cancer. Placer Dome maintains that it is a world leader in social responsibility.

Despite the anti-social behaviour of many corporations there is continued support for a view that corporations have no social obligations other than to make a profit for their shareholders. The person who most famously spelled out the case for this narrow view of business was Milton Friedman, a Nobel Prize winning economist. His 1962 book, *Capitalism and Freedom*, said:

> "In a free economy, there is one and only one social responsibility of business – to use its resources and engage in activities designed to increase its profits so long as it stays within the rules of the game, which is to say, engages in free and open competition, without deception or fraud."

Another writer, Alfred Rappaport, echoed this view in the *New York Times* in 1990 (Frederick, 1992, p 43):

> Corporate management has neither the political legitimacy nor the expertise to decide what is in the social interest. It is our form of government that provides the vehicle for collective choice via elected legislators and the judicial system. Whether corporate social responsibility is advocated by political activists or the chief executive officer, the costs of these expenditures, which don't

increase the value of the company or its stock, will be passed onto consumers by way of higher prices, or to employees as lower wages, or to shareholders as lower returns.

There are many flaws in this argument. One of its problems is that it sees social responsibility as nothing more than donations to charity, so it undermines the idea that companies are ethically accountable for all of their conduct. Philanthropic generosity is just one aspect of corporate social responsibility, and not even the major part. More important is the ethics with which companies carry out their core business.

The important distinction between philanthropy and the ethics of business actions was seen in the sentencing of Ray Williams, CEO of the collapsed Australian insurance company HIH in April 2005. The judge sentenced Williams to a maximum four and a half years' jail term. He had pleaded guilty to charges that included providing misleading information to investors that understated HIH's financial losses by over AU$90 million. The judge noted that Williams had made a "prodigious" contribution to the community through philanthropy, but it did not outweigh his offences, which were "objectively serious and involved a considerable abandonment of duty" on his part.

With respect to acts of charity, arguing that corporations do not have the expertise or political legitimacy to play a role in this area is unpersuasive. There are a range of models that corporations have used to guide and manage their charitable involvements, and expertise can be developed; the critical factor is the will to make a contribution.

As we said at the outset, no one, organisations included, can abdicate responsibility for ethics, because ethics is a lens that can be applied to any activity. Companies may declare that they have no obligations except to make profits, but this is best regarded as an ambit claim. We can nevertheless subject companies to ethical scrutiny and make judgements about them. And in making judgements about their conduct, what we have to conclude is that companies that reject any responsibility towards society are taking the role of a survivalist – they are self-absorbed, self-serving, and inclined to be unprincipled, destructive, cruel and dishonest. We may then decide that it is not healthy for a society to allow such unbridled behaviour.

Ironically, the no-obligation approach to business requires governments to play a more active regulatory role. If businesses do not accept an obligation to be socially responsible, then governments must, more than ever, ensure that their citizens do not suffer as a result. And of course, the cost of increased regulation is borne by everyone, including business. But the no-obligation argument would have far less influence if it did not start by confusing ethics with charity.

2. Paternal/Machiavellian

Charity is seldom associated with organisations operating out of the survivalist world view. They are too interested in self, survival and conquest. But charity is often an aspect of world view 2, the paternal, Machiavellian organisation. There can be several motivations for charity for this kind of organisation:

- it operates as a reward for those who are instrumental to the organisation's success (individuals within the organisation as well as outside individuals and organisations);
- it is useful in obtaining future favours and assistance;
- it contributes to a positive reputation in the community that makes it more difficult for the public to doubt its other (business) actions; or
- it works as an "atonement for sins committed" in the making of profit.

The hallmark of organisations under this world view is the dividing of the world into us and them. Organisations like this have their allies who play by the same rules, looking after each other and exploiting everyone else. Charity plays a part in this game, by creating support in the community and useful allies who are willing to help the organisation – political donations often serve this function.

The problem with the atonement model is that it makes it possible for an organisation to operate in a very unethical way (lying to customers, mistreating its employees) but then think it has redeemed itself by making donations to youth clubs and art galleries (although the thinking is generally unconscious). The further consequence is that it contributes to the view that business is inherently immoral, a view that inhibits the development of belief in the positive possibilities of business.

3. Orderly/Bureaucratic

It is at this stage that some real sense of social responsibility and ethical accountability can be said to emerge. Organisations under this world view constitute a part of society with a recognised role and norms for corporate behaviour based on being a member of society. These organisations are more confident of their legitimacy and ability to sustain themselves.

What emerges in these organisations is a sense of stewardship for the resources at their disposal. There are limits to this sensibility, as this world view is bounded by what is generally accepted in society. For example, supermarkets are now active in encouraging customers to bring shopping bags with them rather than using disposable plastic bags. This reflects society's recognition that waste is an important issue. Until recently, supermarkets tended to regard the shopping bag-toting customer as a nuisance, because it interfered with their efficient cashier routines.

Within these bounds, orderly/bureaucratic organisations recognise that they exist in a matrix of stakeholders and they have responsibilities towards society. Managers may even see themselves as stewards – people in a position of public trust with control over extensive resources. They may recognise that their actions have a significant impact on people's lives, so their interests have expanded from a narrow focus on profits.

A definition of corporate social responsibility that fits well with the viewpoint here is given by a business ethics text (Frederick, Post & Davis, 1992): "a corporation should be held accountable for any of its actions that affect people, their communities and their environment. It implies that negative business impacts on people and society should be acknowledged and corrected if at all possible....The social responsibilities of business grow directly out of two features of the modern corporation: (a) the essential functions it performs for society, and (b) the immense influence it has on people's lives".

There have been some attempts to reconcile ethics and social responsibility with the narrow view of corporations espoused by Friedman. Elaine Sternberg (2000, p 32), restated the case as follows: "The defining purpose of business is maximising owner value over the long term by selling goods or services". She defends this view thus (p 36): "business does not exist to foster employees' physical or psychological well-being; still less is its goal their ultimate fulfilment. Nor is it the aim of business to provide full employment for the nation's labour force or even jobs for local workers.

Business's purpose is not to serve the interests of customers or of managers or of the community. Such positive benefits routinely result from business, but they do not constitute its defining aim".

If this is so, how do ethics come into the picture? Sternberg says there are no special concessions on ethics for the business world. She says business is subject to the same, universal values as individuals in their personal lives. In fact, the same ethical values apply in all areas of life. The only difference is that the types of problems that arise are different, eg ethics in medicine, ethics in computing, ethics in advertising, ethics in architecture etc.

The values she considers to be basic include respect for people and their dignity, decency, fairness and honesty, and the conduct that flows from these values, eg refraining from coercion and violence. But Sternberg puts strict limits on how far businesses should go in exercising values. In discussing environmental issues, she says (p 122): "Business should pursue green objectives only insofar as they help maximise long-term owner value, subject to respecting distributive justice and ordinary decency: business as business has no moral obligation (or right) to do anything else".

As an example of how Sternberg's view plays out in practice, in discussing the environment she bundles all environmental initiatives into the one basket of "green idealism". She does not address the issue of the company's responsibility to limit and rectify any harm that it causes. It could be argued that rectifying harm to the environment is an outworking of distributive justice and ordinary decency – for example, towards the defenceless people of Marinduque Island. If it is not, then the ordinary standards of morality are only being applied in a very impaired way.

In our approach it is also inappropriate to say corporations have no "right" to extend their social responsibility actions. Sternberg's arguments fall under the free economy banner, but they belie that very framework. There surely cannot be limits imposed on what social responsibility actions an organisation takes. In a free market, people can decide whether or not to invest in a particular company, and for some investors, knowing that a company is strongly socially responsible is a persuasive factor in their investment decision.

Beyond these particular objections, it needs to be said that the universal moral values are understood differently by people under different world views. For organisations operating under the orderly/bureaucratic world view, moral values are generally in alignment with society's norms. This is fine up to a point, but where societies have ethical blind spots, these organisations will reflect those faults. Conversely, for organisations that have more expanded world views, moral values will be understood as aspirational ideals rather than as rules with which to comply.

But even under the orderly/bureaucratic world view, organisations have a broader conception of organisational purpose than profit. The perception is that the organisation has a place and a role to play in society and as such it is part of a broad set of mutual obligations. The purpose is to render some benefit to society beyond that of the profit of its shareholders and employees. The purpose will differ between commercial enterprises and other kinds of organisations, but it will invariably be to achieve some legitimate social purpose beyond profit.

Drucker (1955) rightly criticised the enthronement of profit as the primary purpose of organisations more than five decades ago. He argued that to find the purpose of an organisation we have to look at it from the outside, from society's perspective "since a business is an organ of society". He defined the purpose of business as the creation of a customer who sees value in what the business offers. The function of profit is to validate the activities of the enterprise and enable it to continue. Analogous arguments can be put for organisations that are not commercial entities. For all except membership organisations that only provide a service to their own members, organisational activity relates to serving a customer need and obtaining the resources necessary to continue to do so. The scope of this account will broaden as organisations expand their world view.

It is important for leaders in organisations to recognise the beliefs and values that hold sway in their organisation, because it affects how they operate and what they can achieve, regardless of what type of organisation they are in – it could be a commercial enterprise, a government department, a charitable organisation or a recreational club.

4. Participative/Creative

Under this world view, organisations give more emphasis to human values. In some ways this is liberating, while in other ways it is unsettling. Established norms and processes are subject to question, and employees are encouraged to have their say. Hierarchical structure begins to soften, in favour of teamwork and shared decision-making. Whereas orderly/bureaucratic organisations focus strongly on task, participative/creative organisations focus more on human factors.

As organisations undergo shifts in their values and beliefs, the skills embedded in their culture develop (Hall, 1994). The shift from orderly/bureaucratic organisation to participative/creative organisation involves a major shift in the kinds of skills employed. The former organisation requires great strength in instrumental skills – all the technical skills involved in planning, organising, controlling and evaluating operations. In contrast, the latter organisation requires much greater emphasis on interpersonal skills and an increase in system skills (needed to be effective in complex human environments).

There are inherent differences between organisations in the level of relationship required to provide services to customers. Some organisations provide services where customer interaction is minimal; it is task-focused and transactional. Examples are purchasing an item through a website or filing a taxation form. At the other extreme, services require a high level of relationship to be formed; we say interactions are human-focused and relational. Examples might be a financial adviser or a career counsellor. In between, customer interactions can vary across a wide spectrum. A hairdresser, for example, could operate transactionally or relationally, as could a bus driver or doctor.

In participative/creative organisations, the preference is to interact more with customers and to build relationship. The underlying belief that has changed is that situations are seen more as win/win rather than win/lose. The "us and them" mentality has faded and the organisation sees the possibility of success through participation, innovation and openness. It operates out of enlightened self-interest.

Ethically, these organisations are more complex and a measure of uncertainty and ambiguity may be present at times, because different views are being allowed expression and decision-making responsibility has devolved more to the individual level. The attitude towards charity and social responsibility may reflect this complexity. Overall, the view is that the organisation has a social responsibility to deliver some benefits back to society, and efforts are directed to choosing appropriate involvements and beneficiaries.

5. Collaborative/Excellence

Collaborative/excellence organisations are a further evolution of participative/creative organisations. The former are more established in their practices, and the energy of their activities arises out of stakeholder engagement. There is more emphasis on dialogue and partnership but, at the same time, there is more assuredness about the organisation's identity, hence the focus on excellence.

Organisations like this are able to embrace diversity productively because of their inclusiveness. This is reflected culturally and in the flexibility of thinking that informs business decisions. They are likewise clearer – and more explicit – about their values and more adept at problem-solving and conflict resolution. Systems thinking is well-established and the complex connections between different aspects of the organisation and its environment are understood.

One of the misconceptions that arises when people talk about outstanding organisations such as those that operate out of world view 5 is that these organisations are "ethical". The inference is that other organisations are not, and that there is something distinctive about these organisations that can be denoted as ethical.

The danger of this perspective is that it can adversely affect other people (and organisations) who see themselves as not satisfying the criteria that are postulated. A common human reaction in this circumstance is to despair, or to pursue the opposite in defiance. This idea of the "ethical organisation" is an example of the sacred/secular distinction raising its head once again.

The sacred/secular distinction goes back to before the European Reformation period. Christians had come to see things related to the church as being higher than the things of ordinary life. For example, a career in the church was seen as a higher calling than being a tradesperson. There was a sacred sphere and a profane sphere and the two worlds did not meet. The things of God were unapproachable by the common man. The Reformation, with Martin Luther as one of the catalysts, dismantled this view, and societies came to see all aspects of life as being equally capable of reverence.

Similarly, it would be a shame to create a distinction where some companies are seen as ethical and others, by implication, are not. It was argued in Chapter 2 that the concept of ethics is associated with a very diverse range of actions, and it would be exceedingly simplistic to say categorically that a company was ethical or unethical. We might say that a particular action is ethical or unethical, but it is much more difficult to say that an organisation *per se* is ethical or otherwise.

Companies like Anita Roddick's The Body Shop and Ben and Jerry's ice cream business in the USA are often promoted as ethical companies. The problem with this is not with the companies, but with the use of language. These two companies are fine examples of how organisations can pursue high human values and still be commercially successful; and in fact their high ideals are an integral part of their success. But to say they are "ethical companies" leads too easily to the conclusion that there are rigid criteria and standards for being ethical, devoid of context.

What needs to be observed is that:

- there are a multitude of ways of living out core human values in organisational activities;
- organisations have to work from where they are and in their current circumstances, rather than expecting to suddenly leap to some exalted ideal;
- there are two possible orientations involved when ethics is referred to – compliance and aspiration – and in some social contexts, satisfying the former is adequate;
- being labelled "ethical" actually limits organisations, who should always be aspiring to the greater realisation of core human values; and
- being labelled "ethical" also runs the risk of making the organisation complacent.

6. Distributed leadership/Social well-being

Organisations at this stage are distinctive both internally and externally. Internally they have developed a culture where leadership is distributed across the organisation; people have a servant approach to leadership roles and play their part as needed. Ego is subservient to organisational goals and collective well-being. Externally they have a clear role in society – they are an active and responsible corporate citizen.

The idea of the responsible corporate citizen is that the organisation has moved beyond a transactional approach to community involvement and charitable contributions that are strategic to its business purposes. It has established an ongoing relationship with the community and it has a persistent and engaged commitment to society's well-being.

Sustainability underlies both the organisation's external relations and its internal culture. Sustainability is understood as the outcome of being in alignment with natural and human systems. The importance of energy is also understood – success depends on understanding flow and balance. Leaders (who come forward to meet particular challenges) inspire the organisational community through a commitment to core human values and their high aspirations for the organisation as a contributor to society.

Some of the literature of environmental sustainability explores this type of organisation, recognising that organisations that have a highly ecological approach to environmental issues are invariably characterised internally by more open human relationships and servant leadership (Dunphy et al, 2000; Dunphy et al, 2002).

7. Global harmony/Virtual relations

Although few if any organisations could be said to exhibit this world view, the concept is that they understand deeply the way the world is and the need to transform both physical conditions and society's beliefs in line with the core human values of truth, peace, right action, love and insight. Despite the dearth of such organisations, there is nevertheless a need for the ideal. Such organisations would inspire and guide others through their wisdom, harmony and quiet strength, and could exist without the need for much in the way of material supports, although they would be adept at utilising technical means when needed.

It might be thought that church bodies would exhibit the values associated with world view 7. As it happens, the people who are appointed to oversee the fortunes of such organisations, which are "of the world", often display the fears and limitation of vision that are characteristic of people who subscribe to prior world views. Brian Hall (2003), who has consulted to many organisations using the Values Evolution Model (my phrase, not his), discovered in exploring one religious organisation that the values of the leadership council were dominated by the concerns of world views 1 and 2, eg control, self-preservation, security and territory. It is clearly not an easy matter to live out of the perspective of global harmony.

The opening up of people's world views to embrace developmental values is addressed further in the next chapter. The issue is not really a matter of whether or how many organisations there are that exhibit the global harmony world view, but whether development is possible. And it is the purpose of this chapter and the next to show that it is.

The role of leaders

The above brief survey of perceptions of organisational purpose under the various world views implies a wide range of perceptions about leadership. Nevertheless, there is a persistent assumption, particularly under the earlier world views, that organisations require leadership. Bass (1990), in *Bass & Stogdill's Handbook of Leadership*, maintains that leadership is a universal phenomenon among humans. No societies are known that do not have leadership in some aspects of their social life.

Surveys of job satisfaction from the 1920s onwards have illustrated the importance of leadership, and productivity has also been related to employees' favourable attitudes towards the supervisors of work groups. One study of leadership succession in organisations in the 1980s (Day & Lord, 1988) concluded that as much as 45% of an organisation's performance could be explained by the differences between the new and previous executive leaders.

The necessity of leadership is also maintained by systems theory, which observes that organisations, as systems, have order and hierarchical relationships. However, different world views will understand these characteristics in a different way. Under world view 1, leadership will be seen as personal domination of the group, whereas under world views 6 and 7 leadership will be seen as serving to facilitate the communal actions of the system to fulfil human purposes.

The many definitions that exist of leadership reflect the various world views and their allied sets of values. Bass and Stogdill's handbook offers the following alternative definitions of the leader:

- a focus for group processes, an expression of the group's needs and goals
- a personality or a set of skills in influencing and persuading people and achieving social goals
- a power relationship where the leader enforces compliance
- a position and a role within a given social structure, associated with expectations and behaviours
- the initiation and maintenance of social structure through expectations and interactions.

These definitions differ in the level of initiative that is accorded to the leader. Some leaders may be responsible for enormous tasks or challenges. We might think of Napoleon, Churchill or Hitler. On the other hand, leaders may perform a much more modest role, maintaining routine organisational activity within a comprehensive and stable structure. A common thread is that the leader is an agent of change. The leader is the person whose actions affect other people more than the actions of other people affect them.

Our approach to leadership in this chapter is that leaders are indicated by the influence they have on a group or situation, not by formal positional power. Bass and Stogdill observed that being a leader (on this understanding of it) was a function of the both the individual's personal qualities and skills, and situational factors. They stress that it is just as important to examine "followership" as it is to examine leadership.

Kouzes and Posner (1990, 1996) have conducted many studies where they asked people what they looked for in a leader, defined as someone whose direction they would willingly follow. The qualities that consistently ranked most highly were honesty, future orientation, inspiration and competency. Leaders do not become leaders until they are seen as credible. Accordingly, leaders have to be trusted, they have to be clear about direction, be able to engender enthusiasm about those goals and possess relevant knowledge and skills: "If you don't believe the messenger, you won't believe the message".

Kouzes and Posner therefore emphasise the necessity and importance of the leader having a clear set of personal beliefs and values. Along with this, the leader must have regard to the beliefs and values of the group. They say (p 105): "If leaders advocate values that are not representative of the collective will, they will not be able to mobilise the people to act as one. Leaders must be able to gain consensus on a common cause and a common set of principles. They must be able to build a community of shared values."

Where shared values pertain, there are multiple positive effects, as confirmed by Kouzes and Posner's research (1996):

- employees have strong feelings of personal effectiveness
- employees have high levels of loyalty to and pride in the organisation
- consensus is reached about key organisational goals
- ethical behaviour is fostered
- strong norms are created about working hard and caring
- job stress and tension are reduced

- job expectations are clearly understood
- teamwork and esprit de corps are strong.

These research findings indicate what is possible in situations where common values can be attained. Nevertheless, these effects imply a world view that has moved beyond the orderly/bureaucratic (world view 3). Bob Anderson (undated) makes the point that most literature on organisational change and leadership targets the transition from world view 3 to world view 4.

Brian Hall (quoted by Anderson) suggests that over 60% of people operate out of world views 1 to 3, and Anderson argues that "much of what we are trying to introduce through change efforts in organisations is 'over the heads' of those asked to change". What may be truer, however, is that the required change is beyond the leaders asked to implement it. This is more significant than how the change stands in relation to workers, because one hopes that this is exactly what leaders will do – bring workers into an understanding of and commitment to more creative, productive values.

Having said this, we have revealed the essential difficulty of leadership, that is, it involves effecting changes in people's *values*. We know from a wealth of research that it is much more difficult to change people's attitudes and values than it is to teach them new knowledge or skills. And we also know that this language itself is flawed. We do not change others; it is more illuminating to say: we create the possibility of change, we enable people to see better (more productive, more human, more rewarding) ways of seeing and acting.

Anderson goes on to say that the changes most organisations want to institute can only be instituted if the leadership is functioning out of world view 4 or higher. Hall (2003), in reflecting on this problem, concluded that personal growth, and consequently the growth of leadership, is dependent on the individual's explicit awareness of their own values.

Why are the values of world view 4 so important? Hall, along with many others, argues that to remain competitive in a global environment, organisations need to function at the level of collaboration and knowledge creation, with high, transparent ethical standards. Operating out of the mindset of control and force will no longer deliver business success. Dictatorial, hierarchical behaviour is increasingly intolerable and unproductive in a world where innovation and collaboration are the sources of sustainability.

Ch. 8 | Ethical leadership in organisations

The perceptions of world view 4 include:

- authority is now viewed as coming from within rather than being vested in institutions; thus, blind loyalty is replaced by independence in judgement
- law is seen as a guide for action rather than as an inflexible set of rules
- we seek personal meaning and fulfilment rather than merely adhering to an assigned role in the organisation
- we become responsible for our actions and set our own boundaries rather than deferring to the dictates of others; we are no longer so dependent on the approval of others.

These perceptions make possible the leader's intelligent commitment to the development of others. Up to this point, leaders can only monitor and enforce the compliance of their followers to organisational norms and role identities. With leaders who operate out of the authoritarian/survivalist or paternal/Machiavellian mode, the experience can be vicious and demeaning. With leaders who operate out of the orderly/bureaucratic mode, it can be mind-numbing and claustrophobic.

The complex systems or chaos perspective has similar things to say about leadership and followership under evolving world views. Commentators from this perspective argue that the contemporary environment is increasingly complex, and organisations need to recognise and respond to it if they are to be sustainable. Their deliberations on leadership similarly maintain that leadership needs to move away from command and control towards collaboration and the fostering of innovation.

The complex systems view also sees the movement as an expansion rather than a displacement of current models of leadership. Lewin and Regine (1999) say the change required is to augment skills and acquire a new understanding of business. They use the image of the "paradoxical leader" who knows when to be directive and when to let go. The values that are important to the paradoxical leader are a strong sense of direction, a clear sense of self and definitive values. The leader is dealing with a complex, adaptive system. He/she must accept ambiguity and uncertainties and allow answers to emerge. It is the values and the sense of direction that guide leaders when the existing rules and solutions do not work any more.

Lewin and Regine stress that a core quality of the paradoxical leader is caring for their team. Leaders are available emotionally and are not limited to rational thinking. They are attuned to both people and the overall sense of the organisation. Key qualities that ensue are empathy, ability to listen, intuition, good judgement, trust and openness.

There are two aspects of the role of the leader, then, that are in tension. The first is that leaders in the contemporary business environment must aspire to the values and skills that are characterised by world view 4 and higher. The second is that many organisations reflect a belief that the world is dangerous and threatening, with the consequence that leaders act with scant regard for ethics (in any of the three senses – compliance, quality of relationships or development of identity). In these circumstances, is ethical leadership possible?

Leadership in ethics

There is a general symbiosis between organisational types and their members. For example, people who operate out of world view 4 or 5 are unlikely to join organisations operating out of world views 1 or 2, and if they do, they are unlikely to stay there for long. The conflict in values is just too difficult. This suggests that when it comes to leaders in organisations, this symbiosis similarly occurs. But reality is seldom so deterministic and although the general pattern holds, factors are at work that feed the dynamic of change.

For a start, one of the interesting things about the findings of Kouzes and Posner above is that people exhibit a high preference for leaders who are honest, competent, visionary and inspiring. Why is this interesting? Because if most people operate out of world views 1, 2 and 3, these are not qualities that would be expected to be high on the agenda. Ruthlessness might be expected to be admired, or imperiousness, or efficiency.

An explanation for this curiosity is given by Brian Hall (2003), who talks about the attraction of the "omega point". Hall, drawing on the theologian Pierre Teilhard de Chardin, says that human lives have a natural trajectory and they take their form from the omega point. This is a realisation of higher values which pulls us forward into the future. Hall says that modern life handicaps this pull because it elevates opportunity and choice directed towards personal success. In contrast, the omega point concerns realising expansive, creative, inner values and its core image is the development of the mature tree from its small seed.

Stephen Covey (1994) uses the language of chaos theory to describe the same thing. He talks of the "strange attractor", which is the idea that in the midst of what seems like chaos there is order and beauty. Moreover, this order is based on an inner vision which in turn is based on consistent, persistent principles, values and meaning. Covey says that when people live in accordance with faith in the strange attractor, they become self-managing. The strange attractor "lubricates all human interaction" because people then subordinate their ego to a higher purpose.

We know that the strange attractor or the omega point is not without opposition, otherwise evolution, or progress, or development, would be as smooth as the tide. In fact, we live on contested ground, as noted by Hall's comment above on the enticements of modern life. Similarly with leadership, people are attracted both to the admirable leader just described and to the one that plays upon their fears and ignorance. This is summed up in the title of the book, *The allure of toxic leaders* (Lipman-Blumen, 2005). There is indeed an attraction from the harmonic, creative realm, but there is likewise an attraction from the realm of fear, and the latter often holds sway.

It is tempting to look at what the appropriate leadership approach is from the perspective of the various world views. For example, if an organisation operated out of world view 3, how would a leader lead evolution into the more expansive world view 4? But this would create a needlessly complex solution. The *process* of leading the type of change we are interested in, that is, leading the evolution of values, is essentially the same no matter what world views predominate in an organisation.

The common feature of leadership in ethics is the fostering of the development of people and organisational cultures. We have seen in earlier chapters that this development can be viewed in varying levels of complexity. In its simplest form, ethical development is a movement between two states – from compliance to aspiration. We then viewed it as a movement involving three states – (1) ethics as law, (2) ethics as the quality of relationships, and (3) ethics as the realisation of identity and purpose. The Values Evolution Model is the more complex expression of this movement.

We will look first at a model of ethical leadership that reflects our two-state description of ethical development. We will then look at the processes recommended by Brian Hall to foster the evolution of values. Finally, we will examine how the five-dimensional model of the person can provide a guide to addressing the role that leaders can play in fostering ethics, and how this fits with general models of the change process in organisations.

The process of fostering ethics and values

Compliance has become a priority concern of organisations as they face greater scrutiny following the spate of corporate collapses around 2001, and the far more widespread incidence of corporate collapses in 2008 and beyond with the global financial crisis. Legislation such as Sarbannes-Oxley in the USA has increased the emphasis on policing executive conduct and corporate operations. The result is a greater investment in accounting and auditing, and the provision of channels for whistleblowers.

However, some commentators have maintained that an approach that just focuses on rules and policing is both expensive and inefficient. In fact, this viewpoint long precedes the recent scandals. Lynn Sharp Paine (1994) championed the concept of the "integrity strategy" as the alternative to a compliance strategy to prevent organisations from falling foul of the law. She argued that a focus on laws and regulations, lawyers, audits and investigations would be expensive and inadequate: "providing employees with a rule book will do little to address the problems underlying unlawful conduct".

Her integrity strategy aimed at developing an ethos where responsible conduct was fostered. It was based on the assumption that people are "social beings guided by material self-interest, values, ideals (and) peers" rather than individuals who are guided solely by self-interest. Her preferred strategy involves cultivating ethics through an examination of company values and standards, leadership, awareness of social obligations, training and communication, the integration of ethics into company systems, guidance and consultation, identification of problems and review of performance against values.

A study that examined the comparative benefits of the compliance and integrity approaches to ethics management (Trevino et al, 1999) found that the latter is more effective on several dimensions:

- lower incidence of unethical or illegal behaviour
- greater awareness of legal and ethical issues at work
- greater preparedness to seek advice on ethics issues
- more willingness to inform management about problems

- more reporting of ethics violations
- greater integration of ethics into everyday decision-making
- greater employee commitment to the firm.

Paine's model illustrates the shift that leaders can effect from a compliance approach to an approach based on ethical aspiration. Aspiration is reflected in the commitment to the development of individual and group integrity. Learning and growth, combined with the creation of a culture that is supportive of ethical behaviour, are at the heart of this approach.

The process of leading the development of ethics can also be described using the three states: (1) ethics as law, (2) ethics as the quality of relationships, and (3) ethics as the realisation of identity and purpose. We have described these states as being increasingly deeper levels of understanding of what ethics means. This posits a movement from external, social rules (laws), through regard for people (relationships) towards internal realisation. This suggests that leaders facilitate the movement of groups from outer, imposed rules to internalised principles.

But it seems that for this movement to be generated, it has to start from the opposite direction, from inner to outer. We will describe the elements in this process. Stephen Covey's (1992) account of leadership influence takes this approach. He says that organisational transformation has to begin with leaders at a personal level. They must become trustworthy before they can consider influencing others.

Only then can they begin the outward movement of influence. Covey sees this movement in four levels – personal (where the key is trustworthiness), interpersonal (where the key is trust), managerial (where the key is empowerment) and organisational (where the goal is alignment between values and behaviour). We can relate this model to our view of the development of ethics in the following way.

At the inner, personal level, the first stage is your examination of yourself. The establishment of your trustworthiness, one of the foundations of ethics, is the desired outcome of this process. The movement outwards occurs first as the quest to improve the quality of relationships. The establishment of trust between people is the foundation of this phase, and empowerment is the natural flow-on. The outward movement continues as organisations create systems and cultures (the analogue of laws) that support ethical conduct.

Stages of ethical leadership

1. Personal awareness

The first stage of ethical leadership is identified by Hall (2003), Anderson (undated) and Thomas (Thomas et al, 2004) as the realm of the personal. Thomas says it is about "ethics mindfulness", a form of enriched awareness where reflective ethical thinking becomes the foundation for the person's consistent ethical action. Ethics mindfulness is part of the person's self-identity (Aquino & Reed, 2002) and as such it constitutes an enduring and ever-present positive influence on the person's behaviour.

Hall says that ethical leadership begins with our explicit awareness of our own values, which includes an understanding of our underlying world view and the values that inform our day-to-day actions. Bearing in mind Thomas's idea of the moral self-identity, we also need to be aware of the complementary aspects of our identity, namely, the values that pull us back towards the past and values that pull us towards the future.

The values that pull us back towards the past are the foundation values that represent issues that we have not resolved. These may be unconscious, but they influence our choices in certain situations, perhaps where particular kinds of threats or fears present themselves. It is clearly imperative from an ethical standpoint to bring these values to awareness, because they are the ones that will bring us unstuck when faced with a situation where the stakes seem high and a quick decision needs to be made.

It is similarly important to identify the values that represent our vision of the ideal and the fulfilment of our potential. Anderson makes the point that most programs of organisational change fail because leaders treat it as a purely external operation – changing business processes and systems, applying techniques and manipulating rewards. He says that the changes in performance desired invariably require a change in personal consciousness: "there is no organisational transformation without a preceding transformation in the consciousness of leadership".

The above examination of our values presupposes a commitment to honesty and integrity, and a willingness to face our fears with courage. Fairholm (2003, p 262) describes a number of qualities of trustworthy leaders:

- **Integrity** – being honest, authentic and dependable, being open about our motives and feelings, and communicating truthfully
- **Patience** – being prepared to build trust out of the accumulation of experiences rather than expecting it instantly
- **Altruism** – seeing trust as a gift and an act of service to others based on care for them
- **Vulnerability** – recognising and accepting that trust involves vulnerability towards others – risk – and the risk always remains, even when relationships are firmly established
- **Action** – knowing that trust involves action, not rhetoric – a "developing record of authenticated interaction built up in their relations with followers"
- **Friendship** – without ignoring formal organisational relations, trustworthy leaders recognise that mutual trust leads to the same qualities found in friendship, such as compatibility and enjoyment of interaction
- **Personal competence** – having confidence in people's abilities and skills, and willingness to work cooperatively
- **Judgement** – having confidence in people's capacity to make sound, ethical and appropriate judgements.

2. Quality of relationships

The second stage of ethical leadership is to build relationships anew in the organisation. This is a venture in trust, which occurs in two ways: firstly, through the leader modelling ethical behaviour, and secondly, through engaging people in dialogue. Anderson says this dialogue must bring to the surface what is hidden in the organisation's culture and enable personal transformation to translate into cultural and systemic change.

Dialogue is the vehicle for eliciting the engagement of employees, for identifying the prevailing values in the organisation and forging a shared set of values that can inspire both high ethics and high performance. This is not always a simple or painless process, because buried beliefs come to the surface, and some of these we do not want to recognise as our own. Conflicting beliefs also emerge, and a resolution of these is generally challenging.

However, despite the difficulties in achieving trust, it is a necessary element of cooperative action in organisations. It is a key task of leaders to build a workplace community where interpersonal trust is high (Fairholm, 2003). Trust is critical because high performance in organisations nowadays is dependent on the discretionary effort of employees; the changing nature of work means they have more scope for choosing how much effort and imagination they will contribute.

Fairholm asserts that trust in others flows from self-trust, that is, confidence in our own ability and integrity. As noted above, trust becomes established through an accumulation of experiences that demonstrate its efficacy. Jack Gibb (1978) explored the concept of trust at length. He maintained that when trust is high relative to fear, people and people systems function well. Energy is created and mobilised. The converse of trust is fear and, when fear predominates, social processes are impaired.

Gibb sees trust as a liberating force. It allows persons, and organisational groups, to unfold and grow. He proposed the TORI theory to describe this unfolding: Trusting, Opening, Realising and Interdepending. As Covey (1992) holds, trust starts with the self and works outwards to other people to enable high quality relationships. Gibb's four processes consist of:

- Trusting – the initiating act of trust which accepts the self and begins to explore how one can be in the world; it is centring and affirmative

- Opening – the acts of listening, letting the world in, self-disclosing and empathising with others

- Realising – the process of discovering what one can be – asserting, evolving, exploring and finding fulfilment

- Inter-depending – the process of being with others – joining, integrating, participating, sharing and finding freedom in association with others.

Gibb also describes what happens to a person where fear predominates over trust. Each of the TORI processes is stymied. The effects include lack of motivation, energy channelled into defensiveness, a reduced span of awareness, feelings that can be disruptive and dysfunctional, lack of focus in solving problems and inability to imagine solutions, and behaviour that is reactive, congested (not free-flowing) and hindered by fear about consequences. Relationships suffer through these same processes.

The dialogue, conversation and actions that build strong relationships are founded on trust and its outworking, as illustrated in the TORI theory. When the focus has shifted to the quality of relationships in the organisation, the associated values come to the fore and begin to be incorporated into people's actions. If leaders allow this process to flourish, there can be significant shifts in people's values and indeed, the world views that underlie them. Correspondingly, attitudes and understandings about ethics can undergo expansion and evolution.

3. Systems and culture

Continuing to work outwards, the process of change meets organisational systems and culture. Hall (2003) says that the evolution of values depends firstly on the development of awareness about values and secondly on the support of the organisation's culture: "this is a culture that is deliberately created, making all its members explicitly aware of its values priorities". What emerges out of this is a cultural identity for the organisation, made coherent through a common vision.

The focus at this stage is on meaning. Dialogue and conversation can bring values to awareness, but the final test of values is when they characterise the behaviour of a community in a consistent and coherent way. For this to happen, the dialogue of the community has to engage with the meaning of particular actions, otherwise statements of values have no real substance.

Meaning is created through this dialogue and affirmed by the community. This is another form of the process illustrated in Figure 2.3, where an experience or event was seen to be followed by debate on its moral implications and agreement was sought on the appropriate rules and codes to apply in similar circumstances in the future. Events and experiences are continually being assessed against values to affirm or recreate organisational rules and guidelines. And this process likewise illuminates and clarifies values.

Meaning is expressed in organisations through norms, policies, practices, structure and leadership style. Where an organisation has identified positive values and endeavoured to translate them into practice, the effect can be observed in any number of areas, each of which reflects the values:

- **Rewards and recognition** – eg incentives for sales people do not reward "results at any cost": adherence to ethical values is expected, acknowledged and reinforced.
- **Recruitment** – the integrity and values of job applicants are significant factors in the selection of new employees.
- **Communications** – messages to employees from management articulate and reinforce the values and the organisation's commitment to the values is seen to be real rather than opportunistic.
- **Dialogue** – employees are actively engaged in the organisation's business rather than being cast as passive recipients of managerial commands. Dialogue fosters harmony and innovation through inclusiveness and trust.
- **Learning and development** – learning is ongoing for managers and workers, and efforts reflect respect for employees and commitment to the organisation's development of both business capability and human values.

The key concept in the outworking of values in organisational practices is the subjecting of conduct to values. All actions reflect values in some way and the values invest actions with meaning. Kuzcmarski & Kuzcmarski (1995) give some very specific examples:

- start and stop meetings on time – this conveys respect for other people's time and commitments
- provide frequent training to employees that is customised to their needs – this conveys respect for their role in the organisation and their personal need to grow
- establish team bonus programs that reward the value of team contributions and performance – this fosters cooperation over individualism.

The caution that is needed in tackling specifics is that specific actions can convey different meanings to different people, and multiple values can arise out of one action. For example, promptness in ending a meeting may be at the expense of addressing an important issue or allowing a worker to express their views.

The lesson is that in addressing specific actions and how they reflect or embody values, we must keep in mind the overall body of values and exercise judgement. Also, we come back to dialogue: in the example just used, we need to articulate the values at stake and be imaginative in how we find a solution that satisfies the overall body of values. In this case, we might extend the meeting if we have obtained the group's consent, or find another way to satisfy the human values at stake here, perhaps by scheduling another group meeting or continuing the meeting by email.

The ongoing work of bringing values to fruition in the organisation involves moving backwards and forwards between the articulation of values and interpretation of them in practice. This continual process of interpretation, application and review leads to the internalisation of principles among the people in the team and the organisation, and results in improved decision-making skills. This is depicted in Figure 8.1.

Figure 8.1 The relationship between principles and practice

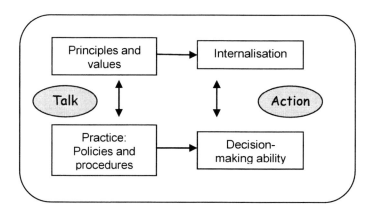

What is happening at this third stage is the consolidation of values among a group of people over time. The work community changes as a result of events, the actions of leaders in response to those events, the interpretation given to actions in terms of the values that have been articulated, and the feelings of members of the community about all of these things. Some behaviour becomes routine (the establishment of norms), relationships take shape and reinforce behaviour (supporting some, discouraging others), and shared understanding of the community's identity grows.

Throughout this process, leadership plays a role in fostering the development of the work community in particular directions. Leadership of ethics starts with the inner person and works outwards to the group. Awareness of one's own values (from survival values to aspiration) is followed by the modelling of trustworthiness, then the establishment of sound relationships, which then form the basis for a robust work community that continually develops its capacities.

The process of growth starts with whatever set of beliefs about the world prevails in the organisation at the time. As we have seen in earlier chapters, values are not set in concrete; at any one time, foundation values sit alongside focus values and vision values and as events occur and the individual deals with them, values evolve. Yet we also saw that the five-dimensional model of the person provides a useful perspective on how we deal with the vicissitudes of life.

5D model and leadership

The five-dimensional model can be applied to the role of the leader. Under any world view, the five core human values have a meaning, and the leader can use the five-dimensional model to cultivate higher purpose and competency, both personally and in the organisation.

Although our immediate concern here is with leadership in ethics, recall from Chapter 7, on decision-making, that there is not one set of rules for ordinary decision-making and a separate set of rules for decision-making on ethical questions. In the same way, what we say about leadership in ethics in organisations is an integral aspect of leadership per se. And in Chapter 7 we recognised, too, that the crucial challenge of personal integrity and of leadership lies in how we integrate the pursuit of organisational survival/success with ethics and values.

The five-dimensional model of the person gives us a way of explaining the full scope of the qualities required to be an effective and ethical leader. It also explains the shortcomings that many leaders exhibit and provides a clear framework to make sense of the many different lists that exist of leadership qualities and competencies. The application of the five-dimensional model to managers and leaders was broached in Chapter 3, where the evolution of management theory over the 20th century was used to illustrate the need for all five dimensions. We will be amplifying that discussion below.

A study conducted by McKinsey (Michaels et al, 2001) on the ability of organisations to retain talented employees found that 70% of the factors in employees' decisions to quit their current job were "push" factors. Push factors refer to the organisation making the employee want to quit, as opposed to the employee being attracted to better offers elsewhere. Moreover, of the push factors, 70% of those related to the employee's negative impression of their immediate manager.

A study by Hudson, the recruitment and HR consulting firm (Hudson, 2004), found widespread perceptions of inadequate people management skills among Australian managers. Its survey of 7,600 managers found that people management skills were regarded, by far, as their major failing. The areas regarded as a failing in order of frequency cited were:

- poor people management, 40%
- poor change management, 16%
- poor business decisions, 15%
- poor customer relationship management, 11%
- poor operational/systems management, 9%
- lack of innovation, 8%.

The report says the results indicate a clear expectation that leaders *should* be good with people, and there is dissatisfaction with the current levels of people skills of Australian managers. An ability to manage and effectively engage colleagues is a core attribute that continues to be undervalued in many organisations. The report cites research by Warren Bennis and Robert Thomas (2002) on the essential skills of leadership. They maintain that good leaders:

- are able to engage others in a shared meaning
- have a distinctive and compelling voice
- have strong values and a sense of integrity
- are adaptive and creative in meeting adversity.

The underpinning capability, according to the report, is emotional intelligence – the ability to identify their own and others' feelings and needs, to appreciate how they influence actions and thoughts, and to understand how they would like themselves and others to feel.

The five-dimensional model picks up on the conclusions of the research cited above, and provides a comprehensive framework for management development. It goes further than an appeal to the need for emotional intelligence. The explanation of why so many managers are tyrannical or otherwise dysfunctional requires coverage of all five dimensions.

What does the model have to say about the dimensions of management? (We will not quibble here about the differences between management and leadership; we assume that there are differences in emphasis as well as areas of overlap, and that what is said below has its application to both.)

Dimension 1: Cognition – skills and knowledge

To be an effective manager, a person must be competent in a set of cognitive, or technical, skills and knowledge. In a particular industry and work environment, this may include knowledge and skills relating to:

- processes and operations for creating the organisation's products and services
- preparing and monitoring budgets and expenditure
- performance and behaviour standards in the organisation
- legal and moral obligations, such as EEO and OHS
- organisational policies and protocols
- administrative procedures.

In addition, it is a pre-requisite that the manager has a thorough understanding of the industry, customers and the products and services offered. Competency in the cognitive area is a minimum requirement for an effective manager. The manager may not need to know how to carry out all of the tasks of the team they manage, but they do need to have a firm idea about what skills and effort are required for workers to fulfil their roles.

Some theories about management do not consider particular knowledge of the industry or the core operational work to be necessary or important for the manager. Instead, these theories maintain that management consists of possessing some generic competencies about management. The discussion above about credibility and trust, however, suggests that managers need to demonstrate that they know what workers are talking about, and what the constraints are upon performance.

Some managers are resistant to going beyond this dimension; they think that only technical skills are needed. A typical assertion from such a manager would be: "We don't want to know about all that 'touchy feely' stuff". But as the Hudson study above might suggest, these are the very people who offend their staff the most.

Dimension 2: Emotions – people skills

The second dimension of the management role is the emotional aspect. It is still true that most managers, particularly at supervisor level, are appointed from among the ranks. And it is still true that they are chosen primarily because of their technical excellence. What this means is that most new managers come to the role with a strong leaning towards the cognitive dimension of tasks, not the emotional dimension that concerns relating to other people.

How do these managers react to the management role? Some common reactions are as follows:

- **They try to carry on as usual** – they try and do all the work themselves, and don't know how to delegate. They don't trust others to do the job as well as they do themselves. As a result, they become frantic and stressed. The workers are sympathetic at first, but they are soon disappointed at the lack of leadership.

- **They become officious or "bossy"** – they suddenly think they have to *make* workers do their work, and exercise power over them. They micro-manage their workers and they focus on rigid rules and compliance rather than enabling and supporting workers. They are often surprised if they find out that their workers neither like nor respect them.

- **They become remote and bureaucratic** – rather than being overt bullies, these managers retreat from their workers and turn the workplace into a machine-like system. They focus on performance standards and productivity, but they are cold and unsympathetic and not nice to work for. And they merely transmit the orders they receive from above to their team; they do not consider the impact of the orders on the team, and they do not support or advocate for the team.

Why do new managers behave in this way? We under-estimate the enormity of the step from worker to manager. When a worker receives a promotion to a higher-level operational role, the change is gradual. The worker may assume wider responsibilities, but essentially they do the same kind of work. But when a person becomes a manager, he/she faces an entirely new set of tasks, not more of the same. And the tasks are different in nature:

- they involve achieving the teams' goals through other people rather than doing it yourself;
- the tasks tend to be manifold and in parallel, so the manager has to switch continually from task to task, juggling them;
- demands from other people are constant, and include contacts within the team, contact with other people in the organisation and external parties;
- the manager has to play many roles, from figurehead to information-processor and decision-maker, combining a comprehensive knowledge of technical issues with a knowledge of people and their motivations.

The emotional leap required in taking on these new tasks is considerable. The challenge is not just intellectual. Consider the emotional maturity required by these aspects of the managerial role:

- assuming and exercising authority
- being responsible and accountable for results
- making decisions under pressure, often when resources, time and information are inadequate
- leading, supporting, encouraging and expressing appreciation for team members' performance, and handling poor performance or behaviour.

The second dimension deals with the emotional competence required of managers – the competence to handle themselves and others so as to achieve productivity and harmony. Goleman (1998) divided the emotional competencies into those concerned with managing oneself, and those concerned with handling relationships:

- **Self-awareness** – recognising and assessing one's own feelings, strengths and limitations
- **Self-regulation** – keeping disruptive emotions in check, being trustworthy and conscientious, and being adaptable and innovative
- **Self-motivation** – striving for achievement, being committed, showing initiative and being optimistic
- **Empathy with others** – understanding others, fostering their development, appreciating diversity, being politically aware and meeting others' needs

- **Social skills** – listening and communicating well, being able to influence others and manage conflict, building relationships, collaborating and leading change.

Goleman also has a lot to say about how EQ can be developed. He insists that the methods have to be broader than classroom-based instruction, and include self-assessment, role playing, and practice combined with ongoing support through coaching and mentoring. He also emphasises the fact that developing increased EQ is a process that takes time – measured in months and years rather than hours and days.

We should also recognise that although Goleman does not highlight this aspect, much of what he says about EQ is about harnessing the ego, and about working in the service of others. New managers who become tyrants fail in this area because: (a) they harbour the generally false assumption that people will not work unless they are forced to, and (b) they are working for their own ends (eg career progression, domination) rather than focusing on doing the job well.

Many commentators, having dealt with the two dimensions of cognition and emotions, finish the discussion here, but some writers are now starting to focus more on the values dimension of management. If we take a closer look at the cognitive and emotional dimensions, we may recognise that we are already dealing with values. A good model of effective management should bring the values aspect to the surface. As managers, we make choices anyway, and we would want those choices to be conscious, consistent and defensible.

And there is another, more significant, reason to move the conversation from emotions to values – the things that arouse our emotions most strongly tend to be related to values. For example, you may experience feelings of outrage when you witness an injustice happening. It doesn't even need to be you who is the subject of the injustice.

The connections between emotions and ethics (morality, values) were discussed in Chapter 4. Brabeck and Gorman (1992) maintain that "emotional development must be included in an integrated theory of morality" and observe that people who uphold given values (in their behaviour) invariably demonstrate corresponding feelings.

Dimension 3: Valuing

Some of the questions implicit in the discussion to this point are as follows:

- Is it acceptable, *ethically*, for the workplace to be cold or hostile?
- Do we always agree with demands placed on us by senior managers, even if they lead to unreasonable or impossible situations for our team members, and even if the demands themselves are ethically questionable?
- Do we strive for fairness and foster participation in our teams? Do we listen to our workers? Do we foster improvement and development?

These questions show the shortcomings of theories of management and leadership that do not explicitly talk about ethics and values. As we saw in the discussion earlier in this chapter, in order to foster positive and ethical values in an organisation, values have to be identified, articulated and discussed explicitly. Values are already implicit in the emotional dimension, but we know that emotional skills can be used for unethical ends (eg manipulation) as well as worthwhile ends.

Managers who are tyrannical or dysfunctional are generally so because they have not resolved issues at an emotional level. Alistair Mant (1997) recognises this in his conceptualisation of leadership when he includes the requirement that leaders should not be psychopathic! He says that psychologically damaged individuals tend to erupt when the complexity of the leadership role becomes too much for them, so that their personal pathologies derail organisational action in moments of crisis. They experience other people as threats and their focus is on themselves rather than on organisational purposes.

The discussion of values in organisations serves to bring out into the open the emotional state of workers and managers. This knowledge is then available for people to work with. The process is not easy, as it can be confronting, but it can be approached with a positive mindset that seeks to affirm what there is in the current situation to appreciate. This approach will be taken up in the next chapter.

It can be helpful to paint a picture of the values-based manager and contrast it with the picture of management when positive and ethical values are absent. We performed a similar exercise for organisations at the beginning of Chapter 2. The value of doing this is that it begins to harness the energy of aspiration – naming positive values taps into deeper desires about ideals, such as "what I would be proud of", what would be liberating and what would be creative. Table 8.2 shows the contrast.

Table 8.2: Values-based management and its opposite

Management where positive values are absent	Values-based management
Applies rigid rules but can also be unfair Serves own interests Uses power to dominate others Uses punishment to assert control	Emphasises meaning and purpose Has integrity Shows concern for people Is fair and just Enables and empowers people Inspires and leads Fosters development

Dimension 4: Energy and spirit

The fourth and fifth dimensions of the model can be understood as being outgrowths of the first three dimensions. As the individual manager develops and internalises the cognitive, emotional and values dimensions, what is interesting is that the manager's development towards expertise begins to produce certain effects in the workplace environment.

The result is an increase in the energy level, which is seen in the building of a sense of community and a strong, values-based culture. It is a result of accumulated momentum, like a flywheel effect. Jim Collins and Jerry Porras (Collins & Porras, 1994; Collins, 2001) discussed this effect as it occurs over the longer term in well-managed organisations.

Energy and spirit are qualities of both the manager and the workplace environment, not something belonging to the manager alone. The features of the energised manager and environment include respectful and warm relationships, enthusiasm, innovation, sincerity, patience, tolerance and compassion.

Dimension 5: Identity

Identity is the final level in the model. Through learning, practice and work upon themselves, managers begin to develop their own personal style. It is based on their firmness and clarity about their values, and their development of skills encompassing people and tasks. It is also about the fulfilment (if such a final thing can be said) of one's potential. This identity is forged through experiences with the community, and it evolves as part of development of the fourth dimension of management.

Hence, this identity is not held by the manager apart from the community but exhibits a healthy interdependence with it. In fact, the community and the manager are each evolving their identity together, and the possibilities of the one are entwined with the possibilities of the other. The work of Collins and Porras, as noted above, again points to this reality.

The identity dimension occurs last because it is the result of experiences in developing skills in the other dimensions. One of the key aspects of that development is the harnessing of the ego. This is the challenge in every dimension:

- in the cognitive dimension, managers must learn to focus on the task rather than upon themselves
- in the emotional dimension they come to terms with ego much more strongly, in learning empathy with others and how to interact with and relate to others
- in the values dimension they learn to honour moral principles over selfishness
- in the energy dimension they must learn to rein in their ego and serve the flow.

In contrast, many contemporary management development programs ask the novice manager to focus immediately on their individual style. This is often done through the use of personality tools such as the Myers-Briggs Type Indicator. The danger of this approach is that it gives style an inflated importance at a time when attention needs to be focused on the fundamental skills and qualities of the first three dimensions.

These personality self-assessment tools may be used as a vehicle for addressing issues in the emotional dimension, eg *how* you relate to others. But effective and ethical management – and leadership in ethics – begins with competence in the first three dimensions. Until competence and awareness is achieved in these areas, the development of individual style is both a luxury and an ego threat.

Perhaps it should also be said, however, that the process of developing as a leader does begin with a commitment to the idea of developing as an individual. This is what was illustrated above in the discussion of stages of ethical leadership. It was seen in the development from inner to outer, from the personal province to relationships and on to organisational systems and culture.

Conclusions

This chapter has presented an account of how people can play a leadership role in fostering ethics in organisations – regardless of whether or not they hold a formal management position. The next chapter will explore the actions that individuals can take to foster their own development and affirm ethical values in organisations.

As indicated at the outset, this chapter has only looked at a narrow slice of what leadership is about, emphasising the values aspect of the role. It has devoted little attention to the area of change management, but leaders who wish to foster ethics in their organisation need to explore the organisational change process and draw on knowledge from that arena.

There is a wealth of literature on change management. Writers such as Kotter (1996) provide a sound basis for addressing the issue of change in organisations. Two other sources that offer a succinct overview of the change management process are:

- Donald Tosti (2000), who presents a framework for undertaking systemic change in organisations
- Lawson and Price (2003), who discuss the psychology of change management.

Leaders play a significant, indeed, pivotal role in fostering ethics. The assertion of Thomas, Schemerhorn and Dienhart (2004) is worth repeating here:

> In the leadership capacity, executives have great power to shift the ethics mindfulness of organisational members in positive as well as negative directions. Rather than being left to chance, this power to serve as ethics leaders can be used to establish a social context with which positive self-regulation of ethical behaviour becomes a clear and compelling organisational norm.

Emphasis has been placed in this chapter on understanding the prevailing world view in the organisation and then exploring how the pull of positive values (the omega point) can be used as a starting point for change and development. Emphasis has also been placed on self-development using the five-dimensional model of the person. Ethics is integrally connected with expansion and development; it is not just about compliance and adherence to rules. We might say that this is a holistic approach to ethics.

However, it may also be useful to provide a set of guidelines for a leader's actions. This is offered below. The focus is on building a team climate where ethics are valued, rather than on structural and formal changes that need to be enacted at the top organisational level.

Ten guidelines for the manager to foster ethics

1. Set the ideal. Articulate it clearly.
2. Make it practical. Not just "We value integrity" but "Sales staff will not make promises to customers on which the company cannot deliver". Be as specific as possible for the context.
3. Model ethical behaviour.
4. Insist on ethical behaviour. Do not excuse unethical conduct.
5. Reward ethical behaviour, formally where appropriate (eg material rewards), and informally (appreciation and acknowledgment).
6. Acknowledge and work through difficult problems with staff.
7. Address rationalisations that allow sub-standard behaviour to persist.
8. Make work roles clear and accountable so that conflicts of interest are less likely.
9. Recognise the work conditions and climate that give rise to unethical conduct.
10. Keep relationships and responsibilities professional but personal.

It should be noted that the emphasis in these guidelines is on satisfying compliance requirements. This is the necessary foundation for ethics, but it needs to be balanced with attention to the development of positive values. Certainly this balance is what managers should be striving for in their application of the guidelines. The benefit of leaders creating a positive ethical environment in the workplace is indicated in Sun Tzu's observation in *The Art of War* (1991), speaking about nations and their rulers: "The moral law causes the people to be in complete accord with their ruler, so that they follow him (or her) regardless of their lives, undismayed by any danger".

9

Personal growth and development

Just as leaders can reframe their concepts, values and behaviour, as discussed in the previous chapter, so too can individuals work on their ideas, beliefs and conduct. We noted earlier the distinction between what we expect of others and what we expect of ourselves. In social contexts it may only be appropriate to expect agreed standards of behaviour from others, eg legal minimum standards or adherence to company policy, rather than higher standards of, say, generosity. This chapter, in contrast, is about what we want from and for ourselves from the perspective of ethics and personal growth.

The Values Evolution Model, described in Chapter 5, tells us that people at any point in time have a certain perception of reality, a set of beliefs, values and attitudes which we have called a world view, and which forms their way of living in this reality. In that chapter we briefly broached the topic of how people's world views evolve. This discussion is the chief concern of this current chapter.

Alongside the framework of the Values Evolution Model we have described a five-dimensional model of the person, which provides us with an approach to understanding and working with ourselves to foster our development. We will be exploring how the five-dimensional model can be used to make sense of your experiences and guide your efforts to survive and thrive as a person of integrity.

This aim is intended to be modest and pragmatic. We are not proposing an all-embracing psychological model of ethical development. We will draw on the work of others as it illuminates our own perspective.

This chapter arises out of the need for something to be written on how to develop personally so that you can live and work ethically. Something more is needed than simply advocating adherence to the ten commandments or some equivalent. To quote an example of this view: "Ethical behaviour simply means adherence to a few common sense principles" – quoted by Steven Kerr (1988). Kerr comments, "It seemed to me as I reviewed the literature that.....the more confident were the prescriptions about how to behave with ethics and integrity, the further removed was the author from the life of the everyday manager".

Like Kerr, we want to illuminate personal ethics in full appreciation of the conflicts and complexities that life throws up, particularly in business and in organisations. Our treatment will expand on the five-dimensional model, placing it in the context of how the individual interacts with the world. Earlier we focused on the five dimensions as providing a comprehensive picture of the person. What we need to do now is include in the model the types of interactions that occur between the individual and the world, because these interactions are what give rise to the individual's need to understand, act and grow.

The reality test of personal development is how our interaction with the world changes and develops as we grow. Accordingly, the concept that underlies this chapter starts with a statement that Eleanor Roosevelt (wife of US President Franklin Roosevelt) made. She said: "It isn't enough to talk about peace [or ethics]. One must believe in it. And it isn't enough to believe in it. One must work at it." But ultimately, we need to add the statement that Gandhi made, because even "working at it" is not enough. Ghandi said, "We must *be* the change we wish to see in the world."

With this concept in mind, this chapter presents a suggested approach to personal development that focuses particularly on ethics. In doing this, we also want to assert that ethics is an essential aspect of personal development, although there is a great deal of material on the subject that does not seem to subscribe to this view. William Doherty (1995), a psychotherapist, addresses this issue, maintaining that many of the problems that surface in psychotherapeutic contexts are, at root, problems of how to make ethical decisions.

Doherty says that "the idea of taking personal responsibility for one's actions is vanishing from the public arena, and....therapists have become magicians who can make moral sensibilities vanish under a veil of psychological rhetoric" (p 5). He urges on us the importance of considering others when making decisions about our future, rather than promoting "the morality of self-interest".

We commence by setting the scene for personal ethical development. If we are going to talk about development, we need to think about what it is that drives it.

Setting the scene for personal growth

What is the question that brings us to the quest for personal development? Following the thread of thought in this book, the question is: how can I live ethically, and develop my understanding and strength to do that well, and become all that I can be? Our line of thinking is the evolution from making sense of ethics as a demand of society and abiding by those values (or complying with those rules), towards embracing ethics in its deeper sense of developing the good in ourselves and the world.

In presenting the five-dimensional model of the person, we asserted that ethics is an integral aspect of the self. As well as perceiving the physical and social world as facts and ideas (cognition), and as well as feeling emotions about those facts and ideas, we evaluate them as good/bad, right/wrong, or desirable/undesirable. Hence values arise and sit together with our views of the world as a configuration of goals, and standards for our actions.

In the Values Evolution Model, we described how people seem to exist at various places along a continuum, which we presented as seven world views. We described what values are at the forefront of people's minds in each of these world views. We also gave a brief account of the skills and understandings people develop under each world view, and how this process of development serves to shift their world view to the next one.

What we did not discuss there, and intend to do now, is what moves people to continually process their experience, make meaning of it and build skills which periodically transform their current views of the world and, along with it, their values. We did suggest in the previous chapter that an influence is at work – what Brian Hall calls the omega point and Stephen Covey calls the strange attractor. We need to return to this concept, because it tells us what people are dealing with when they come up against ethical issues.

There are a number of psychologists who have advanced theories of the life cycle. Sigmund Freud, Erik Erikson, Robert Kegan, Ken Wilber and Clare Graves all had a view of the human life as a series of stages. It is not our intention to enter into the debate between these various theories. Our concern is with creating a set of useful constructs that resonate with the common experiences of people, and illuminate our discussion of ethical development in this way.

We should note too that much of the difference between these theorists is grounded in their focus of attention. Freud was working out of a theory of the individual that saw sexual energy as the primary driver. Kegan and Wilber were looking at development as an expanding consciousness of self in its environment. So, for example, the child learns to distinguish itself from its surroundings as a self with needs, interests and desires.

Our endeavour is also different because the question we want to answer is different to theirs. Our account of personal development is focused on the question: **through the course of our life, what are we trying to do?**

The Values Evolution Model (VEM) described in the earlier part of this book looks at one side of the broader question of human development and the life cycle. VEM looks at what is happening in the person's values dimension, whereas life cycles consider the wider canvas of the person's whole life, the bundle made up of cognition, emotions, energy and identity (insight into self) as well as values.

Discussion of the question: "what are we trying to do?" will enrich our understanding of the positions people take on values. We will present six types of aims that seem to be common to people's life experience, across cultures and societies. These six aims do not correspond to the world views; rather, they relate to aspects of the person that operate through all stages of the model. The six aims are:

1. Pleasure, no pain (Innocence)
2. Mastery, independence (Autonomy)
3. Roles, belonging (Acceptance)
4. Innovation, adventure, beauty (Creativity)
5. Love (Intimacy)
6. Purpose, peace (Meaning).

In some ways these aims are linked to Abraham Maslow's needs hierarchy theory, because the question Maslow was addressing is similar to ours. We differ because we do not describe these aims as needs. Rather, we simply say that these are the common things that people seem to be trying to do as they live their lives. Nor do we present this as a hierarchy, except to accept that aims concerning survival, pleasure and pain generally take precedence over other aims. For the most part, these aims co-exist in the person.

The six aims are also related to the needs that William Glasser (1985, 1998) discussed as part of his control theory, later amended to become choice theory. Glasser said there are five basic human needs:

- to survive and reproduce
- to belong (love, share, and cooperate)
- for power
- for freedom
- for fun.

Although we identify the basic human aims a little differently to Glasser's needs, his exposition is addressing a similar question to ours, and the answers share much common ground. The aim of power, as Glasser sees it, is to have control over one's own self and sphere of action (autonomy), without the inference of control over others.

Following the presentation of the six aims we will discuss the perversions, or deviations, that may occur for each of these aims, including the pursuit of domination over others (ie a deviant form of Glasser's power).

Six aims of human activity

1. Innocence: pleasure, no pain

Beginning with the first world view, we may ask, what kind of experience leads a person to the values of survival and self-interest? And we can probably agree that the most basic distinction in experience is between pleasure and pain. If we think of children, innocent and without knowledge of the world or people, we can understand how it can all be threatening but also a source of wonderment. Life is simple but intense.

What is the person trying to do? The person is trying to obtain pleasure and avoid pain, in the absence of knowledge of how the world works and without power. Although this aim is instinctive rather than conscious, it nevertheless directs action. At its most basic, this drive is for survival. This drive incorporates the basic functions that people carry out to both survive and sustain life, from self-protection to eating. It includes all the things we do for enjoyment too.

The pleasure/pain principle does not disappear as people expand their experience – instead, it is placed in a wider perspective. For example, people postpone pleasure in order to complete projects and achieve goals. Recall that in Chapter 4 we discussed William Kay's model of the development of moral attitudes, and we saw there that prudence and preservation remain a presence in a person's life at later stages.

The pleasure/pain principle is also applied to a wider range of contexts as we develop. As our knowledge and intellect expand and we acquire ideas about many social activities, we experience new forms of pleasure and pain. Our appreciation of music or visual art depends on the sensibilities we have developed, but pleasure and pain lie at their root. Similarly, we feel pleasure or pain in the emotional realm because of understandings and empathy we have developed. We may, for example, be moved by a person's act of kindness.

The ethical question for personal development that arises out of our pursuit of pleasure and enjoyment and our avoidance of pain is: what considerations should modify our efforts?

2. Autonomy: mastery and independence

The second type of aim in people's experience is to gain control over themselves and their circumstances. People make a transition from dependence to independence, autonomy and freedom. They gain knowledge and skills and apply them to acquire proficiency in different areas of their lives. They go through many iterations of this process and, indeed, this process never ends.

Again, it is easy to see this process at work through childhood although, as we say, these drives are at work throughout life. The child is firstly content to be dependent and have things done for them by their parents, for example, being carried from place to place. But then the child takes it on as a project to learn to stand and walk, and the aim is to do it for him/herself, even to the point of rejecting the parent's assistance.

This drive extends to more and more spheres of life – learning to read, leaving home, training for an occupation, pursuing a career – all express this drive. As with pleasure/pain, as we develop, this drive extends into different realms. The first realm is physical, mastering one's own body and mind. Later the challenges may be mental and the challenges become more sophisticated. We learn that gaining control is not just about strength but how to handle strength with grace, how to turn our energy towards a goal.

The aim of autonomy extends into spheres such as work, business and relationships. How do we support ourselves financially? What occupational skills do we develop in order to create a domain in which we are master/mistress? What kind of work situation do we pursue (employee, starting a business etc)? How do we go about establishing and maintaining a home (renting, sharing, buying)? What do we know about finding our way around town?

The key words associated with this drive are words like mastery, proficiency, capability and freedom. The achievement is to be able to do something and get a desired result with confidence, and to have the opportunity to do this. A good image for this drive is the young aborigine who stalks and kills his first wallaby, using all the skills he has learned from the older men – tracking, moving with stealth, knowing the right moment and seizing it, and spear-throwing. He has proved that he has the skills to feed himself (and others) and keep himself alive.

What is the ethical question about the pursuit of control and independence? The question is the same as above – what considerations should modify our efforts to be autonomous, masterful and in control?

3. Acceptance: roles and belonging

The next aim is about the person's relationship to other people in a social sense (society, institutions). As we see in the VEM, especially in world views 2 and 3, the aim of having an identity as a member of social groups can be a major preoccupation of people. And although this aim is to the fore when people subscribe to world views 2 and 3, the aim continues to be present for other people too.

We can see this in terms of Kegan's (1982) and Ken Wilber's (2000) idea of the unfolding identity of the person. At stage 4 in Kegan's theory, the institutional self, people define themselves as a member of institutions (families, school, other organisations). They understand themselves in terms of a role, which provides a set of norms and activities that structure their existence.

This aim draws on other aims of the person, especially the aim of exercising one's skills and knowledge, but here the focus is on the social effect of the exercise of those powers. Thus, the term "expert" can be used now, because it refers not just to skills and knowledge (personal mastery), but to the use of them in the service of institutional aims. One is an expert teacher in a school, or an IT expert who can write a program to control air traffic.

With the aim of acceptance, the person is trying to get other people to accept them as having a legitimate and valued place in the social web. And the ethical question for personal development is the same as above – what considerations should modify our efforts to belong?

4. Creativity: innovation, adventure and beauty

The question now is: have we covered all the things that people try to do, in the broadest sense? We think not. Creativity is an aim that does not seem to be covered by what has been said above. Yes, one learns to master one's environment and oneself, and to develop one's skills and knowledge. However, creativity is more than mastery.

Creativity is about creating something new and perhaps beautiful, or doing something challenging for its own sake. Of course this can be related back to pleasure and/or mastery, but it seems fit to distinguish it from them. When we ask the question, "what is the person trying to do?", it seems worth noticing that people often do things that have no practical value or need. They do them just for the sake of beauty, challenge or innovation. Music, art and all forms of artistic performance are created and appreciated as ends in themselves.

As this list of human aims expands, the scope for tension between aims becomes evident, particularly from our ethical perspective. Am I neglecting people who rely on me in order to pursue my art? Other ethical questions also arise from the aim of creativity. For example, the integrity of my creative pursuits may be an issue – does my work of art further my creative development and expression or is it an attempt to flatter the audience? Am I lazy in my artistic efforts?

5. Intimacy: love

The aim of intimacy can also be distinguished from other aims. It can be seen as an extension of the aim of acceptance/belonging, just as creativity is an extension of the aim of autonomy and mastery. Intimacy is about establishing a close relationship with an individual or individuals, as opposed to belonging to a group.

Intimacy can be described as the enjoyment of being with another person. This enjoyment has a number of features. It implies closeness, openness and sharing. It involves a willingness to take risks in self-revelation and self-expression, and to be vulnerable. Intimacy involves sharing with another person your thoughts, feelings and values. Part of the risk lies in moving from having *transactions* with a person to having a *relationship* with them. We can describe this as experiencing oneself in relationship to another person.

Intimacy may or may not be physical or sexual. It involves accepting the other person and experiencing that they accept you too – for the whole of what you are, as you are, not merely for some particular traits you have. Physical qualities such as beauty may or may not be present, or other qualities such as an engaging personality, valued social role (prestige) or ability to provide goods and services (money, skills and willingness to serve).

The aim of intimacy is to give and receive love. All of the human aims involve the person doing certain things, but in each case the hope is that those actions result in a response. Being intimate involves being open to another, giving of oneself. But one hopes for reciprocity – that the other person knows what you intend and feels the same.

In such delicate country, ethical considerations may assume great intensity. The desire for intimacy may lead to inappropriate efforts to coerce the other person and manipulate their feelings.

6. Meaning: purpose and peace

The final aim of humans is to come to a position of peace about their life. Through an understanding of "who they are" and "what they are here for" they acquire a confidence and awareness about all that happens to and around them. With this understanding comes an aliveness and joy, an acute awareness of their strengths and an acceptance of their limitations.

The aim of understanding one's meaning or purpose is accompanied by a willingness to work with what one has at one's disposal. The daily mechanics of living are not the ceiling of one's experience, but the arena where larger purposes are pursued. Meaning is informed by an appreciation of the finitude of societies, systems and norms.

The emergence of purpose is where the omega factor breaks through all other aims. When purpose crystallises, a sense of harmony with all-that-is prevails. Of all the aims discussed here, the aim of realising or establishing, and then pursuing one's life purpose is probably the one most people can recognise. Regardless of beliefs and ideology, most people can relate to the idea of deciding what it is worthwhile to pursue in their life.

In the chapter on leadership, we suggested that the core idea of identity (ie purpose) is really first on the agenda, and that relationships and the development of systems and culture come as a consequence of that. Here, similarly, we are saying that the aim of knowing one's purpose, or giving meaning to one's existence, is ever-present and infuses all of a person's actions and endeavours in some way.

The six aims and ethics

The six aims are illustrated in Figure 9.1. The figure summarises the above discussion and leads the way into the expansion of the five-dimensional model of the person.

Figure 9.1: The six aims of human activity

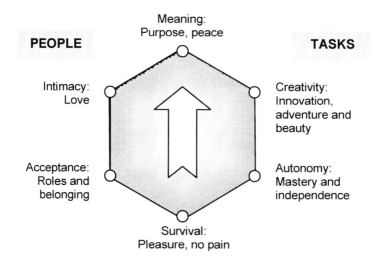

The question that has threaded its way through these aims is: how does ethics get into the picture? The answer goes back to the definition of ethics. We have employed Albert Schweitzer's definition in Chapter 2: "Ethics is the name we give to our concern for good behaviour. We feel an obligation to consider not only our own personal well-being, but also that of others, society as a whole and the natural world."

Ethics emerges the moment we realise that we are not the only person in the world. There are others who are like us – we may wish to survive, experience pleasure and avoid pain, but so do they. In tandem with this realisation, we see that our survival depends on other people. As to the natural world, we learn that our survival depends on it too. We breathe its air, drink its water and eat its food.

From these beginnings, ethics infuses all of the six aims. The choices we make and the way we live our lives rapidly become complex because what is ethical and what is of immediate practical benefit to ourselves do not always coincide. Personal development is therefore about clarifying our choices and firming our resolve to live in an ethical way, knowing ourselves as creatures of the six desires.

Embedded in the context of the world and other people, and the inherent aims of persons, our goal here is to examine how and why we act ethically. Before moving onto the development of the ethical person, however, we need to locate the person in a context.

The four domains of activity

The picture we have of the person so far consists of five dimensions – cognition, emotion, values, energy and identity. The reason we wish to expand this picture is that we want to focus on the interactions that occur between the person and the world. Bearing in mind the above discussion of the six aims, we suggest it is useful to talk about four domains of activity:

- the person's own body
- the physical and natural world
- other people collectively (societies, organisations, families)
- other persons, at an interpersonal level.

Figure 9.2 presents this enlarged model, locating the person in these four domains, an extension of the concepts in Figure 3.1.

Figure 9.2: The person in the world

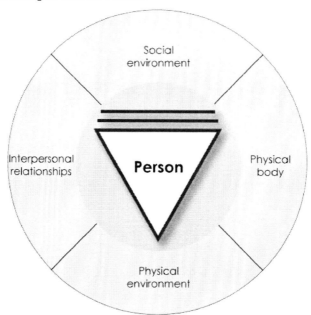

It is not difficult to see that these four domains are where our basic human aims exercise themselves. For example, our quest for autonomy begins with mastery over our own bodies. We do this as a child, from learning to control our emissions to learning how to use utensils to eat and learning to talk. We continue to pursue mastery of our physical self as an adult, perhaps through diet and exercise, yoga or sport.

Similarly we can see how our quest for acceptance and belonging is played out in the domains of the social environment and interpersonal relations. Some of the aims cannot be assigned so readily to a particular domain. Survival/pleasure and avoidance of pain, for example, could be threatened in the domain of the physical environment or through society or interpersonal relationships.

Taking stock of ourselves as part of our personal development means looking at the five dimensions of our person, but we do this through our interactions with the four domains. This is where the core human values take on meaning as we try to fulfil our life aims.

Ch. 9 | Personal growth and development

Processes for growth

The rest of this chapter outlines a process for taking stock of where we are in terms of ethics and values, and determining what we can do to live more closely to those values. This process begins with the exercise of self-awareness and reflection on our life, mindful that we need to look at our actual conduct as well as our ideas and assertions – our rhetoric.

Perhaps the first difficult lesson about living ethically is that we cannot simply decide we are going to live a life of exalted ethics. The Values Evolution Model conveys the idea that people currently work out of a certain world view, and we described seven world views. We described the movement through the world views in various ways:

- there is a movement from world view 1, which is focused on survival and self-interest, through to world view 7, which is a transcendent view of the world as mystery, beauty and harmony;

- this movement is mirrored in ethics as a movement from compliance (rules and laws) to caring for others (relationships) and towards the fulfilment of deep identity (spirit, purpose);

- in our five-dimensional model of the person we saw that the development of the person as a whole requires attention and work on five inter-connected fronts (cognition, emotion, values, energy and identity);

- finally, in this chapter, we have seen that ethics arise as the person seeks to fulfil a number of life aims, and this is an unfolding process throughout our lives.

These perspectives indicate that it is unrealistic to think that living at the "highest level" of ethics is simply a matter of deciding to do so:

> **Our ethics are determined by our values, and our values are determined by our view of the world.**

In this reality, our progress is not magical. Generally it is gradual, perhaps peppered with the occasional breakthrough or sudden realisation. The best analogy is the development of the expert. The expert becomes so through a combination of experience acquired through the practice of their craft or vocation, reflection on that experience, continual learning, imaginative thought, involvement with a community of experts, and feedback from others.

Another analogy is the building of physical strength or fitness. At this moment, we are each capable of doing just so much. If we try to stretch ourselves too far we will damage our body. We know that we can – and need to – stretch ourselves, and in doing so we will build our strength or fitness, but we have to be alert to what is determination and what is foolhardiness.

In the area of ethics, what is the equivalent of over-stretching? This scenario may help to illustrate. Albert lives a frugal life, giving most of his money away to charities, trying to fulfil a life that emulates the saints. But he experiences ongoing gloominess, because he also values being financially secure and providing for his family. His personal finances are always in trouble and his family home is dilapidated.

We have to be careful in interpreting this scenario. No moral judgement is being made about his circumstances or how he uses his money. The point is that his actions and aspirations are out of alignment with his values. It is actually important to him that he experiences being in control of his finances and providing for his family (in a way that is meaningful to himself, not in terms of any assumed social standards).

Using the vocabulary we introduced in Chapter 5, Albert has to consolidate his foundation and focus values before concentrating on his vision values. Note also that each world view has corresponding skills and understandings that enable the person to live out the values that are at the forefront under that world view – instrumental, interpersonal, imaginal and systemic skills.

The analogy of the expert suggests another example to illustrate the need to match our endeavours to our capacities. Suppose we wish to act in terms of world view 7 and promote global transformation. The problem is that our actions are likely to be inappropriate and ill-informed, because we do not have the insight needed to know what is best to do or say from that perspective. We may do more harm than good.

Some writers describe this reality even more strongly. John Sanford (1988, p 23) says: "If we go beyond our natural capacity for love and kindness, we build up an opposing amount of anger and cruelty within us". He urges us to "live, not out of ideals we cannot keep, but from an inner Center which alone can keep the balance. The grounds for the moral life are thus shifted from a striving for the highest moral ideals (though moral ideals are also important) to a striving for self-knowledge, in the belief that *man's moral values and ideals are only effective within the scope of his consciousness"* (italics added).

Self-awareness and reflection

At the same time, it is important to approach ethical development with the belief that development is possible. This discovery from the emotional intelligence realm is applicable to ethical development too. Our understanding, skills and strength as an ethical agent are not fixed or limited. Lennick and Kiel (2008) similarly maintain that development of our moral intelligence is possible, and they chart a course for that development.

The starting point for living ethically and in integrity is striving for self-knowledge. Our tool for reflecting on our personal ethics is the five-dimensional model of the person. As we saw in Chapter 5, we can look at how each dimension is experienced under each of the world views.

To reflect on our performance along each of these dimensions, the following questions can guide us:

- **What critical incidents have occurred in the last month or the last year that have tested how I operate with regard to the given dimension?** This refers to things we have done or witnessed, or how we have responded to situations. A critical incident is one that has made an impression on us – recalling our account of moral emotions in Chapter 4, a critical incident may have aroused anxiety and fear of punishment, guilt, shame, anger and indignation, pride, sympathy, joy in helping others or compassion.

- **What would other people say about my conduct in relation to the given dimension?** This is a tough reality test if we are willing to subject ourselves to it. This does not necessarily involve group exercises, although the use of 360-degree feedback in organisations can be a powerful way of getting beneath the smooth surface of interpersonal dynamics and behaviour. Essentially, this question requires us to be honest with ourselves, asking ourselves how we think others see our behaviour.

The answers to these questions should be matched against the statement describing the given dimension under each world view. When we have completed this personal review, we can look at how to deal with the issues that arise.

Note that no one's conduct across all spheres of their life fits neatly into one world view. The world views are simply a guide to what is most prevalent in our thinking and behaviour, a means of clarifying our current state and aspirations.

Five dimensions of the person and core human values

The five dimensions of the person are addressed below against the framework of the Values Evolution Model. An expanded view of the core value for each dimension is given by naming some of its associated values. The two questions above provide the material from our lives that we are willing to bring into focus.

1. TRUTH: the value associated with COGNITION

The cognitive dimension of the person has the core value of Truth. Other values that are associated with it include:

- honesty
- integrity
- reason
- curiosity
- trustworthiness
- impartiality
- discernment
- knowledge
- learning
- order
- systems thinking

We need to be alert to our tendency to subscribe to one world view (what we espouse) but in practice to act out of another. Adopting the perspective of people that observe our behaviour is one way of disentangling the two. Consider how the truth is seen under the various world views, as described below. Which one explains our behaviour, as it is, the best?

World view 1: The truth is treated expediently. Whatever serves the person's survival ends is what is said and done.

World view 2: The truth is treated selectively, that is, whatever serves the interests of a person's family and friends is what is said and done.

World view 3: The truth is honoured but is filtered through the institutional perspectives that constitute the person's reference groups. The understanding of truth tends to be literal.

World view 4: The truth is pursued in a principled way rather than in an passive or doctrinaire way; this may lead to some conflicts between the person's viewpoint and the institution's.

World view 5: Truth and reality are seen from an expanded perspective, as holistic, incorporating many different dynamics, eg social, political.

Ch. 9 | Personal growth and development

World view 6: Truth merges with peace and love. Until now they have been seen as separate, and sometimes they have appeared to be in tension with each other.

World view 7: Truth is seen from an inner perspective, where external (material) reality is seen as the expression of inner truth.

2. PEACE: the value associated with EMOTIONS

The emotional dimension of the person has the core value of Peace. Other values that are associated with it include:

- caring
- courtesy
- hope
- harmony
- cheerfulness
- dignity
- politeness
- affection
- humility
- discipline

Consider how peace is seen under the various world views, as described below. Applying the questions above to this dimension, which of the world views explains our behaviour, as it is, the best? In doing this, we should pay close attention to the reasons (or justifications) we give ourselves for our behaviour – the object of this exercise is not to deny or invalidate those reasons, but to be sympathetically aware of them.

World view 1: Values directed towards peace (eg caring, cheerfulness, politeness, dignity) are treated expediently.

World view 2: Values directed towards peace are similarly employed selectively.

World view 3: Values directed towards peace are fulfilled in a way that is consistent with the person's commitment to family, authority and institutions.

World view 4: Values directed towards peace are incorporated into enlarged personal goals, in tension at times with other principles, eg when injustice occurs.

World view 5: The person pursues peace as a way of exemplifying the better world they are trying to create.

World view 6: The person has a deeper understanding of how peace and all the other values serve the world purpose.

World view 7: Peaceful action proceeds from insight and a sense of oneness.

3. RIGHT ACTION: the value associated with VALUING

The valuing dimension of the person has the core value of Right Action. Valuing means using our powers of discrimination to assess actions as right or wrong, good or bad – in all the gradations that may apply, not in a simplistic, black-and-white way. Right Action means taking the action that furthers good over bad, or right over wrong, both in terms of our goals and the means we employ to pursue those goals. Right Action manifests through the associated values of:

- duty
- justice
- responsibility
- honour
- respect
- courage
- non-violence
- assertion
- fairness
- reliability
- moderation
- competence

To address the above questions for the dimension of Right Action, we need to be aware that sensitivity about our moral conduct reflects back on emotions and cognition – we tend to have strong emotions when an ethical value is at stake, and our cognitive processes work their hardest when they are trying to sustain our sense of self-esteem under ethical pressure. As was said above, the aim here is to bring our conduct into awareness and understand it, not to deny it, justify it or congratulate ourselves.

World view 1: Right action (eg duty, respect, fairness, responsibility) is regarded with expediency.

World view 2: Right action extends only to a select group of family and friends.

World view 3: Right action is pursued passionately in the context of family, institutions and accepted authorities.

World view 4: Right action is pursued passionately but more from an independent perspective than as an unreflective agent of an organisation.

World view 5: Right action is pursued as the foundation and pre-requisite of human creativity and joy.

World view 6: The person has a deeper understanding of how right action serves the world purpose.

World view 7: Right action is transformed to insight and oneness.

4. LOVE: the value associated with ENERGY/SPIRIT

The energy/spirit dimension of the person has the core value of Love. Love is admitted uncomfortably into the conversation when we are talking about work and organisations. However, when identified through its associated values then its appropriateness, indeed, its necessity, becomes evident:

- enthusiasm
- sincerity
- patience
- tolerance
- sense of community
- collaboration
- compassion
- friendship
- fun
- persistence
- service

This list of values reveals that the energy for activities in organisations, without which nothing happens and no good ideas come to fruition, comes from love. That love is love of people for the shared goals of the organisation, their consideration for each other and their joy in working together on projects. This is strong language, but there is evidence that it is possible and, when it does occur, the organisation's performance is outstanding and the communal morale is wonderful.

Applying the questions above to the energy/spirit dimension may require us to consider both the best and the worst of critical incidents, and an examination of how both can occur and what it means.

World view 1: Values exemplifying love (eg friendship, sincerity, patience) are regarded with expediency.

World view 2: Values exemplifying love extend only to the select group of family and friends.

World view 3: Love is exercised as an aspect of belonging to and being part of family, organisations and institutions. It is conditioned by fears about the world, which may intrude into the person's close circle of friends and colleagues.

World view 4: Love is exercised through the recognition of others as individuals and there is a blossoming of compassion and tolerance.

World view 5: Love is exercised from a sense of the connections between people and the possibilities for community across social and political divides.

World view 6: A greater sense of unity is conveyed to others. The person imparts to them an understanding of inter-connectedness, the need of individuals and communities for each other.

World view 7: Love expressed is palpable and transforming.

5. INSIGHT: the value associated with IDENTITY/PSYCHE

The identity/psyche dimension is the one that takes us into ourselves most deeply, to discover our personal purpose and meaning, hence its core value is Insight. Insight is explained more fully through its associated values of:

- appreciation
- meaning
- equality
- purpose
- awareness
- consideration
- beauty
- being
- forgiveness
- wisdom

At this point we need to be most alert with ourselves, remembering that social desirability leads us all to attest to high personal values. But we have to work with who we really are, not some fond illusion. Some bravery is required to admit what is evident by our conduct and our priorities.

Again, explore the above questions with the confidence that you know more about yourself than you may like to admit. Examine your reactions to incidents at work and what your conduct says about your beliefs.

World view 1: Not applicable.

World view 2: Not applicable.

World view 3: The meaning of reality is understood in terms of social structures, institutions and traditions.

World view 4: Awareness is seen as personal, unshackled from institutional perspectives, although this may be accompanied by trepidation.

World view 5: Insight begins to assume power, informed by an appreciation of the world and by the integration of the value-dimensions of truth, peace, right action and love.

World view 6: Forgiveness, compassion, equality and wisdom come to the fore as the systemic nature of reality becomes clearer.

World view 7: The place of everyone and everything in the overall scheme of things infuses all perceptions and actions: "Humanity's natural state is bliss."

Ch. 9 | Personal growth and development

Dealing with ourselves

Dealing with what we discover about ourselves is often difficult, even disheartening. It may help to approach the situation from the perspective of learning. Peter Honey (Australian Human Resources Institute workshop, Sydney, October 2003), a renowned facilitator of organisational learning from the United Kingdom, maintains that we can approach learning productively with the following attitudes:

1. Everything that happens has learning potential.
2. The quality of learning is improved if the process is made explicit.
3. How you learn is even more important than what you learn.
4. Working and learning are totally compatible, parallel activities.
5. Learning begins with an awareness that we want to do something other than what we are currently doing.
6. Most people need some encouragement or driver to engage in active learning.

There are some important insights here for personal growth in ethics. The first is, having examined ourselves and our situation, not to be disheartened or complacent, but to learn! The second point is to be aware of our learning – the learning process involves reflection on our current behaviour, consideration of new concepts, taking new actions, and reviewing our progress. This process is more effective if we constantly bring it to mind.

Remaining aware of our learning leads to the third point – that embedding the process of learning in the way we live becomes a "core competency", a tool that we use all the time to continually improve ourselves. Thus, how we learn is even more important than what we learn at any particular point in time.

The fourth point, the idea that working and learning are compatible, is important for those who think of learning as somehow separate from ordinary life. But there is a deeper message here too. The message is that personal development is not something that occurs aside from the difficulties and dilemmas of everyday life, as if it were a hobby. In fact, what makes personal development in ethics challenging is that it asks us to resolve the ethical issues that press upon us daily, issues that we may have been trying to ignore.

Our view is that the most serious problems that workers and managers face are not technical, or about resources or logistics, or even "personality clashes". They are about moral dilemmas – feeling forced to do things we believe/know are unethical, or witnessing unethical conduct and feeling powerless to do anything about it. These are the issues that create stress and depression in the workplace.

A study by the Australian consultancy firm Dattner Grant (2005) found that executives felt these pressures just as much as workers. They often felt that they had no control over setting targets, and were forced to implement policies they knew would stretch resources and destroy staff trust and morale. The Dattner Grant report said a significant proportion of executives (around 30% in their study) felt disconnected from their feelings and were often depressed.

The fifth point leads on from the discussion above. Learning begins with an awareness that we want to be more than what we currently are. This can be viewed aspirationally or defensively– we may desire to be more, or better, than we are now, or we may be dissatisfied with what we are currently doing, as the executives described above are experiencing. We will discuss below the different types of learning that arise from this distinction.

The last point is worth bearing in mind because, when we want to change, it may seem that the world conspires to prevent us from doing so. Stephanie Burns (2000), an Australian trainer and researcher, has explored this area at length. She maintains that most instructional material is about goal-setting, and people can become rather good at this. The problem is not so much in setting goals but in having the persistence, techniques and motivation to achieve those goals.

Learning often involves facing the fact that you do not understand something or know how to do something. In the case of seeking to develop ethically, the emotional effort is even greater. Various stages of learning may involve uncertainty, anxiety, frustration, impatience or confusion.

Thus, Honey's last point reminds us to gather support for the changes we want to make. That may mean making connections with other people who will share the journey, or keeping a journal, or establishing a discipline that keeps us on track.

Using the five core human values

How to use the five core human values to start off on the conscious journey of improvement can be summed up succinctly. The following statement speaks to each of the five dimensions of the person:

> People tend to live in the mechanical (rational, cognitive, routine), are governed by the emotional (which drives their conduct) and rarely question their values. They tend not to be open to energy/spirit and therefore do not realise their identity. In the face of this inertia, we should:
>
> - question the mechanical/routine
> - connect with the emotional
> - clarify our values
> - open ourselves to spirit/energy
> - discover our psyche/identity.

In fact, we are being given a constant reminder to do this. We refer to the earlier discussion of the omega point and the strange attractor. There are many other sources that support this view as well. The psychiatrist Roberto Assagioli's (2000) theory of psychosynthesis asserted that the central drama of humanity is the fusion of one's personality with one's higher self.

The inherent drive to make meaning of our lives and fulfil our possibilities is also supported by the work of Victor Frankl (1971), who emphasised the strong need people have to find meaning in their existence, even in appalling circumstances. In management literature the same drive was described in terms of Theory X and Theory Y by Douglas McGregor (1960). McGregor asserted that employees' behaviour is better explained by a natural desire to do good work (Theory Y) than by the assumption that they have to be forced to do so (Theory X).

Figure 9.3 illustrates the drive towards meaning and fulfilment that is naturally at work in a person. This suggests that when we embark on ethical improvement, despite whatever difficulties we may encounter, it is a journey that taps into natural energy.

Figure 9.3: The source of energy for ethical improvement

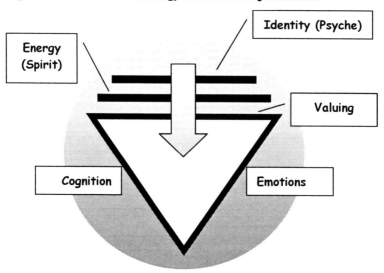

Foundations for ethical improvement

How might an enquiry into one's own ethical progress proceed? Let us focus on an imaginary manager, Peter. In a company of 500 people, Peter is responsible for a group of ten workers. He has undertaken a review of his performance as a manager over the last six months using the five-dimensional model above. He sees that there have been incidents where he is not proud of his actions in terms of truth, peace and right action (as we have defined them), and he would like the working environment to better reflect love and insight.

How to start? As we saw in Chapter 8, personal change begins on the inside and proceeds outwards. Stephen Covey's books, *The Seven Habits of Highly Successful People* (1990) and *Principle-Centred Leadership* (1992), maintain there are three qualities that are the foundation of ethical improvement, or the building of character:

- **Integrity.** This means that we identify our values and we actively live out those values. We are true to ourselves and we keep our promises.
- **Judgement.** This quality (which Covey calls maturity) underpins the other qualities. It means being able to interpret reality in a

balanced way and not being led astray, through enthusiasm, greed, naivety or other emotions. It also means having a sense of appropriateness and proportion.

- **Abundance mentality.** This quality refers to the belief that one is fundamentally safe, provided for and worthy. Covey expresses this as the belief that "there is plenty out there for everybody". In contrast, people focused on survival and power exhibit a scarcity mentality which thinks there is not enough for everyone, so you have to get what you can, and some people have to lose. Recall from the Values Evolution Model that as the world views evolve, the person becomes more and more grounded in the belief that the world, in its mysterious way, nurtures them.

Covey sums up the person of character in this way: "A character rich in integrity, maturity and the abundance mentality has a genuineness that goes far beyond technique. Your character is constantly radiating, communicating. From it, people come to trust or distrust you."

We can consider the three qualities to represent a person's orientation to the past, the present and the future. Integrity represents our commitment to be honest and truthful in the present. Judgement represents the store of our wisdom from past experience, our knowledge of the way the world works. We note, however, that judgement recognises that some of our beliefs are distorted and self-limiting. Judgement here refers to things like natural laws and the social meanings of actions.

The third quality, abundance mentality, refers to the future. It is a choice we make, to put our faith in the worthwhile-ness of living ethically. In making this choice, we open ourselves to the reappraisal of our priorities. We reconsider what is more worthwhile and consider that to be our abundance.

Returning to the core human values

The first test of our judgement is to appraise the situation we are in and our performance to date. We have to determine if this is a situation where we should focus on gradual progress or if we need to make a radical shift. Sometimes we see that we are entangled in situations that make us feel dirty, and we have to consider radical action. At the same time, our voice of judgement might be saying to us, take care how you do this.

We need to be aware not to fall to the naïve desire to fix all the problems of the world in a day. But we also need be aware that we can become inured to bad ethics because it has become easier than confronting it. We can seek advice from sympathetic others, but we also have to remember that we alone are responsible for what we do, and we have to listen to our own wisdom.

One of the first things we notice when we start to examine our conduct in the light of values is how our values rest upon beliefs, some of them well-founded and others not. Appraising beliefs is difficult business, because our view of the world is constructed on beliefs, so to question them is to question the nature of the world. And perhaps the most vexed question of all is: how can we change our beliefs, or in a less confronting way, how do our beliefs change?

Covey contributes a response to this question. He says that character is built on the basis of accumulated experience. We choose to act a certain way, ie adhering to moral principles, and we persist through setbacks and gruelling stages. Through this process we experience times where we can see that what we chose was "right". We prove to ourselves, again and again, that it is worthwhile to be ethical. Eventually, we *know* that it is better to follow right action than to take unethical shortcuts in order to acquire gain, which we know is short-term and ephemeral.

This is true, not only of honesty and integrity, but of all the core human values. To say that they are "core" human values is to say that, in the end, they are unassailable. If we tell a lie, we can go for fifty years and still be found out. If we are truthful, that is unassailably true for all time.

Jean Piaget (1964), the child psychologist and learning theorist, said that children learn about the world by constructing hypotheses and testing them out. This is to say that our beliefs are conditional, not absolute – they are, in effect, hypotheses about the world that we are testing out. It becomes important, then, to construct appropriate hypotheses.

We combine the concept that beliefs are hypotheses subject to verification with the idea that the world becomes what we look for and what we focus our energy on. The journey of evolving ethics is the journey where we come to see and experience that what we thought *should* be true is, in the deepest sense, true.

Facing fears and self-obsession

The major barriers to progress in living ethically are: 1) fear and 2) self-obsession. The open question is whether, ultimately, these are the same thing. We can describe ethical deficiency or deviancy in terms of the six aims of human life. When people are pursuing the six aims legitimately, they are acting ethically. When they are driven by fear of not attaining the six aims, or by selfishness, they act unethically (recall our definition of ethics as being centred in a concern for the other).

One exploration of the impact of fear on people comes from Art Horn (2004). He asserts that "People are, by nature, very insecure. They spend a great deal of their time seeking security and avoiding more insecurity." (p 108) In response, they adopt a number of positions in the world. He suggests there are six types:

- the worrier, who is obsessed with thoughts of what needs to be avoided
- the controller who seeks to maintain security by asserting control over people and situations
- the fake who invents a persona to stand between them and their fears
- the attention-seeker who is compensating for their fears
- the victim who defines him/herself as helpless
- the prisoner who is reacting against a perceived invasion of their consciousness.

The observation from an ethical perspective is that all of these people are driven by fear, which is expressed in a variety of ways and, accordingly, they do not have the emotional reserves to make courageous ethical decisions. Acting ethically requires us to address our fears. As Art Horn contends, our fears may still persist but, to make a change, we have to accept fear as part of the landscape and act anyway.

Fear is one side of our challenge. The other side is self-obsession. Recall that Stephen Covey alluded to the concept of the golden mean – judgement, or balance. The ethical path lies between two extremes. On one side is fear, which leads us to the errors of the powerless. The other side is self-obsession, which leads us to the errors of misuse of power. Table 9.1 shows the six aims and the ethical deviations that occur because of fear and self-obsession.

Table 9.1: Aims of human life and deviations

Deviations due to fear	Legitimate aims of human life	Deviations due to self-obsession
Victim, helplessness	**Innocence, survival: pleasure, no pain**	Violence; annihilation of perceived threats
Dependency; comfort	**Autonomy: mastery, independence**	Domination of others
Isolation; attention-seeking	**Acceptance: roles and belonging**	Manipulation, abuse, demeaning of others
Faking; conformism	**Creativity: innovation, adventure, beauty**	Crushing of experimentation, risk and individuality
Avoidance of closeness or openness; denial of feelings; self-hate	**Intimacy: love**	Conceit; narcissism
Confusion, anxiety, aimlessness	**Meaning: purpose and peace**	Rejection of stillness and contentment

With this framework in mind, we need to go back to the earlier reflective exercise. What were the critical incidents, the hot issues, that you identified when looking at the five dimensions of the person? Do your dilemmas show any of the above self-perceptions? If we are to move towards an ethical life, one of integrity and energy, we need to understand the emotions that drive us.

We also need to understand that the aspects of ourselves with which we are unhappy do have some basis in legitimacy. Table 9.1 places the aims of human life at the centre. These are legitimate aims, and there is an inherent drive in each of us to realise those aims. If we have gone 'astray', it is in allowing our fears or the ego-self to distort our pursuit of these aims.

This perspective gives us the way forward. What is the legitimate aim that we have become removed from? We need to return to that, armed with the three intentions described above – the intention to live in integrity, the intention to exercise judgement (common sense), and the intention to trust in abundance.

This exercise allows us to "dream the possible" instead of berating ourselves for our misdemeanours and shortcomings. It steers us towards restoring the legitimate aims to the centre of our lives. But it also means we have to ponder the inner meaning of each of the aims instead of focusing on the outward signs of success (eg position, power, money).

Further, we need to find a balance among the various aims. One of the curiosities of our lives is that they have multiple aims; not just intimacy or acceptance or adventure, but an amalgamation of all of the aims. At various times, one or the other will be prominent, and awareness and judgement will tell us what the important focus is for us now. Over time the emphasis will change.

Building the ethical person

There are a number of propositions that lie at the heart of the personal development of ethics. They need to be taken together and reconciled, because at first glance they may appear to conflict. Consider these statements:

- Ethical development is about our intentions, not about external achievements.
- Ethical development is about our actions, not our theories and thoughts about ethics.
- Ethical development is about acknowledging our fears and still having the courage to act ethically.
- Ethical development is about acting for the common good without any fear.
- Ethical development is about developing good habits of right conduct.
- Ethical development is about breaking habits to make decisions that lift our ethical standards.

Taken together, these statements provide a balanced approach to our personal development of ethics. The previous chapters have presented the complementary actions we need to pursue. For example, in Chapter 6 we looked at habits, scripts and the social context in ethical conduct, and in Chapter 7 we looked at decision-making processes. Each aspect complements the other, and the bridge between them is our judgement, knowing when each is appropriate.

Having determined to develop ourselves ethically, we can see how it unfolds in the model James Rest offered, which was described in Chapter 4. He identified four components of moral conduct:

- **moral sensitivity** – being aware of the ethical import of situations
- **moral judgement** – reasoning intelligently about ethical options
- **moral motivation** – being committed to following through on our decisions with ethical actions
- **moral character** – building habits and an ethical sense of self through courage and consistency in our actions.

This is also known as the development of virtue. The terms 'character' and 'virtue' are somewhat out of favour, perhaps because they became identified with stereotypes from inward-looking cultures. Virtue may have become identified with narrowness and social conformity rather than living on the basis of universal principles (core human values). Note that Covey uses the term 'habits' instead.

Unfortunately, when we interpret virtue as simply obeying social rules, we lose its deeper sense. The term that the ancient Greeks used was 'arête', which combined the ideas of doing right and being excellent. This is important in the Values Evolution Model because the model describes how these two ideas belong together. In describing the model we have shown that the ethical path leads from compliance towards aspiration – excellence.

The development of virtue or character can be likened to other processes with which we are familiar. In Chapter 7 we explored the notion of the expert (which could be in fields as diverse as carpentry, engineering or dance) saw that there are qualities that commonly distinguish experts from novices. We could also explore the establishment of change in personal habits (eg diet, fitness and overcoming addictions).

Development of expertise

These areas can give us a richer sense of how we can develop personally in the area of ethics. We noted in Chapter 7 that we may have reservations about the concept of the "ethical expert" because it may imply that the expert is "a better person" than someone else. But we also acknowledged that devoting attention to a topic, whether it is fire-fighting or ethics, is likely to result in the development of relevant skills and understanding.

In discussing the skills of the expert, we drew on Gary Klein's work (1999). Experts are not merely defined by having more knowledge than others. They can:

- see patterns in situations that others do not notice
- detect anomalies (eg things that should have happened but didn't) that indicate something is amiss
- place actions in a larger framework and understand how things operate, the hidden processes
- see opportunities to take effective action, including improvisations
- perceive the flow of events, even if they have not been direct observers, so that they can see the direction in which things are headed
- understand their own limitations.

All of these aspects are applicable to acting ethically. Each aspect is a skill that comes from giving it time and attention. The skills fit into James Rest's model of the components of moral conduct. For example, reflecting on situations at work, particularly on repeated patterns of unethical conduct, will enable us to see what is driving those patterns. In doing this, we are honing our moral sensitivity and judgement. We can then look for opportunities to take effective action, exercising our moral commitment and character.

Our focus here has been on how we can use the five-dimensional model of the person, and the corresponding five core human values, to pursue an ethical life. Whoever we are and whatever our history, we can tap into the core human values, find their meaning in our current situation, and commit to living in accordance with those values. The complementary aspect is that, as we do this, we are developing our understanding and our skills in living ethically, and our view of the world is affected. As we argued in Chapter 5, as we consolidate our skills in living our values, our world view evolves.

Changing habits

The other area we can use to gain some insight into how we develop ethically is the area of changes in personal habits. James Prochaska (1992) has carried out extensive studies on the process of personal change, addressing habits and addictions such as smoking, alcohol, overeating and toxic relationships. He has described the stages of change and what support is appropriate at each stage:

- **Reflective (or contemplative) stage** – individuals are not intending to change their behaviour in the near future, for many reasons, eg uninformed about the consequences of their behaviour, lacking in confidence. Information is given to encourage recognition of the issue.

- **Preparation stage** – individuals intend to take action in the near future. They have goals and an action plan and have rehearsed skills and strategies to put in place.

- **Action stage** – behavioural changes are put in place and they are measured and evaluated.

- **Maintenance stage** – this stage could extend for six months from when behaviour was changed. At this stage, tools and techniques are used to prevent regression, until the problematic behaviour is no longer an issue.

This depiction of the change process gives a good sense of the concerted and persistent effort that may be involved in initiating and establishing significant personal changes. The effort is emotional as well as cognitive. The person will experience a range of feelings about the problem they are addressing, and they may need to gain feedback on the impact of their behaviour (new and old habitual behaviour) on others.

Prochaska's model is a therapeutic one. We can apply it to ourselves in addressing ethical issues. The nature of the model alerts us to the factor of support. Deep personal changes require us to have ways of reinforcing the change, perhaps through the sympathetic support of other people. Note that Prochaska's model has been adopted in workplace coaching and life coaching as an effective tool for change.

Ethical development: sudden or gradual?

In discussing the role of judgement earlier, we commented that in a given situation we may conclude we need to change either radically or gradually. We have also noted that it may be nice to imagine we could suddenly be "perfect", but we are in fact located in a specific context with a given history and an imperfect bag of beliefs and skills. Sustainable change is for the most part gradual, and our ethical actions often involve compromises.

Nevertheless, there are times when making immediate or drastic changes is what we need to do (according to our own judgement). An example of drastic change from the corporate world is Ray Anderson, the CEO from Interface, a US carpet manufacturer, who was featured in the movie, *The Corporation* (Achbar, Abbott & Bakan, 2004). Anderson was a successful businessman who had not given much thought to the environmental impact of his enterprise. His transformation came when his research director asked him to address a staff meeting on an environmental vision for the company.

Anderson realised that his enterprise was ecologically delinquent, and made a public commitment to change. He vowed to make his business sustainable, to make it a "restorative" enterprise – one that puts back more than it takes from the earth. Later, he said the speech "surprised me, stunned them (his staff), and galvanised us into action" (Meadows, undated). Since Anderson's declaration, "the company has reduced its environmental footprint by one third, redesigning processes and products, pioneering new technologies and reducing or eliminating waste and harmful emissions while increasing the use of renewable materials and sources of energy" (*The Corporation* website).

Whether we perceive the changes that we have to make as drastic or gradual, the measures we need to apply to ourselves are the same:

- Are we clear about the purpose we are pursuing?
- Are we using our best efforts to work towards this goal?

Drastic change generally occurs when we see that we are pursuing the wrong goals or, as in Ray Anderson's case, pursuing goals in the wrong way. Bringing the ecological issue to consciousness was sufficient for him to launch himself in a more desirable direction. Notably, he has pursued his new course, not by asking whether sustainability is possible, but by holding to the conviction that he will *make* it possible.

The two questions above mirror the two aspects of ethics that have been presented in this book – compliance and aspiration. The questions reinforce the idea that there is often a threshold aspect to ethics – we see that some things are clearly right or wrong, but then there is a continuum aspect – *how much* are we doing to foster the good? Distinguishing these two aspects enables us to avoid much confusion that is generated by ethical discussions.

Stories of sudden realisations and radical change are heartening, but not always applicable to our situation. Sometimes the proper path is quieter and gradual, and it may involve compromises in organisational contexts. It is difficult to stand outside situations and say something definitive about what a person should do.

We have stressed the importance of judgement and personal accountability. In organisations we encounter a variety of ethical and unethical purposes in other people, and these purposes are joined to varying degrees of power, as when managers insist on us doing something that is dishonest. We know that we have choices, we try to act with integrity, but we have to consider all the consequences of our actions, which may include losing our job and being unable to feed our family next week.

We have looked at this situation from the perspective of moral imagination, looking for innovative ways to make progress and elevate the common understanding of ethical values. But sometimes even this much appears to be a distant goal. And we have also emphasised that it is little use being an armchair ethicist – being ethical means acting to further the common good, not being satisfied with thinking nice thoughts.

A way into discussing this problem is given by the six aims of life. One of these is autonomy (mastery and independence). As Glasser argued in control theory, the only behaviour we can control is our own. This means that we may not control our external circumstances, but we can master how we see those circumstances and how we react to them, including how we feel. So, it is not avoidance that leads us to consider our inner environment before taking action in organisations, but good sense.

Glasser's approach gave rise to reality therapy, the purpose of which was to support people so as to build up their inner strength, by showing them what they could have control over – their internal space, thoughts and feelings. On this basis, clients could then make different decisions and learn how to live in the world with more power, dignity and peace. In the same way, we need to address our inner space before contemplating external action to enhance ethics in organisations.

Earlier in the chapter we suggested that we can work through the five core human values to make a start on personal development of ethics. Although each of us is at a different place, and different perceptions of the world influence our actions, the core human values are universally applicable.

We have looked at these in their expanded forms, but we can summarise them to use as a guide for getting a sense of our inner environment, as in Table 9.2.

Table 9.2: Getting in touch internally

Dimension	Quest	Values to foster	Behaviour to be alert for
1. Cognitive	To question current routines and circumstances	Honesty, integrity	Lies, deceit, ignorance, confusion
2. Emotional	To connect with our emotions	Caring, trust, peacefulness, cheerfulness	Depression, anger, bullying, domination, resentment
3. Valuing	To clarify our values	Fairness, justice, reliability	Capriciousness, favouritism, selfishness
4. Energy/ spirit	To open ourselves to spirit, energy	Enthusiasm, compassion, perseverance	Rigidity, meanness
5. Identity/ psyche	To discover our purpose	Meaning, personal purpose, appreciation	Anomie, fickleness, delusion

The aim of this exercise is simply to gain a sense of our control over our inner space, which is true even in difficult organisational environments. The Jewish psychotherapist Viktor Frankl, reflecting on his experiences in the Nazi concentration camps, said, "everything can be taken from a man but one thing: the last of the human freedoms – to choose one's attitude in any given set of circumstances, to choose one's own way" (Frankl, 1984).

We remember too that there is a natural positive energy at work, which we showed in Figure 9.3. The message is that cultivating personal power and virtue keeps harm away. We can act to curb our anger and resentment, treating them as entanglements that hobble our positive energy.

We can inquire into our motivations and find our strengths and our personal purpose. This imposes a direction on things and changes the flow of energy. We can hold true to that purpose and allow it to unfold, trusting that it will sustain us. We can constantly remind ourselves that curbing bad ethics in organisations is the small game; the real game is to foster larger purposes.

For ourselves, we can gather our strength to enable our own larger purpose to unfold. When this experience is common among people in an organisation, then the organisation itself gains a sense of larger purpose. And we need to be aware that it is no small thing for organisations to gather this sense of purpose. In *Built to last*, Jim Collins and Jerry Porras (1994) found only a small number of organisations that sustained such a vision over time, after examining thousands of organisations to find this quality.

Personal development requires us to cultivate the core human values every day, to stabilise our practice of those values and to constantly correct ourselves. This will mean acting with integrity and fostering relationships so that trust can build among the people around us. As well as remaining true to these values ourselves, we need to recognise them in those around us and honour right conduct.

The five-dimensional model has shown us that ethical conduct is in harmony with competent and productive work, because the core human values are about the integrated development of all our capabilities. Ethics merges into purpose, competence and achievement.

Once we are established in our inner sense, we can consider how to deal with external circumstance. Joseph Badaracco (2002) maintains that reality in organisations is not neat and we cannot prescribe simple rules to govern our actions. Ethical issues do not present neatly defined and free of messy complications; they are "embedded in the very fabric" of everyday life.

In this milieu, ethics is very much a matter of judgement. Actions that at first flush seem to be simple and necessary in order to uphold the right quickly throw up unintended consequences. Innocent people may be harmed by our well-intentioned acts. And we ourselves are not pure in motive. For example, actions that seem to promote the common good may at the same time offer us personal windfalls. Our motives are frequently mixed.

Badaracco recounts a number of stories about managers who accepted the complexity of their situations and worked out a course of action that, in all the circumstances, was both prudent and furthered the common good or set limits around harm. He calls these people quiet leaders. They combine ethics with intelligent strategising, in order to achieve the most feasible positive outcome.

Within the bounds of specific circumstances, Badaracco's quiet leaders seek to live out the core human values. They exercise judgement; they understand that the best outcome countenances all five of the values – it is not just about honesty, or just about fairness, but a holistic appreciation of what is most important overall, remembering that ethics is, at its heart, about valuing people.

Acting to foster ethics in organisations, whether it is from the position of a manager or a worker, is subject to constraints and may involve compromise. Yet the idea of compromise is inadequate. At any point in time, we should aim to achieve the most that is possible, and this may represent a compromise on what we would like.

Yet, if we shift our focus from compliance to aspiration, our framework is larger – any decision is just a point along the road, and we are always moving towards a greater understanding of the core human values and how they play out among people in the material world. We build energy and commitment towards the realisation of our higher possibilities. A concrete example is what Ray Anderson at Interface committed the company to – turning a typical corporation that degrades the environment into a restorative, ecological enterprise. Compliance is necessary, but it is still only the small game.

Given that situations in organisations are complex and we cannot rely on simple rules of behaviour, what do we rely on? We have to come back to principles. Action is guided by a deep understanding of what the core human values mean, combined with a serious examination of the situation. We seek to understand what is motivating the people involved, and know as much of the facts as possible. We need to cultivate our moral imagination as well, so we have the best chance of determining the action that will further the good. This is the challenge.

Badaracco discusses taking time (instead of jumping in), building allies and delving deeper into the layers of the situation. Sometimes we have to craft a solution rather than make a grand gesture. The paradox of quiet leaders, ie people who are trying to live ethically, is that their personal development is an upshot of forgetting about self and doing what needs to be done in the situation. As Schweitzer said, ethics is about a concern for the well-being of others.

Summing up ethical development

In the previous chapter we maintained that effective leaders combined the qualities of the five dimensions of the person – they were competent in a cognitive sense, they exhibited the qualities of emotional intelligence, and they were ethical; as an outcome of these qualities, they generated positive energy and enabled teams and organisations to discover and realise great purpose. Similarly this is true of individuals who seek to improve themselves ethically.

Personal development of ethics embodies the paradox that the person is focused on the common good rather their own "progress". However, personal development is characterised by a willingness to examine and reflect on our actions and motivations, and to work at seeing the core human values fostered in personal and communal life. This work engages our intellect, our emotions and our moral judgement, our persistence and our desire to live a life of integrity, creativity and purpose.

Our belief that it is worthwhile to pursue ethics and integrity is central to our efforts, as Stephen Covey asserts. In this we need to constantly steer our thoughts and actions, subject as we are to fears and ego, to work at "strengthening our virtue". But there is also a natural tendency at work in our lives, urging us to develop and live in integrity. In that sense, our endeavour is to tap into that flow.

The core human values are available to all of us, to apply in our situation as we are and where we are. The meaning of the core human values expands as we focus on them and seek to live in accord with them. Through experience, our skills and insight develop and our view of the world undergoes evolution.

In the next chapter we will address some issues about personal development that linger. Some more will be said about how to distinguish between ethics and "style", and how to continue with the ethical course when we experience setbacks and unfavourable circumstances, and we are feeling discouraged. We will also revisit the question of the relationship between ethics and success.

10

Coda: present perfect

The purpose of this book has been to set out how it is possible for people in organisations to live ethically when they are not in positions of great power, although we have noted that even CEOs often feel the tension between ethics and what business success seems to require. We have put forward an approach based on core human values, and have seen that this approach integrates two aspects that are generally treated separately – compliance and aspirational purpose.

The previous chapter dealt with how we can foster our personal development of ethics using the core human values, the values that relate to each of the five dimensions of a person. We realise that this is a challenging process, because it is a different focus from figuring out how to be a "success" in life. Sometimes it seems that the ethical choice is precisely the opposite of the path to success.

Nevertheless, we also cautioned against opting for the heroic acts of the martyr. The bold stance of rebellion and opposition may sometimes be necessary, but it can also be an empty gesture, and counter-productive in the larger situation. What is generally more productive is a twofold approach:

- a steadfast commitment to our own integrity, manifested as constant effort to exhibit high human values in our own conduct; and

- communal action that promotes those values, using astute strategy and clear articulation of values, exercising our judgement about what is appropriate in the situation.

This chapter does not extend the models that have been presented earlier. Rather, there are some issues that may be suggested by the material that deserve comment. Hence the chapter is called a coda. And in finishing, it is apt that we return to the question of how ethics and worldly success relate to each other. We explore the concept of success and link it to the core human values. In doing so we suggest there is a sense in which we need to recognise the present as being "perfect".

We acknowledged in the previous chapter that personal development of ethics can be fraught with difficulty. This chapter will add some further comments on that issue – how we deal with discouragement. The chapter also looks at some aspects of personal development that it is helpful to distinguish from ethics, aspects that pertain to style rather than core human values.

Personal style and human values

A great many tools exist to explore and categorise individual preferences and qualities. The second half of the 20th century saw such tools proliferate. These tools examine different aspects of the self – personality, motivations, types of intelligence, ability to work in teams and the like. Some examples are:

- **Myers-Briggs Type Indicator (MBTI)** – this tool, based on the ideas of Carl Jung, maps the preferences of individuals on four dimensions: extraversion/introversion, sensing/intuition, thinking/feeling and judging/perceiving.

- **Brain preferences** – Walter Lowen (1982; discussed in Colins & Chippendale, 2002) built on the MBTI framework, investigating people's preferences for processing information and interacting with the world. To the MBTI he added two more dimensions: people/things and concrete/abstract.

- **Multiple intelligences** – Howard Gardner (1993, 1999) developed the idea that there are many types of intelligence other than cognition (IQ). He maintains that there are nine types of intelligence: linguistic, mathematical-logical, visual, auditory, kinaesthetic-motor, interpersonal, intrapersonal, naturalistic and philosophical.

There are many other such tools (eg DiSC, TMI). Of particular interest in the context of this book is A Values Inventory (AVI; 2004) from Paul Chippendale and The Minessence Group, as this tool specifically looks at the framework of values we have adopted. Colins and Chippendale suggest there are some links between brain preferences, the MBTI dimensions, and values. Our question is: does this have any implications for people's ethical conduct?

Multiple intelligences raise another question. Gardner describes philosophical intelligence as recognising and assessing the principles regarding human behaviour, especially moral, spiritual and ethical development. If so, does this mean that some people are more inclined, by natural disposition, to be ethical?

Brain preferences, ethics and values

The research of Colins and Chippendale (2002), combined with that of Lowen, demonstrates a correlation between a person's brain preference and the person's priority values. Lowen used the MBTI and looked at the kinds of occupations towards which people of each type would gravitate. Colins and Chippendale compared MBTI profiles with values profiles obtained from the AVI.

To illustrate, consider a person strong in Sensate-Thinking (ST; low in Feeling and Intuitive). Lowen describes a number of occupational types that ST people would prefer – implementer, organiser, operator and moulder:

- Implementers like to work with established procedures to create order, achieving harmony through systematic processes, eg project manager, bureaucrat.

- Organisers like efficiency and order and they work to maintain these qualities, eg stock controller, accountant.

- Operators focus on categorising what they perceive with their senses and this is critical in their work, eg mechanic, surgeon.

- Moulders gather information through their hands, developing high levels of hand-eye coordination, eg crafts person, masseur.

The priority values that Colins and Chippendale found were correlated with ST people included administration/control, productivity, work/labour, duty/obligation, criteria/rationality, efficiency/planning, hierarchy, uniformity, rules/accountability.

What are the ethical implications of having a particular MBTI profile? We can look at this question through the lens of the ST profile just described, and apply the five core human values and the Values Evolution Model.

Firstly, the core human values – truth, peace, right action, love and insight – are intended to offer a framework for all people and conduct. Persons of the four occupational types described above should look to these ethical values as much as people in any other type of occupation. In practice, we would expect them to be particularly conscious of ethical rules and norms. However, we may be less confident about their awareness of ethics in the areas of relationships and less tangible issues.

The core human values represent a holistic view of the person in the world. They tell us that acting ethically involves consideration of social rules and structures on the one hand and, on the other hand, sensitivity to people's feelings and dignity. The connection between "personality style" and ethics, then, is that everyone has some kind of bias – they are more aware of and more adept at some aspects of life than others.

The holistic model tells us that the five dimensions of the person each have an ethical aspect and given our biases we will have to work harder to be conscious of some of these aspects. An ethical issue may be a matter of cognition, eg truth and integrity in processes, but it may also be a matter of emotions and relationships, eg listening to others and respecting their views.

Colins and Chippendale go on to talk about the differences between men and women. They list the seven top priority values for men and women, as in Table 10.1.

Table 10.1: Value priorities of men and women

(*Source:* Colins & Chippendale, 2002, p 40)

Women	Men
1. Sharing, listening, trust	1. Decision, initiation
2. Intimacy	2. Sharing, listening, trust
3. Knowledge, discovery, insight	3. Productivity
4. Rights, respect	4. Adaptability, flexibility
5. Decision, initiation	5. Rights, respect
6. Productivity	6. Knowledge, discovery, insight
7. Life, self-actualisation	7. Intimacy

The priority of the values indicates that men (generally) will be quicker to make decisions than women, but women's decisions may be better grounded on consultation with and consideration of others. (Of course, this is just indicating a general bias based on the data.) The list indicates the higher task focus of men and the higher people focus of women. We have seen that ethical issues embrace quality of relationships between people as well as compliance with social rules and laws.

The quality of relationships between men and women in organisations depends on their awareness of their different biases in style and their efforts to accommodate each other and to see the value of both sides. The area of engagement in organisations is generally around the balance between task (getting the job done) and people (maintaining harmony), remembering that the breakdown of harmony can quickly lead to the inability of a group to complete tasks.

The conclusions?

- Style is a bias factor, rather than a determinant.
- As a bias factor, style does tend to make us stronger in some aspects of ethics than others, as we have defined it through the core human values model of the person. The challenge for people is to properly countenance all five aspects of ethics, remembering

that this view of ethics takes us from compliance towards human development and aspiration.

- In terms of compliance with social or organisational rules and laws, personal style is not a factor, or an excuse, in ethics. Whether we have a bias towards Sensate-Thinking or some other profile, ethics apply impartially.

Moral intelligence?

Multiple intelligences, particularly the addition of an intelligence (philosophical) associated with ethics, pose the question of whether some people are more disposed than others to be ethical. This challenges the expectation that all people in society are equally subject to ethics, in terms of both sanctions (eg do not steal) and acts of initiative (eg saving a person in peril).

Gardner (1999; discussed by Joyce Martin, 2001) is at pains to point out that philosophical intelligence refers to awareness of and interest in issues of principle and meaning, and the capacity to discuss and evaluate such issues. There is no implication that such people are more ethical; the intelligence itself is morally neutral.

Joyce Martin says that philosophical intelligence is characterised by:

- Awareness and curiosity about moral and ethical issues. We could contrast this propensity with someone who is focused on financial matters.

- Application of philosophy as part of assessing problems, seeking solutions and evaluating outcomes. There is a focus on 'why' as well as 'how' and 'what'.

- Willingness to discuss and debate values and examine assumptions.

- Appreciation of and respect for differences between points of view. Underlying principles are probed.

- Engagement in regular self-review of moral standards. The person is not necessarily "more moral" but spends more time thinking about moral choices.

- Deriving energy and satisfaction from engaging in activities related to moral, spiritual or ethical development.

Gardner did not at first include philosophical intelligence in his catalogue of intelligences (1993) but came to the conclusion that it was identifiable and distinct from the others after further research (1999). Although Gardner is addressing a different question to the five-dimensional model of the person, it is at this point that the two schemes come closest together.

Gardner's definition of philosophical intelligence is close to what we are talking about in the valuing dimension – in both cases the central focus is the process of valuing things in a moral sense. This kind of valuing is not reducible to anything else, either in the cognitive arena or the emotional arena or, in Gardner's scheme, any of the other eight kinds of intelligence.

The problem with discussing philosophical intelligence is that the traditional notion of intelligence is of something fixed by birth and for life. Unless we amend this notion, we would still be left feeling that some people are more likely than others to be ethical. However, Gardner constructs his catalogue of intelligences on quite a different notion of intelligence.

Instead of intelligence being a fixed factor that is determined by some mysterious internal genetic quality, Gardner defines intelligence as a capacity evidenced by actions. For example, saying a person has high linguistic intelligence is to say that the person exhibits strengths in such areas as story-telling, report-writing, analysis of written materials and humour. This capacity is socially defined (eg social standards for good reports), that is, it is not defined in isolation from social mores.

Most importantly, intelligences, according to Gardner, are capacities that can be developed; they are not fixed. As Joyce Martin (2001, p 39) says, "the model acknowledges that genetics endows us with different propensities but stresses that the development of these propensities is dependent on nurture and opportunity".

Another aspect of intelligences that is significant here is Gardner's view that the exercise of an intelligence that we prefer is not exhausting. Instead, it refreshes and renews the mind. Thus, a person who is high in interpersonal intelligence will be refreshed after spending time with friends. This view resonates with what Jung and subsequent researchers said about personal preferences – the introvert will be energised by interaction with the inner world, while an extravert will be energised by interaction with the outer world.

We may accept that people have inherent preferences and biases and yet feel that some attention to certain areas would be beneficial. Nowhere is this more so than with ethics. A person high in mathematical/logical intelligence may pursue a career as an engineer, but ethics applies to everyone. We recognise that we are talking about more than Gardner was – we are talking about moral conduct, whereas Gardner's focus of interest was readiness to discuss ethics. Thus we wish to explore what the multiple intelligences school has to say about developing philosophical intelligence.

Joyce Martin found that occupations where people rated highly on philosophical intelligence included judges and magistrates, psychologists and sociologists, union organisers, religious ministers and arbitrators. Occupations where people tended to rate low included scientists, engineers, accountants, computer technicians and stockbrokers.

She comments that many people practising the latter occupations "assume that these endeavours are value-free". Their only measure is whether their acts are legal. Another sort of person who has low interest in philosophical intelligence is people who are racist, sexist or bigoted. Such people tend to have an authoritarian and rigid approach to life, because they do not put their ideas to the test of whether they are principled.

Martin maintains that development of intelligences in which we are not strong may be required if we are to be effective in our situation. In the workplace, our job role may require us to interact with people and establish respectful, trusting relationships with them – this is even true of managers who are responsible for staff who have a strong task focus, such as scientists, engineers and technicians. Senior managers need to think about the vision of the enterprise and the values attached to that. Lack of awareness of this aspect, or unwillingness to think about it, leads to confusion, lack of motivation and resentment among staff.

According to Gardner and Joyce Martin, the multiple intelligences are universal. They are present in some degree in all people. Martin (2001, p 39) says: "This assumption means that it is the responsibility of all members of a team to encourage the discovery and expression of all intelligences as a basis for communication and respect".

This view is not just a diversity perspective. The diversity argument is that everyone has a strength or viewpoint that plays a part in organisational endeavours; diversity enriches life. The argument for cultivating multiple intelligences is even stronger than this – it is saying that all the intelligences (and in our context, particularly philosophical intelligence) are necessary for the healthy functioning of the whole.

The core human values model takes a similar view. All the intelligences are relevant to a balanced life, just as all five dimensions of a person are necessary. In the core human values model we have given a prominent place to right action (valuing), because it informs our cognition (ie it influences the purposes to which we apply our cognition) and it is a major factor in our emotions (eg our feelings about fairness and justice). Events at these levels flow through to affect our energy and our psyche.

The Values Evolution Model combines with the five-dimensional model of the person to assert that our personal development of ethics requires us to bring values issues into awareness and to reflect upon ethical questions. This includes being aware of our natural preferences (our intelligences) and how they affect our view of the world. Taking this step opens the technical world to the moral dimension.

An example is given by the carpet firm of Ray Anderson, Interface (Lau et al, 2001). When they were designing a new facility in Shanghai, there was a certain process that required a pump of 95 horsepower. This process was evaluated from a new perspective – how could energy use and pollution be reduced? This new approach led to a redesign where a pump of only seven horsepower was required.

In this instance the solution resulted in savings on running costs as well as positive environmental outcomes. The company was not assuming that environmentally friendly solutions would always be readily found, but it did find that its engineers began to look beyond the solely technical to include the environment as a moral imperative in the design process. In the Values Evolution Model this is an illustration of how tasks aimed at maintaining the institutions of society are expanded to incorporate a broader sense of moral purpose.

Colins and Chippendale also recommend that we develop our capacities in order to become balanced. In describing personal style and the different brain preferences that people exhibit, they talk about people having various levels of brain preference. They may be strongest in Sensate-Thinking (ST), for example, but they exhibit other styles in some measure. Moreover, they assert that spending some time in activities associated with styles where we are weakest has significant benefits for the person.

The area where a person is strongest is called their primary work mode. The area where they are weakest is called their creative mode, and is opposite to the former. Thus an ST person will have FN (Feeling-Intuitive) as their creative mode. The focus of each of these personal styles is contrasted below:

- ST – competence, rationality, productivity, responsibility, efficiency, planning, work, family, belonging
- NF – expressiveness, honesty, search, meaning, insight, integration, human dignity, joy.

Colins and Chippendale would maintain that this person should look to occupations that allow them to express their ST brain preferences, but they should engage in activities that enable the expression of NF brain preferences for their own enjoyment. They argue that this approach enables a person to work with their brain preferences but also to develop their values and insight.

Summing up this discussion, we can bring the question of style, personal development and ethics back to the idea of the aims of human activity. We saw in Chapter 9 that each of the six aims had its legitimate expression, and that the role of ethics is to remind us when we have deviated, either through fear or self-obsession (hubris, conceit). This is a constant exercise in self-correction.

Determining what to do and how to go about it involves judging whether our proposed action is part of the legitimate and balanced pursuit of the aims, or a manifestation of fears or self-obsession. Style is part of the picture because our knowledge of our strengths and natural preferences is the basis of our integrity and it must provide the direction for our development of the fifth dimension, the fullness of our identity.

Discouragement

In Chapter 9 we looked at how to go about developing ourselves – in particular, from an ethical perspective. We discussed how this was generally a question of "gradual progress" rather than dramatic transformation. We also referred to Stephen Covey's concept of the abundance principle as an essential factor in our perseverance. However, we sometimes experience times of discouragement, and this is an issue that invites further discussion.

Ch. 10 | Coda: present perfect

The title of this chapter refers to the present as perfect. We know the ways in which this is not true – we can sit down and write a list of all the current imperfections in our own life and the life of the planet. So, in what sense is the present perfect? If we can identify this, we can begin to understand why discouragement is ultimately an enemy of effective power.

The current imperfections in our life can be turned into goals. Our society is very efficient at defining goals and strategies to achieve them. Goals pervade our lives from schooldays onwards. The workplace is replete with goals – organisational goals, team goals, individual targets. We are rewarded for achieving goals and we may be punished for falling short. But not every aspect of our life at work is organised around goals, and this is even truer at home.

Consider the goal aspects of our work life. If we take the example of a teacher, they have certain goals that are measurable – getting students to learn the course and pass exams, maintaining order in the classroom, fostering the scholastic achievements of both boys and girls, and boosting the performance of talented students. However, there are aspects of the teacher's work that fall outside of the list of goals. What are they?

The non-goal aspects of work are related to our satisfaction. What makes the teacher show up each day, apart from the contractual obligation and the salary? It may be the challenge and pleasure of interacting with and guiding young, exploring minds. For the engineer it may be the satisfaction of finding a clever and innovative solution to a design problem.

These aspects do not fit into the goal paradigm. We do not keep score except in a very general sense. We do not consider at a certain point that we have "achieved that goal" and can move onto something else. As Lewis Richmond (1999, p 113) describes it, the non-goal aspects are "simply a deep, authentic part of who you are". In fact, Richmond says that these intentions can be so deeply embedded in us that it may be difficult for us to articulate them or even know what they are.

The point that Richmond goes on to make is that if we understand the distinction between goals and our deeper intentions, we can avoid sinking into discouragement. Why? Because we understand that the important thing is to sustain our intention, not to expect to fulfil it in any particular action or strategy. The intention itself becomes the goal.

Being aware of our deeper intention, then, is our "present perfect". It is the inherent power of the sixth aim – purpose and peace – to uplift us in the present. Richmond says that regularly reminding ourselves of this intention becomes enjoyable in itself, and enables us to persevere when external progress seems blocked. In terms of the five dimensions of the person, Richmond is saying that cultivating the values of the fifth dimension (psyche – awareness, appreciation, meaning) flows through to positively affect the other dimensions.

Discouragement is an ailment of the emotional dimension. Note that among the values associated with this dimension are cheerfulness, discipline and hope. These qualities can be directly cultivated, but they are also nurtured by the appreciation that comes from the dimension of the psyche, the insight that, in a significant, personal sense, the present is perfect.

Richmond provides support for this insight from Buddhism, with two assertions. The first is that thoughts are real and are the source of all actions; everything that exists in the external world was first of all a thought. The second assertion is that everything is connected; the effects of our thoughts, feelings and actions do not disappear, but radiate outward like ripples in a pond.

Richmond says that developing this kind of confidence results from paying close attention to what is going on around us, but not becoming too attached to any particular outcome or achievement. The important thing is the larger intention and our constancy in adhering to that. Because everything is connected and our thoughts have power, spiritual intention can stir up events. We get a boost from the outer world.

The boost is the fourth dimension of the person, spirit/energy, in operation. Our efforts sometimes come back to us in energy from others. Other people catch the spirit of our intention and respond. The morale of a team lifts, attitudes towards standards improve, hope instead of cynicism infuses actions. We have all seen this happen, although we may need to see this many times before we can sustain our confidence in situations where there is no apparent progress.

Discouragement is a good adversary, because it strikes at our emotions, but it needs to be faced in all five dimensions of our person. If we just seek to combat discouragement at the level of our emotions, it is a raw battle between it and cheerfulness. Facing discouragement in the cognitive dimension is also needed – we need to remind ourselves that worldly achievement and success are in any case ephemeral. In the values dimension we need to affirm that regardless of the apparent outcomes, it is worthwhile to continue to be ethical.

But it is in the dimension of the psyche that the real commitment is made, and this flows down into energy (ie it energises us) and the other dimensions. In the face of discouragement we have to return here, to affirm the wisdom of powers we do not understand or control. In the end, we know that the only way to be is to do right and foster the good. Or, in Buddhist terms, to have compassion, which is to return to Schweitzer's idea that ethics is about considering the well-being of others.

What is success?

We have just looked at discouragement, and it appears that discouragement arises primarily in relation to reaching goals. This brings us to the question of success, and how it relates to ethics. We have argued strongly that outward success is not the measure of "good ethics".

At this point it is appropriate to deconstruct the meaning of success. Once we accept the assertion that life is meaningful only in terms of the five dimensions of the person, the core human values, the various aims of human life and the Values Evolution Model, we need to redefine success.

In ordinary conversation we are apt to accept the socially defined conception of success as outwardly evident achievements and possessions – a highly paid executive role in an organisation, entrepreneurial success, an important or influential job, financial wealth and its accoutrements (house, car, clothes and exotic holidays), fame, social standing, an attractive, healthy and sane spouse and family, and personal health and fitness.

When people are asked to define goals for their own success, the goals are usually drawn from this set. The problem with goals is that, in themselves, they are silent on values. Values remain implicit and unexamined. Yet we know they are important.

Suppose my goal is to win an Olympic gold medal. Without the counsel of values there is no reason why I should not consider using performance-enhancing drugs in my quest for gold. However, most of us would reject the idea that this is an acceptable strategy, and if we won a gold medal in this way we would feel guilty and ashamed.

Similarly, many of us would modify a quest for wealth if it meant stealing, cheating or subjecting other people to abuse and mistreatment. We would accept the role of values to modify our means, and even the goal itself if necessary.

Organisations went through a similar process in the 1980s and 1990s. First they recognised the value of mission statements and statements of goals and strategies. Later many realised that a statement of values was also necessary, and was distinct from the other statements.

Once values enter the picture, our ideas about success have to be modified. We accept that we do not want the gold medal if it means cheating. Moreover, when we articulate this as a value in our life and establish it in our conduct, we accept the stronger admonition, that we will not cheat even if others do.

Our efforts are then modified to support this value. In this case it may mean dedication to greater effort and discipline, a focus on better techniques in our given sport and advocacy of more rigorous methods of catching cheats. Tracing the steps in this example, where has the acknowledgment of ethical values taken us? Our pursuit of success has changed in the following ways:

- The external goal remains, but another goal has taken precedence – an ethical value – which regulates the means we are prepared to use in pursuit of the external goal. Two comments can be made about this: 1) we have shifted from a goal that is defined by external achievement to one that is defined by an internal standard, and 2) this second "goal" is more like the broader intentions we described above in the discussion on discouragement. It is part of who we are.

- Ethical values have become an integral and explicit part of our definition of success. We resist the superficiality of public acclaim that just looks at externals without considering the integrity and morality of the players. In Australia we remember how people fawned over Alan Bond and Christopher Skase at their height in the 1980s before their illusory empires crashed. In the USA we can point to the cheap euphoria that accompanied the apparent brilliance of the Enron executives before their charade disintegrated.

- Our success is established, first of all, in our personal conduct. Whatever success we experience in the external world is a product of personal consistency in habits and conduct, and clarity about our values. This aspect reminds us of the development of leadership from inner to outer, from being trustworthy to building trust with others. Perhaps it should be added that this discussion is about sustainable success rather than ephemeral success.

- Finally, in pursuing outward success, we are prepared to work at redefining the public perception of success. We articulate and advocate the ethical foundations of sustainable success. We do this, not from a position of moral superiority, but from the perspective that we are all travelling down the same road. For example, Anita Roddick of The Body Shop led by example, as has Ray Anderson of Interface, advocating for values-based business.

Another way in which our conception of success needs to change is in its singular focus on one goal. People often choose one goal and pursue that. The classic instance is the executive who gets to the top of the tree but loses all sense of joy and meaning. Laura Nash and Howard Stevenson (2004) suggest that this single-focus perspective is responsible for burn-out, satisfaction that is short-lived, and unethical conduct.

Nash and Stevenson conducted a study with hundreds of professional and personal high achievers to determine a more sustainable framework for success. Central to their framework is the principle that success can mean very different things for people in different times and situations. They proposed four components for enduring success that are the same for everyone:

- happiness (feelings of pleasure or contentment about our life)
- achievement (accomplishments that compare favourably against similar goals others have strived for)
- significance (the sense that we have made a positive impact on people we care about)
- legacy (a way to establish our values or accomplishments so as to help others find future success).

They advocate that people set reasonable goals for themselves in all four areas, and in pursuing those goals to balance their efforts across the four areas. This strategy is based on the authors' view that unless people hit on all four categories with regularity, they will remain dissatisfied.

Nash and Stevenson's approach has much in common with our concept of six aims of human activity. If there are six aims, it makes sense that we should not define our success in terms of one goal. The happiness component partially corresponds to our survival aim; the survival aim takes a broader view. A comparison of the other aims and components requires some discussion.

The six aims distinguished between aims that concerned things and aims that concerned people. Two aims concerned things – autonomy (and mastery) and creativity (and innovation), and two aims concerned people – acceptance (and belonging) and intimacy (and love). People tend to lean more towards aims to do with things or aims to do with people, but there is a need to reach a healthy balance between the two over time.

In Nash and Stevenson's scheme, achievement is somewhat like our aims concerning things. Perhaps we would not make the definition of achievement so dependent on comparisons with other people, but on the other hand we should recognise that our individual perceptions of autonomy and creativity are to a great extent socially constructed.

Significance in Nash and Stevenson's scheme is like our aims concerning people. In acceptance and intimacy the success of our aim is indicated by the depth and quality of our relationships, social and personal, which certainly includes having a positive impact on people we care about.

Legacy is to be compared with our aim of purpose and peace. While the two are not equivalent, they could be described as compatriots. Nash and Stevenson's further discussion of balanced success echoes other features we have discussed above. Two assertions they make resonate with our discussion of ethics and success:

- identity (who we are and what we stand for – our values) is as essential as achievement and performance, and
- being satisfied with oneself (happiness – present perfect) is as important as achieving something "out there in the world".

Working from core human values

The initial and continuing challenge of success is to shift from an external focus, being dependent on social definitions of success, to an internal focus, defining success on the basis of the core human values and the legitimate aims of human activity. Living ethically does not guarantee success in any worldly sense, but it points us to a way of living that is ultimately the only worthwhile way to live. A simple test is, on our death bed we would not want to be clutching the gold medal with the knowledge that we had cheated to get it.

The five-dimensional model of the person provides both a starting point and a framework for moral conduct and personal development (Figure 10.1).

Figure 10.1: The five-dimensional model

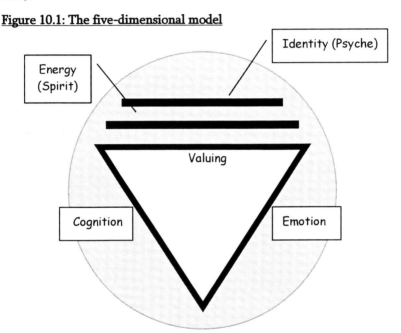

The model provides a starting point for ethical conduct in this way:

- **Cognitive dimension** – we choose to live in honesty and integrity;
- **Emotional dimension** – we establish peace with ourselves and with others (for Daniel Goleman, this is emotional intelligence; for Stephen Covey it is maturity);
- **Valuing dimension** – we determine to live according to right action, having faith that it is worthwhile to do so (Covey's abundance principle);

- **Energy dimension** – we observe that when we apply ourselves to living with integrity and furthering the good that the universe sometimes conspires to help us, and even when external validation is not in evidence, we become clearer, firmer and more satisfied about what we do, and a sense of community with others often arises;
- **Psyche dimension** – we accept that there is purpose and meaning for our life that is still unfolding (the "present perfect" aspect) and this infuses and balances all our efforts.

The Values Evolution Model then provides us with a picture of what our current values are and what values it is productive for us to focus on, remembering the thought from John Sanford (1988) in Chapter 9, that our moral values and ideals are only effective within the scope of our (current) consciousness. The essence of personal development of ethics is to work through the core human values to enlarge the scope of our consciousness.

One of the key thoughts behind the core human values is the idea that ethics and aspiration form an integrated whole. Most people avoid discussion of ethics because they think all it concerns is what we should *not* do. Hence it must involve self-righteous people trying to make us feel guilty. Ethics, on this perception, takes us away from thinking about what we *want* to do.

We have placed ethics within a larger framework, where ethics and aspiration lie on the same continuum. What holds them together is the idea that development, or evolution, is the process of expansion, of enlarging our perception and understanding.

Thus, when ethics as compliance tells us not to do something, the larger picture shows us why. In the larger picture ethics is not just a constraint, it furthers the greater good. As Schweitzer said, ethics is our way of thinking about the well-being of all, of the whole, and in this book we have sought to translate that thought into the five dimensions of the person.

The ideas in this book have been informed by several of the world's major philosophies and religions. The following two quotations from Chinese Tao sum up what it is hoped this book will offer to the reader – a meaningful fusion of the pragmatic and the sublime.

Ch. 10 | Coda: present perfect

Finally, the best way to combat evil is to make energetic progress in the good.

— *The I Ching*, Hexagram 43, Breakthrough (Wilhelm/Baynes, 1951)

It is better to just live one's life,
realising one's potential,
rather than wishing
for sanctification.

When one rediscovers reverence and love
there is no need of ethical teaching.
When cunning and obsession with profit are renounced,
then stealing and fraud will disappear.
Ethics, kindness, even wisdom,

are not in themselves sufficient.
Better by far to see
the simplicity of the given,
the beauty of the natural,
to be one with oneself and with others.
Develop selflessness,

and temper desire
with compassion.

— Lao Tzu, *Tao Te Ching*, 19 Returning to naturalness (Feng & English, 1972)

References

—, *The I Ching or book of changes*, 1951, Richard Wilhelm translation, rendered into English by Carey Baynes, Routledge and Kegan Paul, London.

Achbar, Mark, Jennifer Abbott and Joel Bakan, 2004, *The corporation*, movie.

Anderson, Bob, undated, "The spirit of leadership", online at www.theleadershipcircle.com. Accessed 14 April 2005.

Aquino K and A Reed, 2002, "The self-importance of moral identity", *Journal of Personal and Social Psychology*, vol 83, no 6, pp 1423-1440.

Assagioli, Roberto, 2000, *Psychosynthesis: A collection of basic writings*, Synthesis Center, Amherst MA.

Badaracco, Joseph, 1997, *Defining moments: when managers must choose between right and right*, Harvard Business School Press, Boston MA.

Badaracco, Joseph, 2002, *Leading quietly: an unorthodox guide to doing the right thing*, Harvard Business School Press, Boston MA.

Bandura, Albert, 1977, *Social learning theory*, Prentice-Hall, Englewood Cliffs NJ.

Bass, Bernard, 1990, *Bass & Stogdill's handbook of leadership: theory, research and managerial applications*, 3rd ed, The Free Press, New York.

Bassi, Laurie and Daniel McMurrer, 2004, "Developing measurement systems for managing in the knowledge era", White Paper at www.mcbassi.com.

Benedict, Ruth, 1934, Anthropology and the abnormal, *Journal of General Psychology*, vol 10, pp 72-74.

Bennis, Warren and R Thomas, 2002, "Crucibles of leadership", *Harvard Business Review*, September, pp 39-45.

Bird, Frederick and James Waters, 1994, The moral muteness of managers, in J Drummond and B Bain (ed), *Managing business ethics*, Butterworth Heinemann, Oxford, pp 91-106.

Blanchard, Ken and Michael O'Connor, 1997, *Managing by values*, Berrett-Koehler, San Francisco.

References

Boss, Judith, 1998, *Ethics for life: an interdisciplinary and multicultural introduction*, Mayfield, Mountain View CA.

Brabeck, Mary and Margaret Gorman, 1992, "Emotions and morality", Chapter 5 in Richard Knowles and George Mclean (ed), *Psychological foundations of moral education and character development: an integrated theory of moral development*, 2nd ed, The Council for Research in Values and Philosophy, Washington, pp 89-124.

Burns, Stephanie, 2000, *The emotional experience of the adult learner*, PhD thesis, University of South Australia, Adelaide.

Butterfield, K, Linda Trevino and Gary Weaver, 2000, "Moral awareness in business organizations: influences of issue-related and social context factors", *Human Relations*, vol 53, no 7, pp 981-1018.

Carter, Rita, 1998, *Mapping the Mind*, Weidenfeld & Nicolson, London.

Claxton, Guy, 1994, *Noises from the darkroom: the science and mystery of the mind*, Aquarian, London.

Colins, Clare and Paul Chippendale, 2002, *New wisdom II: values-based development*, Acorn, Brisbane.

Collins, Jim and Jerry Porras, 1994, *Built to last*, HarperCollins, New York.

Collins, Jim, 2001, *Good to great*, HarperBusiness, New York.

Covey, Stephen, 1990, *The seven habits of highly effective people,* The Business Library, Melbourne.

Covey, Stephen, 1992, *Principle-Centred Leadership*, Simon & Schuster, London.

Covey, Stephen, 1994, "The strange attractor", *Executive Excellence*, August, pp 5-6.

Dalai Lama, 1999, *Ancient wisdom, modern world: ethics for the new millennium*, Abacus, London.

Dattner Grant, 2005, *Purpose and spirit in the workplace*, Dattner Grant, Eltham, Victoria, Australia.

Day, DV and Lord RG, 1988, "Executive leadership and organizational performance: suggestions for a new theory and methodology", *Journal of Management*, 14, pp 453-464.

Doherty, William, 1995, *Soul searching: why psychotherapy must promote moral responsibility*, Basic Books, New York.

Drucker, Peter, 1955, *The practice of management*, William Heinemann, London.

Dunphy, Dexter C, Andrew Griffiths and Suzanne Benn, 2002, *Organizational change for corporate sustainability*, Routledge, London.

Dunphy, Dexter C, Andrew Griffiths, Jodie Benveniste and Philip Sutton (ed), 2000, *Sustainability: the corporate challenge of the 21st century*, Allen & Unwin, Sydney.

Ethics Resource Center, 2004, *PLUS – a process for ethical decision making*, online at www.ethics.org

Ethics Resource Center, 2009, *2009 National business ethics survey: ethics in the recession*, Ethics Resource Center, Arlington VA.

Fairholm, Gilbert, 2003, *The techniques of inner leadership: making leadership work*, Praeger, Westport CT.

Fishbein, Martin and I Ajzen, 1975, *Belief, attitude, intention and behavior: an introduction to theory and research*, Addison-Wesley, Boston MA.

Frankl, Victor, 1984, *Man's search for meaning*, Pocket, New York.

Frederick, William, James Post and Keith Davis, 1992, *Business and society: corporate strategy, public policy, ethics* (7th ed), McGraw-Hill, New York.

Friedman, Milton, 1962, *Capitalism and freedom*, University of Chicago Press, Chicago.

Friedman, Milton, 1990, "The social responsibility of business is to increase its profits", *The New York Times Magazine*, 13 September 1970. Reprinted in W Hoffman and J Moore (ed), *Business ethics: readings and cases in corporate Morality*, McGraw-Hill, New York, pp 153-157.

Freud, Sigmund, 1930/1961, *Civilization and its discontents*, Norton, New York.

Garden, Annamaria, 2000, *Reading the mind of the organization: connecting the strategy with the psychology of the business*, Gower, Aldershot England.

References

Gardner, Howard, 1993, *Multiple intelligences*, Basic Books, New York.

Gardner, Howard, 1999, *Intelligence reframed*, Basic Books, New York.

Gardner, Howard, Mihaly Csikszentmihalyi and William Damon, 2001, *Good work: when excellence and ethics meet*, Basic Books, New York.

Gibb, Jack, 1978, *Trust: a new view of personal and organizational development*, The Guild of tutors Press, Los Angeles CA.

Gilligan, Carol, 1982, *In a different voice*, Harvard University Press, Cambridge MA.

Glasser, William, 1985, *Control theory: a new explanation of how we control our lives*, Harper Collins, New York.

Glasser, William, 1998, *Choice theory: A new psychology of personal freedom*, Harper Collins, New York.

Goldman, Alvin, 1993, "Ethics and cognitive science", *Ethics*, vol 103, no 2, January.

Goleman, Daniel, 1998, *Working with emotional intelligence*, Bloomsbury, London.

Grace, Damian and Stephen Cohen, 1995, *Business ethics: Australian problems and cases*, Oxford University Press, Melbourne.

Guy, Mary, 1990, *Ethical decision making in everyday work situations*, Quorum Books, New York.

Haigh, Gideon, 2006, *Asbestos House: The secret history of James Hardie Industries*, Scribe, Melbourne.

Hall, Brian, 1986, *The genesis effect: personal and organizational transformations*, Paulist Press, New York.

Hall, Brian, 1994, *Value shift: a guide to personal and organisational transformation*, Twin Lights Publishing, Rockport MA.

Hall, Brian, 2003, "Classifying 125 values", available online at www.valuestech.com/sub

Hall, Brian, 2003, "The omega factor: a values-based approach for developing organizations and leadership", paper presented at 2003 Servant Leadership Forum: Serving Students and the Common Good, online at www.georgiahumanities.org

Hawley, Jack, 1993, *Reawakening the spirit in work: the power of dharmic management*, Berrett-Koehler, San Francisco.

Henderson, Michael and Dougal Thompson, 2003, *Values at work*, HarperBusiness, Auckland New Zealand.

Henderson, Verne, 1990, "The ethical side of enterprise", in W Hoffman and J Moore (eds), *Business ethics: readings and cases in corporate morality*, McGraw-Hill, New York, pp 69-79.

Hill, Ivan, 1976, "The meaning of ethics and freedom", in Ivan Hill (ed.), *The ethical basis of economic freedom*, American Viewpoint, Chapel Hill NC, pp 3-20.

Hills, Ben, 2004, "Sins of the fathers", *Sydney Morning Herald*, Business & Money, 2-3 October, p 39.

Hinman, Lawrence, 1994, *Ethics: a pluralistic approach to moral theory*, Harcourt Brace Jovanovich, Orlando FL.

Hofstede, Geert, 1984, *Culture's consequences: international differences in work-related values*, Sage, London.

Horn, Art, 2004, *Face it: recognizing and conquering the hidden fear that drives all conflict at work*, AMACOM, New York.

Hudson, 2004, *The Hudson report: employment and HR trends, Australia*, Hudson, Sydney, October-December.

Johnson, Mark, 1993, *Moral imagination: implications of cognitive science for ethics*, University of Chicago Press, Chicago.

Kant, Immanuel, 1963, *Lectures on ethics* (trans. Louis Infield), Harper Torchbooks, New York.

Kant, Immanuel, 1994, "The categorical imperative", in Peter Singer (ed), *Ethics*, Oxford University Press, Oxford, pp 274-279 (first published in 1785).

Kay, William, 1968, *Moral development*, George Allen & Unwin, London.

Kegan, Robert, 1982, *The evolving self: problem and process in human development*, Harvard University Press, Cambridge MA.

Kerr, Steven, 1988, "Integrity in effective leadership", in Suresh Srivastva (ed) *Executive integrity: the search for high human values in organizational life*, Jossey-Bass, San Francisco, pp 122-139.

References

Klein, Gary, 1999, *Sources of power: how people make decisions*, MIT Press, Cambridge, MA.

Knowles, Richard and George McLean, 1992, *Psychological foundations of moral education and character development: an integrated theory of moral development*, 2nd ed, Council for Research in Values and Philosophy, Washington.

Kohlberg, Lawrence, 1984, *Essays in moral development, Vol. II: The psychology of moral development*, Harper & Row, San Francisco.

Kotter, John, 1996, *Leading change*, Harvard Business School Press, Cambridge MA.

Kouzes, James and Barry Posner, 1990, "The credibility factor: what followers expect from their leaders", *Management Review*, January, pp 29-33.

Kouzes, James and Barry Posner, 1996, "Seven lessons for leading the voyage to the future" (Chapter 10), in Frances Hesselbein, Marshall Goldsmith and Richard Beckhard (ed), *The leader of the future*, Drucker Foundation Future Series, Jossey Bass, San Francisco CA, pp 99-110.

Kraft, William, 1992, "A phenomenological approach toward the moral person", in Richard Knowles and George McLean (ed), *Psychological foundations of moral education and character development: an integrated theory of moral development*, 2nd ed, Council for Research in Values and Philosophy, Washington, pp 21-44.

Kuczmarski, Susan Smith and Thomas D Kuczmarski, 1995, *Values-based leadership*, Prentice Hall, Englewood Cliffs NJ.

Lao Tzu, *Tao Te Ching*, 1972, translated by Gia-fu Feng and Jane English, Vintage, New York.

Lawson, Emily and Colin Price, 2003, "The psychology of change management", *The McKinsey Quarterly*, online at www.mckinseyquarterly.com

Lennick, Doug and Frank Kiel, 2008, *Moral intelligence*, Wharton School Publishing, Upper Saddle River NJ.

Lewin, Roger and Birute Regine, 1999, *The soul at work: unleashing the power of complexity science for business success*, Orion Business Books, London.

Lipman-Blumen, Jean, 2005, *The allure of toxic leaders*, Oxford University Press, Oxford.

Lowe, Anthea, 2009, "Bullying", in *Australian master human resources guide*, 7th ed, CCH Australia, pp 1,011-1,033.

Lowen, Walter, 1982, *Dichotomies of the mind: a system science model of the mind and personality*, John Wiley & Sons, New York.

Mant, Alistair, 1997, *Intelligent leadership*, Allen & Unwin, Sydney.

Markkula Center for Applied Ethics, 2004, A framework for ethical decision making, online at www.scu.edu/ethics/practicing/decision/framework.html

Martin, Barbara, 1989, *A checklist for designing instruction in the affective domain*, available online at: http://plaza.v-wave.com/kegj/mar.html (accessed 3 May 2001)

Martin, Glenn and Klaas Woldring, 2001, Ready for the mantle? Australian human resource managers as stewards of ethics, *International Journal of Human Resource Management*, vol 12, no 2, pp 243-255.

Martin, Glenn, 1997, "HR takes a bet each way on ethics", *HRMonthly*, November, pp 27-29.

Martin, Glenn, 1998, "Once again: why should business be ethical?" *Business & Professional Ethics Journal*, vol 17, no 4, pp 39-60.

Martin, Joyce, 2001, *Profiting from multiple intelligences in the workplace*, Gower, Aldershot, England.

McCrone, John, 1993, *The myth of irrationality: the science of the mind from Plato to Star Trek*, Macmillan, London.

McGregor, Douglas, *The human side of enterprise*, McGraw-Hill, Kogakusha.

Meadows, Donella, undated, "A CEO responds to a spear through the heart", online at www.sustainer.org, Sustainability Institute.

Michaels E, H Handfield-Jones and B Axelrod, 2001, *The war for talent*, Harvard Business School Press, Boston MA.

Morgan, Gareth, 1986, *Images of organization*, Sage, Beverly Hills CA.

Myers, David, 2001, *Exploring social psychology*, 2nd ed, McGraw-Hill, Boston.

References

Nash, Laura and Howard Stevenson, 2004, "Success that lasts", *Harvard Business Review*, February, pp 102-109.

Nonaka, Ikujiro and Hirotaka Takeuchi, 1995, *The knowledge-creating company: how Japanese companies create the dynamics of innovation*, Oxford University Press, Oxford.

Paine, Lynn Sharp, 1994, "Managing for organizational integrity", *Harvard Business Review*, March-April, pp 106-117.

Paine, Lynn Sharp, 2003, *Value shift*, McGraw-Hill, New York.

Peacock, Matt, 2009, *Killer company*, ABC Books (Harper Collins), Sydney.

Petrick, Joseph, Robert Wagley and Thomas Von der Embse, 1991, "Structured ethical decision making: improving the prospects of managerial success in business", *SAM Advanced Management Journal*, Winter, pp 28-34.

Piaget, Jean, 1932, *The moral judgment of the child*, Harcourt, New York.

Piaget, Jean, 1964, *Judgment and reasoning in the child*, Littlefield Adams, Paterson NJ.

Posner, Barry and Warren Schmidt, 1992, "Values and the American manager: an update updated", *California Management Review*, Spring, pp 80-94.

Prochaska, JO and CC Di Clemente, 1992, *Stages of Change in the Modification of Problem Behaviors*, Sage, Newbury Park CA.

Rachels, James, 1993, *The elements of moral philosophy*, 2nd ed, McGraw-Hill, New York.

Richmond, Lewis, 1999, *Work as a spiritual practice*, Judy Piatkus, London.

Ritchie, Sheila and Peter Martin, 1999, *Motivation management*, Gower, Aldershot, England.

Rokeach, Milton, 1973, *The nature of human values*, Free Press, New York.

Rokeach, Milton, 1979, "Change and stability in American value systems, 1968-1971", Chapter 7 in Milton Rokeach, *Understanding human values, individual and societal*, The Free Press, New York, pp 129-147.

Rokeach, Milton, 1979, *Understanding human values: individual and societal*, Free Press, New York.

Sanford, John, 1988, *Evil: the shadow side of reality*, Crossroads, New York.

SBS Television, 2004, *Unholy orders*. Documentary filmed by Geraldine Gandolfo. See also, story online at http://www.talkaboutparenting.com/group/alt.parenting.spanking/messages/128675.html, accessed 21 Nov 2004.

Schein, Edgar, 1998, *Career anchors: discovering your real values*, Pfeiffer & Co, New York.

Schwartz, Shalom, 1992, "Universals in the content and structure of values: theoretical advances and empirical tests in twenty countries", *Advances in Experimental Psychology*, vol 25, pp 1-65.

Schwartz, Shalom, 1994, "Are there universal aspects in the structure and contents of human values?" *Journal of Social Issues*, vol 50, no 4, pp 19-45.

Schweitzer, Maurice, Lisa Ordonez and Bambi Douma, 2004, "Goal setting as a motivator of unethical behaviour", *Academy of Management Journal*, vol 47, no 3, pp 422-432.

Senge, Peter, 1992, *The fifth discipline: the art and practice of the learning organization*, Random House, Sydney.

Sexton, Elisabeth and Tony Stephens, 2004, "Lives in the dust", *Sydney Morning Herald*, News Review, 25-26 September, p 27.

Sims, Ronald and Johannes Brinkmann, 2003, "Enron ethics (or: culture matters more than codes", *Journal of Business Ethics*, vol 45, pp 243-256.

Singer, Peter (ed), 1994, *Ethics*, Oxford University Press, New York.

Singer, Peter, 1993, *Practical ethics*, 2nd ed, Cambridge University Press, New York.

Skinner, B.F., 1971, *Beyond freedom and dignity*, Knopf, New York.

Smith, Hyrum, 2000, *What matters most: the power of living your values*, Simon & Schuster, London.

Sprinthal, Norman, Richard Sprinthal and Sharon Oja, 1994, *Educational psychology: a developmental approach*, 6th ed, McGraw-Hill, New York, p 190.

References

St James Ethics Centre and Beaton Consulting, 2009, *The 2009 annual business and professions study: business ethics study*, St James Ethics Centre, Sydney.

Steiner, Rudolf, 1982, *The roots of education*, Rudolf Steiner Press, London.

Sternberg, Elaine, 2000, *Just business: business ethics in action*, 2nd ed, Oxford University Press, Oxford.

Sun Tzu, 1991, *The art of war*, trans. John Cleary, Shambhala, Boston MA.

The Corporation, 2004, website for the movie, at www.thecorporation.com.

The Minessence Group, 2004, *A Values Inventory*, Brisbane, Australia.

Thomas, Terry, John Schermerhorn Jr and John Dienhart, 2004, "Strategic leadership of ethical behavior in business", *Academy of Management Executive*, vol 18, no 2, pp 56-68.

Tosti, Donald, 2000, "Systemic change", *Performance Improvement*, vol 39, no 3, pp 53-59.

Trevino, Linda Klebe and Katherine Nelson, 1995, *Managing business ethics: straight talk about how to do it right*, John Wiley & Sons, New York.

Trevino, Linda and Michael Brown, 2004, "Managing to be ethical: debunking five business ethics myths", *Academy of Management Executive*, vol 18, no 2, pp 69-81.

Trevino, Linda Klebe, Gary R Weaver, David G Gibson, and Barbara Ley Toffler, 1999, "Managing ethics and legal compliance: what works and what hurts," *California Management Review*, vol 41, no 2, Winter, pp 131-151.

Ulrich, Dave, 1996, "Credibility x capability", in F Hesselbein, M Goldsmith and R Beckhard (eds), *The leader of the future*, Drucker Foundation Future Series, Jossey-Bass, San Francisco, pp 209-220.

Walton, Clarence, 1988, *The moral manager*, Ballinger, Cambridge MA.

Watson, Don, 2004, *Watson's dictionary of weasel words*, Knopf, Sydney.

Weiss, Joseph, 1994, *Business ethics: a managerial, stakeholder approach*, Wadsworth, Belmont CA.

Werhane, Patricia, 1999, *Moral imagination and management decision making*, Oxford University Press, USA.

Wilber, Ken, 2000, *Integral psychology*, Shambhala, Boston.

Williams, Robin, 1979, "Change and stability in values and value systems: a sociological perspective", Chapter 2 in M Rokeach, *Understanding human values: individual and societal*, Free Press, New York, 1979, pp 15-46.

Woldring, Klaas, 1996, The ethics and performance criteria of Australian executive remuneration packages, in K Woldring (ed), *Business ethics in Australia and New Zealand: essays and cases*, Thomas Nelson Australia, Melbourne, pp 145-158.

Wolfe, Donald, 1988, "Is there integrity in the bottom line: managing obstacles to executive integrity", in Suresh Srivastva & Associates (ed) *Executive integrity: the search for high human values in organizational life*, Jossey Bass, San Francisco, pp 140-171.

Zohar, Danah and Ian Marshall, 2000, *Connecting with our spiritual intelligence*, Bloomsbury, New York.

About the author

Glenn Martin B.Bus.(Hons), M.Ed., FAITD, CAHRI

Glenn is an Australian writer who writes on management, human resources, employment law, learning and development, compliance issues and business ethics. He has many years' experience writing commentary and articles for professional publications and subscription-based information services.

He has been the editor of CCH Australia's *Master Human Resources Guide* and he has contributed several chapters. He has also contributed chapters to CCH *Master Guide* books on workplace relations and occupational health and safety.

Glenn has written and edited training courses and manuals on human resource skills, coaching and mentoring. He has presented at many conferences and seminars.

Glenn was National President of the Australian Institute of Training and Development (2006-2007) and was a Fellow of the Institute and the editor of its publication, *Training & Development in Australia* from 2006 to 2010. He is also a Certified Practitioner of the Australian Human Resources Institute.

Prior to being a business writer, Glenn had many years of experience in management roles. He has also been a high school teacher, psychiatric nurse, a coordinator of adult education and a community development officer. He has held leadership roles during times of rapid development and change, and he understands the central role of values and integrity in management and leadership.

Glenn is also the author of *The Ten Thousand Things*, a novel which is the story about a man's endeavour to conduct himself ethically in a leadership position, amid a host of pressures and threats from some unscrupulous stakeholders. For more information, see www.glennmartin.com.au.

Contact Glenn at info@ethicsandvalues.com.au

Glenn's ethics website: www.ethicsandvalues.com.au

Index

Abbott, 255
Achbar, 255
Adler, Rodney, 18
aims of human activity, 226, 227, 270
  ethics, 232
Ajzen, 91, 96
altruism, 41, 91, 92, 207
Anderson, Bob, 200, 206, 207
Anderson, Ray, 255, 259, 269, 275
Ansett, 3, 17, 18
Aquino, 206
Aristotle, 89, 175
Arthur Andersen, 4
Asch, 26, 27
Assagioli, 245
attitude, 38, 52, 67, 91, 93, 243
Badaracco, Joseph, 149, 161, 170, 180, 258
Bakan, 255
Bandura, 85
Bass, 198
Bassi, 141
beliefs, 29, 66, 68, 126
Benedict, 82
Bennis, 213
Bird, 29
Blanchard, 58
Boss, Judith, 82, 88, 91
Brabeck, 217
brain preferences, 262, 263
Brinkmann, 188
Brown, 153
bullying, 54, 153
Burns, 244
Butterfield, 154
career anchors, 60
Carter, 93
change management, 213, 221
chaos theory, 203
Chippendale, 69, 99, 111, 116, 262, 263, 264, 269
Claxton, 93
code of ethics, 29, 187
Cohen, 161
Colins, 69, 99, 111, 262, 263, 264, 269
Collins, Jim, 74, 219, 220, 258

compliance, 2, 8, 18, 23, 30, 37, 47, 53, 72, 104, 123, 187, 196, 201, 203, 222, 235, 259, 266, 278
corporate social responsibility, 22, 46, 187
Covey, Stephen, 139, 144, 145, 172, 203, 205, 208, 225, 246, 252, 260, 270, 277
Csikszentmihalyi, 153
culture, 94, 122, 138, 146, 194, 205, 207, 209, 219
  of denial, 128
Dalai Lama, 42, 89, 91, 109
Damon, 153
Dattner Grant, 244
Davis, 25, 191
Day, DV, 198
decision-making, 122, 138, 146, 156, 170, 205, 212
  Integral Model, 156, 165, 178
  intuitive approach, 149, 155, 173, 176, 178
  psychological aspects, 161, 170
definition
  corporate social responsibility, 191
  ethics, 34, 41, 140, 232
  situation, 155
  value, 61
denial of ethics, 125, 126
dialogue, 122, 195, 207, 209, 211
Dienhart, 221
discouragement, 270
Doherty, 224
Drucker, 193
Dunphy, 197
Durkheim, 58
duties
  Kant, 145
  of employees, 134
  of employers, 132
duties of employees
  ethics, 135
emotion, 75, 85, 86, 89, 93, 215, 239, 277
emotional intelligence, 73, 93, 141, 153, 213, 260, 277
emotions, 7, 11, 50, 89, 217, 240, 272

Index

Enron, 2, 3, 17, 18, 29, 31, 132, 188, 274
Erikson, 86, 226
ethical criteria, 158
Ethical criteria, 159
ethical development, 84, 125, 141, 203, 224, 225, 226, 251, 254, 260, 263, 266
ethical dilemma, 8, 125, 147, 159
ethical leadership, 184, 203
    stages of, 206
ethical standards, 30, 42, 55, 80, 104, 115, 123, 131, 161, 200
Ethics Resource Center, 19, 24, 32, 160, 162
expertise, 100, 155, 173, 230, 235, 252
Fairholm, 73, 206, 208
Fishbein, 91, 96
focus values, 111, 112, 114, 115, 130, 212, 236
foundation values, 111, 112, 116, 206, 212, 236
Frankl, 245, 257
Frederick, 25, 188, 191
Freud, 84, 226
Friedman, Milton, 188
Garden, Annamaria, 69, 74, 184
Gardner, 153, 262, 266, 267, 268
Gibb, 208
Gilligan, 88
Gioia
    scripts, 139
Glasser, 227, 256
Goldman, 171
Goleman, 73, 93, 141, 144, 145, 216, 217, 277
Gorman, 217
Grace, 161
Graves, 226
Guy, Mary, 159
habits, 82, 122, 139, 246, 251, 252, 253
Haigh, 127
Hall, Brian, 11, 67, 69, 98, 109, 112, 115, 116, 194, 197, 200, 202, 203, 206, 209, 225
Hartshorne, 95
Hawley, 74
Henderson, 51, 59, 73, 117

HIH, 3, 17, 18, 29, 132, 189
Hills, 127
Hinman, 42
Hoffman, 85
Hofstede, 88
Horn, 249
Hudson, 213, 214
human values, 3, 9, 39, 60, 66, 72, 105, 184, 196, 238, 245, 262, 276
Hume, 89
identity, 39, 43, 70, 76, 144, 161, 206, 219
imaginal skills, 114, 115
instrumental skills, 113
Integral Model
    decision-making, 156, 165, 178
integrity, 1, 2, 3, 6, 9, 11, 13, 31, 70, 77, 79, 83, 106, 138, 143, 144, 160, 163, 204, 207, 213, 219, 222, 223, 230, 237, 238, 246, 256, 257, 277
Interface, 255, 259, 269, 275
interpersonal skills, 113, 194
James Hardie, 127
Johnson, 149, 171
Johnson & Johnson, 129, 139, 174
judgement, 19, 35, 41, 48, 49, 52, 67, 83, 86, 94, 162, 169, 173, 189, 201, 207, 211, 246, 252, 254, 258, 262
Kant, Immanuel, 5, 140, 148
Kay, William, 92, 94, 96, 104, 116, 228
Kegan, 226, 229
Kerr, 224
Kiel, 79, 139, 237
Klein, 148, 174, 175, 177, 178, 253
Knowles, 85
Kohlberg, 11, 55, 86, 87, 88, 89, 90, 91, 92, 95, 96, 109, 171, 184
Kotter, 221
Kouzes, 172, 199, 202
Kraft, 84
Kuczmarski, 58, 73
law, 4, 31, 35, 52, 75, 87, 94, 106, 124, 131, 157, 201
Lawson, 221
leadership, 59, 142, 172, 183, 196, 198
    5-dimensional model, 212
    ethics, 202
Lennick, 79, 139, 237

Lewin, 201
Lipman-Blumen, 203
Lord, RG, 198
Lowe, 54
Lowen, 262, 263
Mahatma Gandhi, 109, 172
Mant, 114, 218
Manville Corporation, 127
Markkula Center for Applied Ethics, 160
Marshall, 74
Martin Luther, 195
Martin, Barbara, 93
Martin, Glenn, 19, 29, 34
Martin, Joyce, 266, 267, 268
Martin, Peter, 61, 63, 64
Maslow, 11, 64, 65, 66, 227
May, 95
MBTI, 262
McCrone, 93
McGregor, 245
McKinsey, 213
McLean, 85
McMurrer, 141
Meadows, 255
Michaels, 213
Milgram, 26, 27
Minessence Group, 263
moral development, 55, 84, 89, 184
    cognitive approach, 86
moral imagination, 149, 171, 256
moral intelligence, 79, 139, 237, 266
moral muteness, 29
moral philosophy, 6, 10, 159, 161
Morgan, 184
Mother Theresa, 109
motivation, 45, 89, 117, 216, 252
multiple intelligences, 263
Myers, 26, 91
Myers-Briggs Type Indicator, 220, 262
Nash, 275, 276
needs, 64, 227
Nelson, 96, 138, 153, 180
Nonaka, 141
O'Connor, 58
omega point, 202, 221, 225, 245
One.Tel, 3, 17, 18, 28
organisations
    psychological aspects, 184

Paine, 29, 127, 128, 129, 164, 204, 205
Peacock, 127
perceptions, 52, 67, 80, 94, 103, 115, 151, 184, 201
performance appraisals, 162
personal style, 219, 262
Petrick, 184
philanthropy, 189
Piaget, 86, 248, 287
Placer Dome, 188
Porras, Jerry, 74, 219, 220, 258
Posner, 59, 172, 199, 202
Post, 25, 191
Price, 221
Prochaska, 253, 254
psychological needs, 64
Rachels, 42
recognition-primed decision model, 176
Reed, 206
Regine, 201
relationships, 3, 23, 35, 38, 43, 63, 70, 113, 124, 139, 153, 180, 207, 258, 265
Rest, 88, 252, 253
rewards, 28, 63, 85, 136, 206
Richmond, 271, 272
Ritchie, 61, 63, 64, 71
Roddick, Anita, 196, 275
Rokeach, 60, 98, 143
role model, 85, 130, 172
Rousseau, 82
Sanford, 236, 278
Sarbannes-Oxley, 132, 204
Schein, 7, 60, 63, 64, 65, 66, 68
Schemerhorn, 221
Schmidt, 59
Schwartz, 60
Schweitzer, 42, 43, 44, 109, 115, 136, 137, 232, 259, 273, 278
scripts, 122, 138, 146
Senge, 114, 155, 179
Sexton, 127
Sims, 188
Singer, 42, 89
Skinner, 85
Smith, 59
Smith, Adam, 65
social influences, 26

Index

Socrates, 6, 83
Sprinthal, 88, 95
St James Ethics Centre, 31
stakeholders, 18, 40, 113, 156, 166
Steiner, 125
Stephens, 127
Sternberg, Elaine, 191
Stevenson, 275, 276
strange attractor, 203, 225, 245
success, 3, 5, 41, 78, 126, 141, 187, 202, 212, 251, 261, 273, 277
Sun Tzu, 222
sustainability, 197, 255
systemic skills, 114, 115, 236
Takeuchi, 141
Teilhard de Chardin, 202
The Body Shop, 196, 275
The Corporation, 255
Thomas, 206, 213, 221
Thompson, 59, 73
Tosti, 221
Trevino, 96, 138, 153, 154, 180, 204
trust, 52, 58, 205, 207
Ulrich, 172
unethical behaviour, 21, 25, 54, 137, 180
Unholy orders, 152
values
conflicts between, 84, 148, 150, 162, 175
instrumental, 61
terminal, 61
Values Evolution Model, v, 11, 12, 13, 71, 79, 84, 86, 88, 99, 103, 105, 110, 119, 126, 131, 148, 180, 184, 185, 197, 203, 223, 225, 226, 235, 238, 247, 252, 264, 269, 273, 278
values-based management, 219
Velasquez, 160
virtue, 85, 175, 252
vision values, 111, 115, 130, 212, 236
Von der Embse, 184
Wagley, 184
Walton, 25
Waters, 29
Watson, 154
Weaver, 154
Weiss, 127
Werhane, 149
Wilber, 226, 229
Williams, Ray, 18, 189
Williams, Robin, 66
Woldring, 28, 29
Wolfe, 163
world view, 67, 99, 102, 105, 109, 201, 235
Zohar, 74